Endorsements

"*Project Career Quest* is a practical guide for people transitioning in life. Whether the change is by choice or due to decisions beyond their control, this book will allow them to find new opportunities to use their God-given gifts, talents, and abilities. It is filled with best-practices, stories, strategies, and techniques to educate, inspire, and empower job seekers to find meaningful employment. Kerry masterfully blends her experiences in the field of project management and career coaching to create a guide that will undoubtedly help thousands of people navigate the challenging journey known as *career transition*. Whether you are looking to stay on the same career path or move from your day job to dream job, I highly recommend *Project Career Quest* and Kerry to guide you in this process."

—**Kary Oberbrunner, Author of *Elixir Project, Day Job to Dream Job, The Deeper Path*, and *Your Secret Name***

"I found *Project Career Quest* to be a game changer in learning how to treat the process of looking for a new job or transitioning to a different career as an actual project! For so many job seekers, job searching can quickly turn into an endless cycle of activity with little return to show for the time and energy invested. As a project management professional, Kerry has done an excellent job of combining project management concepts and human aspects (such as understanding and leveraging your personality profile) with actionable job seeking advice that will lead to concrete results if followed through. Kerry has a heart of gold with a clear passion for helping others—it shows in this book!"

—**Kimberley Parker, Ph.D., PMP, Chemical Engineer/Mompreneur**

"Kerry is an expert in her field! As a frequent speaker at Colonial Job Seekers, she is in her wheelhouse when it comes to helping professionals in transition identify their full potential and their job search challenges. From a unique project management perspective, *Project Career Quest* guides the reader through a practical career transition method that can easily be put into practice. As an experienced career coach and trainer, Kerry knows her audience and through *Project Career Quest* she provides highly effective tools for a productive job search that can lead to the perfect job. I highly recommend it!"

—**Paula Bryan, Career Coach and Volunteer Director of Colonial Job Seekers, Cary, North Carolina**

"Not only does *Project Career Quest* break down the logistical steps of the job search process, it also addresses the emotional ups and downs that many job seekers will experience. This book is relevant for both entry-level and seasoned professionals. It will motivate and empower job seekers. As an employer, I also found insightful the discussion regarding best practices in the hiring process."

—Li-Chen Chin, Ph.D.
Assistant Vice President - Intercultural Programs, Student Affairs
Duke University, Durham, North Carolina

"Kerry is genuinely dedicated to helping you find your best self and hidden talents. Her positive yet direct feedback and encouragement was exactly what I needed to navigate my last job search. Besides hiring Kerry as my career coach, she also taught several project management classes for my former employer including PMP Exam Prep. Her teaching style is collaborative and entertaining filled with first-hand experiences, real world examples, and case studies. I know *Project Career Quest* will be an invaluable tool to anyone in transition and/or navigating important career decisions."

—Elizabeth Crisp, PMP, Senior Project Manager/Pharmaceutical Industry

"Kerry has been an exceptional mentor for the past three years and has been instrumental to my professional success. She knows when to challenge her mentees, when to encourage them, and offers a unique knowledge of project management, career transition, and professional growth. She always seems to have the right advice to give at the right time! Her book is a must-read for anyone going through career transition, as it provides a clear method to finding the perfect job. It helped me get the results I was looking for during a particularly challenging career transition. I highly recommend it!"

—Emilie Smith, Ph.D., PMP, Business Intelligence Developer

"Although I graduated from college with a strong academic record and high confidence in my ability to succeed in the workplace, I had little idea about how to tackle the job search. Every application felt like a shot in the dark. After a frustrating attempt to find employment on my own, I hired Kerry to help me in my career transition. She helped me identify some of my roadblocks and then to map out a strategy to move forward. With renewed confidence, I moved to Boston and began my job search. Using her advice, I was able to network effectively and find a job quickly in my field of study. The tools and strategies Kerry shared with me were vital in clarifying my goals and taking action. I am thankful to Kerry not just for helping me find my first job, but because I believe her advice will help me with any career transitions I make in the future."

—Nathan Shepherd, J.D. Candidate, 2019
University of Virginia School of Law

"Kerry spoke many times to the career transition support group I co-founded and co-led in Raleigh, North Carolina for a number of years. Her background was an excellent fit for our group with her knowledge and training in project management, resume writing, and LinkedIn. Her presentations were always informative, empowering, and encouraging to the job seekers. She knew how to engage the audience and always left them with tools and strategies to enhance their ability to conduct a successful job search. In *Project Career Quest,* she shares many of those same tools, strategies, and her knowledge using a project management approach to deliver successful projects. This book will help those individuals who are in transition, as well as those seeking to make a career change, to navigate their career quest with confidence."

—Robert (Bob) Gates, Retired AT&T International Executive

"In my 39 years of supporting the production and sales of electric power, I have consulted and been trained by many leadership and project management professionals. Only one stands out heads and shoulders above the rest—Kerry. The material she has compiled in *Project Career Quest* is invaluable to those who are experienced, those in pursuit of a new career, and every stage in between. With her vast knowledge, she provides useful tools, sound advice, and a sensical and easily understood methodology for success. She is a master in conveying real life examples that are easily applicable to a wide variety of interests. This book is a *must-have* resource from a talented and wise professional that everyone should consult often and recommend to others in their pursuit of genuine joy in their lives."

—Linda Mann, PMP, Project Manager
Electric Utility Industry

"God equips each and every one of us with unique talents and gifts for various kinds of work, to add value to others and create an internal sense of purpose and meaning. But sometimes we struggle to identify that greater purpose and run against obstacles and roadblocks that seem to keep us from making progress in our career. Through her book, *Project Career Quest*, Kerry empowers the reader with tools, techniques, and strategies to identify new opportunities where they can apply their unique talents and gifts. She shares inspiring stories and her real-world experiences to help the reader address and overcome the obstacles and challenges they may face as they transition from one job to another or one phase of their career to another. Kerry's vast experience as a leader, trainer, career coach, and project management professional gives her the unique ability to guide the reader through a structured, focused, and disciplined approach to making a successful career transition and perhaps even finding their *why* along the way. Regardless of where you are in your career, let Kerry be your guide on your quest to find more meaningful and purposeful work."

—Joan L. Turley, Author of *Sacred Work in Secular Places:*
Finding Joy in the Workplace

"This book is an invaluable resource for anyone trying to figure out how to translate their skills and passion into a fulfilling job. It breaks down the daunting process into easily attainable goals that can be accomplished even amid a busy schedule. I highly recommend *Project Career Quest* both for those just graduating college as well as for those who, like me a short time ago, are looking to make a transition mid-career. In the 20-year span since the last time I started a new job, the job-seeking process has undergone many changes, and I appreciate the help this book has given me in navigating the current job market and finding a place where I truly belong."

—Beverly deSouza, Mentee/Women in Bio
Graduate Student at Duke University

"Kerry shared Chapter 14 on interviewing with me before an important career-changing job interview that would require relocation. After reading the chapter and taking notes, I felt very prepared and confident. I used the method she describes to prepare answers to the many potential questions she lists. My answers seemed to be exactly what the employer was looking for, and I received very positive feedback during and after the interview. Her advice on how to communicate with the hiring manager to follow-up was also critical and, most importantly, I received a great job offer!"

—Emily Vaughn, Regulatory Medical Writer

PROJECT CAREER QUEST

Navigating the Journey to New Opportunities Waiting

Kerry Ahrend, M.S., PMP

Published by Author Academy Elite
P.O. Box 43, Powell, OH 43065
www.AuthorAcademyElite.com

ISBN 978-1-64085-912-8 (Softcover)
ISBN 978-1-64085-796-4 (Hardcover)
ISBN 978-1-64085-913-5 (eBook)

Library of Congress Control Number: 2019913378

Available in hardcover, softcover, eBook, and audiobook

DISCLAIMER

Any Internet addresses that have been shared in the book are offered as a resource to the reader. Their inclusion does not in any way imply an endorsement by the author or the publisher nor do they vouch for the content or permanence of the sites.

DEDICATION

I dedicate this book to my father, **Charles Walter Ahrend**, better known to others as Chuck, or Chuckles, as I liked to call him. He was always trying to get a chuckle out of people with one of his corny jokes and one-liners, aka "Chuckisms." I had hoped he would see the finished product of my book, but sadly he passed away June 24, 2019 before I could hand him the signed copy I had promised him. At 92 years old, he certainly did not need a book on career transition. However, he served as a good example of how we can transition successfully from career to career and find fulfillment in our chosen vocation.

My Dad spent his working career doing things he loved. Raised on a vegetable farm in Staten Island, New York (yes, can you believe it), he spent his entire career in the field of agriculture. After high school and a short stint in the U.S. Navy, he attended Cornell University where he studied Horticulture before embarking on a nearly twenty-year career with Campbell Soup Company. He eventually found his way back to a farm in Virginia, where he raised livestock for twenty years. When he retired from farming, he continued his journey by supporting the farmers of Rockingham County Virginia. He served as an elected official on the Board of Supervisors for yet another twenty years. Even after getting off the Board, he continued to serve the people of Rockingham County, in the beautiful Shenandoah Valley, through his extensive volunteer work. He loved what he did and did what he loved. Oh, good and faithful servant, you have left a lasting legacy.

Dad this book is for you because I believe everyone should do what they love and love what they do. My hope and prayer is that through *Project Career Quest* I can help my readers find fulfillment in their work and understand the importance of serving others. Thanks for the inspiration. Love you and miss you Daddy Chuckles—even your corny jokes.

CONTENTS

ACKNOWLEDGMENTS

I want to acknowledge all the people who supported, inspired, and kept me focused on this journey. Writing and publishing a book has long been on my bucket list. Through my volunteer work with various career transition groups in my area, I realized my book would be to meld my knowledge of project management with the need so many have to find a job, and more importantly, a meaningful and purposeful career.

To Kary Oberbrunner, David Branderhorst, and the entire Igniting Souls Tribe, I thank you for your support and encouragement. Author Academy Elite is literally changing lives by helping people realize their dream of writing, publishing, and building a career around their message and content. The energy, enthusiasm, collective wisdom, and support of this group are second to none!

Thank you Paula Bryan and Bob Gates for giving me the opportunity to share with the local career transition groups. I learned so much from helping job seekers on their journey. And thank you to all of the job seekers I've encountered along the way. I learned something from each of you—from your questions, your experiences, your struggles, and your successes.

Thank you to my beta readers, contributors, and supporters for your insight, feedback, encouragement, and for sharing your own experiences. Sincere thanks and gratitude to Kimberley Parker, Emilie Smith, Zoma Childe, Beverly deSouza, Bob Gates, Paula Bryan, Susan Lankford, Scott MacLean, Gail DiPreta, Nancy Borst, Linda Mann, Carol Linden, Shawn Ramsey, Li-Chen Chin, Joan Chartier, and Bryon Spells. I also want to thank fellow Igniting Souls tribe members and authors Teri Capshaw, Donna Reiners, and Joan Turley for supporting and encouraging me through the process. You were all a part of my journey and for that I am forever grateful.

And last, but not least, thank you to my coaching clients, private and corporate, for allowing me to come beside you and be part of your journey. It's both an honor and a privilege to be able to serve you—to help you recognize your special talents and gifts to meet your challenges with confidence.

INTRODUCTION

Whether you've lost your job, you're looking for a job for the first time and are totally lost in the process, or you're about to lose your mind and know it's time to find a new job, what you need is a roadmap and a guide to help you on this journey. There are **N**ew **O**pportunities **W**aiting (**NOW**) for you if you know where to look and how to approach the job market. I will guide you through the job search process, providing you the information, resources, tools, and strategies you need for a successful transition and to help navigate your journey to **N**ew **O**pportunities **W**aiting.

If you've recently graduated from college, gotten out of the military, or you're re-entering the job market after a long absence, you will find there is much to learn and much work to be done to find meaningful employment. If you've been in the job market and recently lost your job, then you will need help looking for a job and perhaps dealing with the emotional aspects of losing a job.

Losing a job is never easy. Work is a big part of our identity. It's how we pay our bills. It's a reason to get out of bed in the morning. It's why you spent years going to school. It's something you enjoyed, or maybe not so much. Whatever your job was to you, it was *your* job—until you lost it, for whatever reason.

NOW What?
How do you get started?
Where do you go from here?
What are employers looking for?
Who do you know who can help you?
What should your resume look like?
What information should be included?
What will you be asked in a job interview?
How do you find out who's hiring?
How will you get an interview?
Where do you begin?
NOW What?

So many questions and uncertainties. Quite frankly it can be overwhelming. And, depending on your emotional state, you may not want to face the reality of looking for a job. How long has it been? Five years, ten, twenty, or more? How times have changed! The job market is not the same and neither are the expectations of employers. Technology, social media, and resources available continue to change and impact how we look for and find employment. To be successful in landing a job, you will need to educate yourself so you can use your time and resources efficiently and effectively.

WHY I WROTE THIS BOOK

I deliver courses to my corporate clients who have been laid off to help them transition successfully from one position to another. However, I realized there is very little support available to those who work for smaller companies or companies who choose not to support their employees with a transition package. While there are job seeker and career transition groups in many communities, it can take months of attending meetings to figure out how to approach the job search process, develop an effective communication strategy, and pull together all of the other activities necessary to enable someone to obtain meaningful employment.

I decided to write this book to fill the ever-increasing need to educate people on how to find a job, change careers, or find employment that is more fulfilling, challenging, and engaging. Writing this book aligns with my passion to help people: people who are struggling to figure out their next career move, people who lack clarity about their career goals, people who want to discover their passion, people who want more out of life than a routine nine to five job that simply pays the bills but offers no real excitement or future potential. My hope for each and every person who reads this book is that I can educate, equip, empower, and encourage you to achieve your career goals with confidence and find success in your Career Quest.

"CAREER QUEST" APPROACH

Project Career Quest will guide you step-by-step through the process of finding a job, or perhaps even a new career if that is your desired outcome. This book takes a project management approach to navigating your job search/career transition.

A *project* is a temporary endeavor undertaken to create a unique product, service, or result. *Project management* is the discipline of initiating, planning, executing, controlling, and closing to achieve specific goals and success criteria. Looking for fulfilling employment and/or changing careers is truly a project that requires a structured approach to achieve your goal(s) and find success.

To get the results you want, you will need to follow a disciplined approach, especially if you want your job search/career transition to be a temporary endeavor. Using a project management approach and applying best practices and lessons learned is exactly what you need to be successful on this journey.

By definition, a project has a beginning and an end. If you've lost your job or have been notified that your position will be eliminated in the near future, your project has already begun. If you are unhappy in your current position or career, then it's time to kick off your project.

My goal is to guide you through the transition process so you will have more control over the results and the length of your project. If you organize your project, creating a plan and executing the plan based on *best practices*, you will be able to successfully close out your project much quicker and the journey and outcome will be much more rewarding.

WHY A PROJECT MANAGEMENT APPROACH

To be successful finding a job or changing careers takes dedication and focus. Sending out an occasional resume and attending a networking event here and there will not, unless you are extremely lucky and well connected, land you the job of your dreams, nor any job for that matter. It takes having a plan and working the plan. It takes using a structured approach, completing certain essential activities, and surrounding yourself with people to support your efforts.

I cannot think of a better way to approach your job search or career change than using project management best practices. If you don't know much about project management, no worries. I am here to teach, guide, mentor, and coach you throughout this journey.

Besides my role as a career coach, I am also a certified Project Management Professional (PMP®)[1] and have been teaching project management courses and best practices to corporate clients all over the world for over twenty years. I will show you how to turn your job search into a successful project where you meet your objectives and deliverables. Using a project management approach will expedite your efforts and get you focused and on target for success.

HOW TO APPROACH THE BOOK

How you approach the book will depend on your learning style, your objective, your time frame, and a number of other factors. *Project Career Quest* is a hands-on book with a lot of work to be completed to help you see clearly where you want to go, to chart your course, and move toward your intended destination with confidence.

There is no right or wrong way to approach the book—do what works best for you. Much of your approach will depend on how long you have been in the job search process and your immediate needs. However, I would suggest first skimming the table of contents to understand the big picture of what's included. Do a quick overview of the entire book and then use one of the approaches suggested below:

1. Start with Chapter 1 and work through the material one chapter at a time, completing the activities before you move onto the next chapter. This will be especially effective if you have been recently laid off or you are looking for your first professional position. If you have been looking for a while and still lack clarity and direction, you may also want to start with Chapter 1 and then move forward.

2. If you have been on your job search journey for a while and you need something specific, such as help with interviewing, start there and then go back to the other chapters as needed. Even if you have a resume (for example), you will want to carefully read the chapter on Communication Strategy to ensure you have developed your resume with a focus on adding value to the prospective employer. I see far too many people who are struggling to make progress in their job search because their resume is not focused on the position for which they are applying and the resume is not accomplishment-based.

Whichever approach you use, be sure to complete all of the exercises and Action Items found in each of the chapters for maximum benefit. The exercises are intended to help you articulate and be confident in your goals, objectives, accomplishments, strengths, value proposition, etc. All of these things are needed to influence the decision makers and close the deal. Get a notebook or journal to take notes and complete the Action Items. Write things down!

IMPORTANT: READ THIS

To help facilitate your journey, I have created a set of tools and templates entitled **Career Tools.** Throughout the book you will be prompted to go to the Career Tools section and complete an activity to create awareness and understanding of your Career Quest goals and deliverables and how to achieve them. Use the tools also to track your progress and performance.

You will see a hammer (tool) every time a career tool, template, or sample document is referenced. You can find the **Career Tools** at **www.ProjectCareerQuest. com**. When you land on my website, click the button for **Project Career Quest Tools**. You will then need to enter the password **EAGLES4031** to access the fifty plus (50+) tools available to you for your **Career Quest** journey.

The tools are listed by topic, in alphabetical order, to enable me to add more after the book's publication. As I come across additional tools that may be helpful on your journey; or reader's share some of their tools, templates, and examples; they may be added to the toolbox as additional resources.

Every successful journey begins with a vision and a roadmap to get you where you want to go. I will guide you step-by-step through the job search/career transition process. Let the journey begin!

> "Life is a journey, not a destination."
> —*Ralph Waldo Emerson*

NOTE: Although the primary focus of the book is for those who have been in the workforce for a period of time and are now unemployed or under-employed, the content also applies to college students and others entering the workforce for the first time, people returning after a hiatus, or anyone wanting to make a change in their current career situation. Throughout the book I will refer to the job search process and career transition, often using the terms interchangeably. While some of you may be looking for a new job, others will be seeking a new career.

PART 1

INITIATE

Preparing for the Journey

CHAPTER 1

THE EMOTIONAL SIDE OF CAREER TRANSITION

If you are reading this book, I can only assume that you are in transition as it relates to your career. Perhaps you recently graduated from college (or are getting ready to) and are looking for your first professional job. Or maybe you are in a position that is less than satisfying and have made the decision to start looking for something else that is more challenging or fulfilling. Or you, like a lot of people who will read this book, are out of work because your position was eliminated, outsourced, or acquired by another company. Regardless of why you picked up this book and what your circumstances are, few people are ever really prepared for the ups and downs of the journey ahead.

If you follow the *project management approach* outlined in this book; complete the activities, use the tools provided, and adhere to the *best practices* and *lessons learned* I share throughout; your job search or career transition project (call it what you want) will gain traction and move you in the right direction—closer to your ultimate goal.

Change, transition, and uncertainty are never easy. You will have to deal with a plethora of emotions along the way. So, before we jump into the meat of the book, I have devoted the first three chapters to discussing the emotional side of career transition, job search realities, and the challenges you will face on your journey to discovering your dream job or landing meaningful employment. I cannot possibly foresee the surprises and twist and turns you will encounter on your journey. I can, however, help you anticipate some of the issues you are likely to face and to help you be more prepared to deal with them effectively.

Since I believe a majority of the people reading this book are in search of a job or a new career; not because they chose to but because that decision was made for them; I will start with that audience. If you are entering the job market for the first time, or the first time in a long time, or you are looking to make a career change, please read on because you too will face many of the same emotions and challenges at some point.

RANGE OF EMOTIONS

People are rarely prepared for a job loss. To lose a job you enjoyed and looked forward to, most days, is extremely difficult and charged with emotions. And even if you did not love your job (or even like it), this does not necessarily make things any easier. The fact is you now need to find a new job and, hopefully, meaningful and satisfying work.

Losing one's job is an emotional event and can run the gamut from anger, shame, embarrassment, fear, frustration, shattered confidence, to low self-esteem. It can lead to apathy, depression, and withdrawal. All of these are natural and predictable feelings associated with the loss of a job. Although there is likely no reason for you to be embarrassed or ashamed about losing your job, it is a natural reaction. Even if you choose to leave your job to seek something more fulfilling, you are still likely to experience most, if not all, of these emotions somewhere along the way.

WHY ME?

The "why me" syndrome kicks in for many people. "What did I do wrong? Why was my position eliminated? I had the largest territory and some of the company's most influential and important clients. Why didn't they select (so and so)?" If you fixate on "why me," you will get stuck and bitter. Don't do it!

Decisions have been made that you cannot change. You do not need to know the rationale for the decisions, nor will you get very far if you seek answers. It is what it is! So, move on with your life.

If you find yourself getting stuck, then I advise you to seek professional help. Many organizations offer their employees assistance through their Employee Assistance Program (EAP). If you do not have access to an EAP from your former employer, then seek professional counseling through a community-based group (e.g., a church) or professional organization. Getting stuck will not help you find another position and get you back to work.

Please try to remind yourself during this transition process that although your life is changing, it's *not* over. You still have plenty to give and value to offer. Far too often we tie our identity to our jobs. Losing a job can leave people feeling worthless and without purpose. Where you will land is unknown at this point, but if you do the work you will land somewhere in time. In fact, as hard as this might be to believe at this moment, you may actually enjoy your new job or situation better than your previous position. Time will tell. I only ask you to be open to the possibilities and approach things with a positive mindset.

KEEP IT POSITIVE!

You can't find a job if you keep it a secret. For starters, let your friends, neighbors, former colleagues, and family members know that you are "in transition and looking for your next career opportunity." Keep it positive! Let people know so they can support you on your journey. You need to get on the "radar screen" and enlist the help of others.

Are you going to have to work hard during this transition period? Absolutely! Wallowing in sorrow and regret will gain you nothing. No one wants to see a friend or family member lose a job, but if you do not approach the job search process with a positive mindset you will find it very difficult to get others to engage with you. Building a support team is critical to your success. Your friends and family members want to help you and will help if you approach them with a positive attitude. I am not trying to make this sound easy—it isn't. But at the same time, you do not want to alienate those who can help with your job search and career transition. I have seen it happen many times over the past ten plus years that I have been working with job seekers. People who love and care about you do not want to see you going through a difficult time. They will often withdraw themselves because they do not know how to help the situation, how to deal with your emotions, or how to cope with their own feelings of inadequacy. If you keep things as positive as possible, you will gain much more support and traction in your job search.

"Life is 10% what happens to me and 90% of how I react to it."
—*John C. Maxwell*

ENGAGE OTHERS

It is important that you deal with your own emotions: fear, anger, frustration, or whatever you are feeling. Do not try to bury and ignore them. Ignoring your feelings will hinder your productivity. My suggestion is that you find a support group to help you work through your emotions. There are many career transition support groups that exist in communities. Many are through churches and you do not have to be a church member, a churchgoer, or even a person of faith to attend. An online search for "career transition support groups," or "job seekers" is a good place to start. If there are none in your area, you may consider starting one. Chances are there is a need.

A large majority of job losses these days are due to business decisions and have little or nothing to do with job performance. Perhaps your location is being closed or your position eliminated due to a merger, buyout, outsourcing situation, or other business decisions. Jobs are being consolidated and relocated or eliminated altogether due to technology and other emerging issues. Do not be afraid to let people know you are looking for employment. You will not find a job if you are not communicating your need with others. To get started, let people know you are looking for your next career opportunity and ask them if they can help you network and find potential job leads.

"Being challenged in life is inevitable, being defeated is optional."
—*Roger Crawford*

THE 3 P'S TO SUCCESS

The job search process will challenge you, but defeat is optional. You choose! If you are to be successful in your career transition, I suggest you employ the three P's: *Persistence, Perseverance,* and *Patience*. In time, the right opportunity will come along, but you must be persistent, persevere, and be patient. **Create a plan and work the plan**. Allow others to help you but do not relinquish responsibility for your own destiny. Read on and I will give you the knowledge, tools, and strategies needed to be successful!

☑ CHECKLIST - BEFORE YOU MOVE ON

☐ Have you begun to deal with your emotional issues regarding your job loss?

☐ Do you need to seek counseling?

☐ Do you know where you can find support in your community to help you with your career transition needs?

☐ Have you informed your friends and family members with a positive attitude?

☐ Are you ready, willing, and committed to taking on the career transition challenge?

☐ Will you commit to making a plan and working the plan?

Lessons Learned: *Keep it positive and let people know you are looking for your next career opportunity and ask for their support. Do not isolate yourself and seek help as needed.*

CHAPTER 2

JOB SEARCH REALITIES

Before we get into the specifics of your job search project, let me take a few minutes to discuss some things you will encounter along the way, four things specifically. I share these four things so you will have a clear understanding of what to expect and, thus, be more prepared as you experience these job search realities. The realities include:

Reality #1 - Roadblocks
Reality #2 - Potholes
Reality #3 - Gremlins
Reality #4 - Benefits

REALITY #1 – ROADBLOCKS

Along your journey you will encounter some roadblocks, maybe many. A roadblock is something that is real and must be addressed; it's a barrier to your progress. For example, let's say you are applying for a job that requires you to have a specific certification (PMP, CAPM, CISM, CPA, CTP, MCP, CCNP, PE, SPHR, etc.)[1] and you do not have the certification. That's a ROADBLOCK. Does it mean you should not apply for the position? Maybe, but then again, maybe not. But if it is required, you will need to make a decision. Do I forget this position and move on or do I work towards getting the certification, if qualified? You may have to wait to find another position that requires that certification, or the hiring manager may still consider you for the position because you are working on the certification (and you best be working on it!) You will need to decide how to handle your roadblocks: turn back, go around, or bust right through.

Other roadblocks you may encounter might be things such as: "You are too qualified for the position." This could be interpreted as, "you are too old," or "you will cost me too much." If you are too qualified for the position, be prepared to address the employer's concern (e.g., that you may quickly get bored and move on). Share why you want the position and what you will do to bring value to the employer's organization.

Another potential roadblock is when you think you are under-qualified for the position. (Note: most job descriptions today expect you to be Superman or Superwoman! With that in mind, most of us would be under-qualified.) If you are interested in the position and you match up with a majority of the qualifications, go for it! You never know unless you try.

I recently had a client who applied for a job that required someone with a Master's degree or Ph.D. She had neither. Actually, she has a B.A. in Arts but is a certified Project Management Professional (PMP®) and had fifteen years-experience in the field. Although she did not meet the minimum educational requirements, she felt she was otherwise qualified for the position and so she applied. She got a phone interview, a face-to-face interview, an offer, and the job.

One of your biggest roadblocks to finding meaningful employment may be staring you in the face—look in the mirror. Yes, that's right, YOU might be your own biggest obstacle. Realistically, a few of you reading this book (I hope only a few) may have already determined that you will not be able to land a new position. "I'm too old" is one of the reasons I hear far too often. So, let's get it out there and address some of the reasons why job seekers convince themselves they are no longer employable.

- "I am too old; no one will hire me at my age."

- "I have never worked in that industry. I have no experience."

- "I can't get a job if I don't have a job."

- "They recently downsized, they won't be hiring."

- "I never went to college."

- _____ (Fill in the blank, what's your excuse?)

If you approach your job search with a negative mindset, already having convinced yourself you are unemployable, then it is likely you will find yourself unemployed. Think *Law of Attraction*![2] As James Allen said in his book *As a Man Thinketh...*[3]

> "As he thinks, so he is; as he continues to think, so he remains."
> —*James Allen*

"YOU'RE TOO OLD"

Okay, let's discuss the age issue. What I have heard way too often is "I am over fifty, I will never find a job again." Maybe it's forty, maybe it's sixty—like they say, "Age is only a number."

Your age should not limit your ability to be effective in a position. What may limit you is your attitude or the attitude of the hiring manager. Now I know what you are probably thinking, or at least I think I do. "Yes of course, it's the hiring manager who won't hire me because I am too old."

Does discrimination happen? Absolutely! Anyone who says it doesn't is either lying or in denial. Still, the most effective way to overcome someone's prejudice or perception that someone over fifty (or forty) is too old to perform and deliver effectively the responsibilities of the job is to prove them wrong.

To prove them wrong, you will need to focus on your skills, core competencies, and your experience, not your age. You will want to approach the interview with enthusiasm and confidence. You need to demonstrate flexibility and the willingness to learn new things. Keeping a positive attitude, knowing your value, and selling yourself effectively will keep you in the game.

Often the perception that may come with hiring an "older worker" is that they may not fit into the ever-changing culture of an organization. Or they may be too set in their ways and change-resistant. I heard it a lot myself when I first started my corporate career back in my twenties. Older co-workers of mine would say things like "That won't work; that's not the way we've always done it." Or, "Here's how we always did it at XYZ Company." They seemed focused on the past and resistant to change to meet the current circumstances. I personally found it very annoying and frustrating and can understand why some hiring managers may have the perception that an older worker might be set in their ways and fear that this would hold the team back.

As a general rule, when the economy is in a downturn, recruiters will tend to hire predominantly younger, less experienced workers as a way to cut costs for the employer. As the economy improves, company recruiters are often directed to hire more experienced workers (with fifteen-twenty plus years of experience) who can help the organization grow. So again, focus on your experience, the value you bring to an organization, and how you can help them grow and succeed—not on your age!

"YOU HAVE NO INDUSTRY EXPERIENCE"

A colleague of mine had a client who wanted to enter the field of energy management with no prior experience in that industry. He had seventeen years of experience with a major technology company where he did inside sales. This man was discouraged by many who told him he would not be able to enter that field without prior industry experience. Fortunately for him, he did not listen to the naysayers.

This individual was determined and took action to move forward and get what he wanted. He went back to school to obtain a certification in facilities management and immediately joined an associated professional organization where he volunteered to be on both the membership and programs committee. Eventually, he was also asked to serve on a Board that gave him access to a lot of good contacts in energy management. He committed himself to networking within the industry. He attended a national conference and soaked up as much knowledge as possible and was able to network with energy industry professionals from all over the U.S.

In the end, he got two very attractive job offers in energy management, the field he was told he would not be able to break into because of his lack of direct experience. Did I mention he is in his fifty's? He was determined, unstoppable, and received some good coaching from my colleague as well. He set a goal and achieved it because of his attitude, his persistence, perseverance, patience, and belief in himself. He did not let others deter him nor did he listen to the naysayers.

"I CAN'T GET A JOB IF I DON'T HAVE A JOB"

Everyone else who is currently unemployed is in the same boat (so to speak) and people are finding jobs and successfully transitioning every day. Don't let this be your excuse. Put in the effort, do the work, and you will eventually find employment.

"THEY RECENTLY DOWNSIZED. THEY WON'T BE HIRING"

While this seems logical to conclude, the reality is that even companies who have recently laid off employees are still hiring somewhere within the organization. Vacancies occur due to retirements, employees relocating, resignations, promotions, taking a leave of absence, and a variety of other reasons. Don't assume a layoff means a company is not hiring. If you are interested in a particular company or organization, follow them on social media and check their website for employment opportunities. And most importantly, network with people in those organizations so you can find the unadvertised positions (known as the "hidden job market"[4]). Connect with hiring managers so when a desirable position becomes available you will be ready to seize the opportunity.

"I NEVER WENT TO COLLEGE"

This can be a barrier; no two ways about it. If this is your situation, networking will be critical to opening doors for a job you may otherwise be unqualified for based on the educational requirements. You may have the experience and knowledge, but without the degree your resume will not pass the applicant tracking systems (ATS).[5] Network, network, network! I helped a friend get a position that was filled primarily with professionals holding master's degrees and above. She did not go to college but had great experience and was otherwise qualified. Had it not been for my recommendation and getting her resume into the hands of the hiring manager, it is doubtful she would have been considered for the position.

ATTITUDE MATTERS

I am guessing you do not want to remain unemployed, so be aware of your thoughts and attitude during this journey. Your attitude and state of mind can be your single greatest roadblock in your job search project or your greatest asset. You *can* transform your life and find meaningful employment. But remember—your reality begins in your head! Your mindset is the primary factor that will determine whether you succeed or fail in your job search and in your approach to life. Go forward with an attitude of abundance. Think about what you do have and not about what you don't. Focus on your strengths, not your age. Focus on what you can do and not on what you can't. Be sure to allow your friends to support you on this journey. With the right attitude and approach, they will!

"Our attitude can give us an uncommonly positive perspective."
—*John C. Maxwell*

QUESTIONS TO EXPLORE

What's your attitude and state of mind as you enter this time of transition? What are your excuses? Have you tested them or are they assumptions and negative talk? Where are you putting your focus? On what you can do or on what you can't do? On what you do have or on what you don't? Be very aware of your belief system because it will create your reality. Sometimes our belief system is nothing more than BS!

Action Item #1

If you have never kept a **gratitude journal** now would be a good time to start. At the end (or beginning) of each day write down three to five things you are grateful for. Look back on your life and appreciate all that you have done and accomplished. Re-live those moments. Remember those moments and allow those moments to help you find joy in the journey you are now on, and build the confidence you need to be successful.

"Our greatest freedom is the freedom to choose our attitude."
—Viktor Frankl

I highly recommend you read Viktor Frankl's book *Man's Search for Meaning*.[6] This is a book of survival, perseverance, meaning, and purpose. Viktor Frankl, an Austrian neurologist and psychiatrist, survived the prison camps of World War II when many perished. It wasn't the strength of his body that sustained him, but rather the strength of his mind. If you have not read his book yet, you should. It will change the way you see yourself and your circumstances.

"We who lived in concentration camps can remember the men who walked through the huts comforting others, giving away their last piece of bread. They may have been few in number, but they offer sufficient proof that everything can be taken from a man but one thing: the last of the human freedoms—to choose one's attitude in any given set of circumstances, to choose one's own way."
—Viktor Frankl

Lessons Learned: Y*our thoughts will influence your attitude, your attitude your behavior, your behavior your results. Maintaining a positive mental attitude is critical to success.*

REALITY #2 - POTHOLES

Potholes, as I define them, are bad habits that you can easily fall into if you are not careful during a time of transition. For example, I am a procrastinator—okay, I said it! Yes, I do procrastinate and tend to put off those things I would rather not do. Looking for a job is something many of you may rather not do, but putting it off will not help you find employment. That's why having a plan and working the plan is the best course of action.

Another bad habit is going online to do your job search and spending hours on social media chatting with friends instead. Oops, not a lot done today.

The inability to say "no" can delay and derail your job search project. It is very important to set boundaries with key people in your life when in transition. If you don't, your project will drag on for a very long time. Few of us want to disappoint others, but saying "yes" to doing this and that (whatever that may be) will not be a good use of your time and will significantly increase the length of your project. During career transition, it is critical that you establish boundaries, allowing you to stay focused on your goal of finding meaningful employment.

Setting boundaries and learning to say "no" to lesser things, will allow you to say "yes" to greater things. Setting boundaries will protect those things that will help you be productive and successful in your job search and will keep the wasteful and unimportant activities out. Create a schedule for your job search project and stick to it. Discipline and commitment to your project will make it easy for you to say "no" to things that keep you from achieving your goal(s).

"The difference between successful people and really successful people
is really successful people say no to almost everything."
—*Warren Buffett*

QUESTIONS TO EXPLORE

Potholes are bad habits or behaviors that hold you back and keep you from making progress. What are your bad habits? What potholes are you likely to fall into along the way if you do not have a plan of how to avoid them? What can you do to ensure you will keep on track and avoid the potholes?

At the end of this chapter, take time to write down your potential potholes and create a strategy to avoid them. In project management lingo, we refer to this as doing your "risk assessment" to identify possible threats to your project's success, and then creating a strategy to mitigate the risk.

REALITY #3 – GREMLINS

The negative voices you will hear speaking to you during your time in transition are what I call your "gremlins." Some of those voices will be from friends and family, but most will be from inside your own head. You know what I am talking about, "You can't do that," "you're too this," and "you're too that." The negative voices can start early and keep going unless you cut them off and shut them down. Your gremlins might include:

- Doubting yourself
- Low self-esteem
- Fear of change
- Fear of failure
- Fear of rejection
- Fear of the unknown
- Fear of success

DAVID VS. GOLIATH

Many of you have heard the Biblical story of the young shepherd boy named David who slew the Philistine giant Goliath. Goliath was a mighty warrior who stood six cubits and a span (approximately 9 feet 6 inches tall or 2.9 meters). For forty days Goliath and the Philistine army stood on one side of a mountain while the Israelites stood on the other, with a valley between them that they both wanted to control. For forty days Goliath shouted to the Israelites to send a man to fight him and whomever won would control the valley. All of the men of Israel fled from him and were very much afraid except one, David. While others doubted and discouraged him, David was confident in his ability to fight the mighty Philistine.

For years, David had kept his father's sheep safe from lions and bears and he was confident he could deliver Goliath to King Saul along with control of the valley. King Saul gave David armor to protect him. Instead David chose five smooth pebbles from the brook and his slingshot as his weapon of choice. And as the story goes, it only took one pebble for David to take down the giant Goliath. David would have never been able to slay Goliath if he had listened to the naysayers and doubters or allowed personal insecurities (such as his size) to get in his way.

As with the story of David and Goliath, most peoples' discouraging or negative comments are not meant to be harmful. They mainly don't want to see you fail or they are voicing their own fears. If you are to succeed, you cannot listen to negativity whether it comes from inside your own head or the mouth of others. You will encounter many giants during your career transition project, with many seemingly impossible to slay. You can run from your giants or you can face them head-on. To be successful you must believe in yourself and your abilities and approach your giants with confidence.

SLAY YOUR GIANTS

Negativity will not allow you to meet your goal of finding new and meaningful employment. You must maintain a positive mental attitude, engage in positive self-talk, and surround yourself with positive people who will support you in a positive way. A career coach, a mentor, a positive role model, inspirational speakers (live or pre-recorded), can help keep your attitude, thoughts, and beliefs in the right place.

Do not, I repeat, do not listen to the gremlins. Don't let the gremlins become your roadblocks. Don't let the gremlins derail your job search project. Squash the gremlins and slay your giants.

QUESTIONS TO EXPLORE

What are your gremlins saying to you? What strategy will you use to squash the gremlins and focus instead on accomplishing your goal(s)?

REALITY #4 – BENEFITS

One other thing I want to talk about before we move on is something that few people think about, and that is the benefits and positive situations that you will encounter along the journey known as a career transition. Seeing the benefits at first can be difficult, but they will emerge as you get further into your job search project. There are four major benefits that I have outlined below, although plenty more exist if you look for them.

> Benefit #1 - You will learn a lot about yourself
> Benefit #2 - You may end up in a better place, a better job
> Benefit #3 - You have the opportunity to reinvent yourself
> Benefit #4 - You might decide to pursue your passion

Benefit #1 - First and foremost, *you will learn a lot about yourself.* If you are going to be successful you must be clear about who you are, what you want, and what value you have to offer. This can be one of the most challenging aspects of the job search process, but it is essential to be able to *sell* yourself. Like selling a product, you must know yourself inside and out and be able to share with others, particularly hiring managers. What value do you have to offer, why you are the best candidate for the job, and what separates you from other applicants. (If you choose the entrepreneurial route, you will need to articulate your value to potential clients.)

One of the first requests you are likely to get in a job interview is, "Tell me about yourself." Could you respond to that right now, as you are reading this book? If not, you have a lot of work to do. Most people will struggle with that request and critical questions like: "Tell me what you want to do next?" "What things are important to you?" "What are your priorities?" "What are your values?" "What's your leadership style?"

We will work on getting to know you better when you get to Chapter 6 entitled **Getting to Know Yourself.** If you want people to help you in your job search you must be able to give them an idea of what you want to do, what's your career objective, your core competencies, and a whole list of other things. Taking the time to examine your strengths, core values, and current priorities will provide insight into the direction you want to take your life.

A job loss can give you new perspective and can help you see yourself and your future more clearly. Overall, getting to know yourself better will benefit both you and others who will support you in the process.

Benefit #2 - Another benefit of losing your job might be that *you end up in a better place, a better job that is a better fit.* Too often people stay in dead end jobs, or jobs they are unhappy in, because they are afraid to move on. They are afraid there is nothing else out there for them. They are afraid they cannot learn new things, they are afraid of the unknown, or they have become complacent and lazy—better the known than the unknown.

Have you heard of the "Boiling Frog Syndrome"?[7] A frog placed in a pot of boiling water will jump out immediately. However, a frog placed in a pot of room temperature water with the heat slowly turned up will stay in the pot as the heat increases and starts to boil. The frog will ultimately perish! Could that have been you in your previous position (or current position)? If so, then the fact that you lost your job (for whatever reason) could actually be a blessing in disguise. If you haven't lost your job, but you're feeling like the frog in the boiling pot, it's time to take action so you don't perish in an unfulfilling job or career.

"Every situation comes bearing a gift."
—*Marianne Williamson*

Several years ago I worked with a client at one of the major universities in my area. Her job was eliminated due to funding (many of the jobs are grant-funded). She completed my workshop and proceeded to look for another job. Several months later I ran into her at a local non-profit event. She told me she was able to secure another position with the university, which had been her goal. The real story here is that not only was she able to stay at the university, but that she had landed a position that was eight pay grades higher than the position that had been eliminated. Wow! It took over two months to get approval due to the circumstances. Now she looks back with gratitude for her layoff.

For many of you reading this book, it may have been time to move on to another job or another career, but you would not for whatever reason. A secure job (or the perception thereof) that pays the bills, but is not satisfying nor challenging, for many people is better than taking a risk to find something more meaningful. I personally believe in divine intervention and that things happen for a reason. Some of you may have needed a "kick in the pants" to get you moving onto bigger and better things.

My wish for all of you reading this book is that your job search journey will lead you to new and exciting adventures and opportunities far beyond what you may have thought possible. My advice to each of you is to do your best to enjoy the journey. Build new relationships, discover new things about yourself, and stretch yourself to learn new skills along the way.

"Death isn't the greatest loss in life.
The greatest loss is what dies inside of us while we live."
—*Norman Cousins*

Benefit #3 - During the career transition process *you have the opportunity to re-invent yourself.* You do not have to be defined by your previous position(s) or work you have done in the past. Naturally you will draw from your experiences and transferable skills. But you can completely reinvent yourself if that is your desire.

Think of the corporate executive who decides it's time to leave the "rat race" and move to the country or a small town to open a restaurant, an art gallery, or buy a franchise totally unrelated to her corporate job. The skills gained in her corporate job such as leading, managing, budgeting, communicating, and relating effectively with others are transferable and will serve her well in a new and unrelated field/business.

How will you brand yourself? What's your area of expertise? For what do you want to be known?

"Life isn't about finding yourself. Life is about creating yourself."
—*George Bernard Shaw*

In my corporate career, I was many things—a paralegal, a technical writer, an editor, an organizational effectiveness consultant, a warehouse engineer, a project manager, a contract manager, and a manager of training and professional development. When I left the corporate world, having earned a Master's degree in Human Resources Training and Development, and a Master's Certificate in Project Management, I re-invented myself as a Project Management trainer and consultant. Since that time, I have continued to learn and develop new skills and now I brand myself as an author, speaker, trainer, coach, and Project Management Professional (PMP®). Now is a good time to start thinking about what you want your brand to be, what you want to be recognized for, and then create a growth strategy to get you there.

One of my mentors is John C. Maxwell, an internationally known speaker and best-selling author of books on leadership, communication, and personal growth. (John has sold over 26 million books in fifty languages.) One of the things John firmly believes is that having goals is good, but it is more important to have a *growth strategy*. Goals are finite and once achieved you are done. However, growth is an on-going process.

The times we grow most in life are not when things are going well, it's during times of adversity. Tribulation brings about perseverance and perseverance develops character.

Benefit #4 - This might be a good time to explore and *pursue your passion.* Is there anything you have dreamed of doing but pushed it aside for more practical pursuits? After working for years doing something that may not have been fulfilling, now might be the right time to pursue your passion and see if you can turn your passion into a full-time gig—day job to dream job! If you are not sure what your passion is, check out Chapter 7 entitled **Discover Your Passion**.

WHAT'S YOUR GROWTH STRATEGY?

Do you have a growth strategy? Many people stopped growing a long time ago. Those who have, will find the job search process much more challenging and restrictive than those individuals who are constantly challenging themselves to learn new skills and attain new knowledge. What's your growth strategy to ensure you don't become stagnant and to help you reach your full potential?

"Successful and unsuccessful people do not vary greatly in their abilities.
They vary in their desires to reach their potential."
—*John C. Maxwell*

QUESTIONS TO EXPLORE

What are you learning about yourself that will help you better navigate the career transition process? What do you need to know about yourself to define and share your goals with others? What's the blessing in your current situation? How will you reinvent or rebrand yourself moving forward?

 If you are interested in personal and professional growth, let me introduce you to John Maxwell's book entitled *The 15 Invaluable Laws of Growth*.[8] Reading and implementing the strategies and ideas John offers in this book will be invaluable to your future success.

"When life kicks you, let it kick you forward."
—*Kay Yow*

Action Item #2

Write down your **roadblocks**, **potholes**, **gremlins**, and the **benefits** you may/do encounter during your career transition project. A blank template can also be found in the **Career Tools** section at **www.ProjectCareerQuest.com.**

ROADBLOCKS/POTHOLES/GREMLINS/BENEFITS

ROADBLOCKS	POTHOLES
GREMLINS	**BENEFITS**

Action Item #3

Refer to your list of **potholes** (bad habits and non-productive behaviors) that could have a negative impact on your ability to succeed in your career transition project. Now brainstorm strategies to overcome or avoid your potholes. A blank template is available in the **Career Tools** section at **www.ProjectCareerQuest.com**.

POTHOLES & MITIGATION STRATEGIES

POTENTIAL POTHOLE	MITIGATION STRATEGY

Action Item #4

Keep a list of the **benefits** you encounter during your job search project. A template is available in the **Career Tools** section at **www.ProjectCareerQuest.com** to capture this information. Some of the things to include:

- Things I have learned

- People I have met

- Opportunities or experiences I have had

- Discoveries I have made about myself and others

- Doors that have opened

"Opportunity often comes in the form of misfortune or temporary defeat."
—*Napoleon Hill*

 # CHECKLIST - BEFORE YOU MOVE ON

☐ Have you done an assessment of the roadblocks you will face on your job search journey?

☐ Are you aware of the potholes that may get in the way of your success?

☐ Are you engaging in positive self-talk? Are you approaching your job search project with a positive mindset? Are you surrounding yourself with positive, supportive people?

☐ Do you need to reach out to someone to help you deal with the obstacles and emotions you are facing during this time of transition?

 Lessons Learned: *Be aware of the roadblocks, potholes, and gremlins you will face on your journey to find meaningful employment and have a plan to address them. Also look for the benefits along the way, there are many!*

CHAPTER 3

JOB SEARCH CHALLENGES

You will face many challenges on your journey to finding meaningful employment. No two peoples' journey will be exactly alike, nor will their challenges be the same. However, after working with job seekers for ten plus years, there are some recurring themes that I have noticed. Here are the *top five challenges* I have identified that many job seekers experience.

Challenge #1 - Gaining Clarity
Challenge #2 - Staying Focused
Challenge #3 - Negative Mindset
Challenge #4 - Lack of Support
Challenge #5 - Patience and Sustainability

CHALLENGE #1 - GAINING CLARITY

The greatest challenge many job seekers face is *gaining clarity*, figuring out what they want to do next. "NOW what?" After working for years, perhaps decades, and then getting laid off, it can seem like a daunting task to determine "What's next?" Emotionally you may not want to deal with it, and secondly you may not know where to begin. Even if you are currently working and looking to change jobs, change careers, or upgrade your current career through professional development, you may not know where or how to begin the process.

Or perhaps you graduated from college or got out of the military and you are ready to enter into the workforce. While some people have clarity about what they want to do next, many (if not most) do not.

When I graduated from college I had no idea what I wanted to do. I majored in Political Science, just because—no reason other than I had to choose a major and that seemed generic enough. "Now what?" "Where do I go from here?" "What do I do with my life?"

Those were but a few of the questions I was asking myself. If I had clarity when I was in college, my transition may have been much easier. But I didn't have clarity and my transition wasn't easy. If I had had a good coach or advisor, maybe that would have helped, but I didn't! And I am not the exception. Many others have and will follow in my footsteps.

In Chapter 6 I will walk you through *discovery activities* to help you gain clarity. There is no easy way to figure this out. You have to do the work! You must dig deep inside yourself for the answers. You must seek answers to tough, probing questions if you are to gain clarity on the direction of your journey.

In Chapter 8 we will discuss potential paths you could follow in your career with multiple options on each path. Many of the job seekers I have coached over the years struggle answering the million-dollar question, "What do I want to do when I grow up?" Or perhaps your question is, "What's my encore career?"[1] Until these questions are answered, the job seeker will struggle to pull together an effective communication strategy. It is hard to get others to help you find your dream job if you don't know what it looks like yourself.

Personally, it took me years to figure out what I wanted to do when I grew up. Eventually I did—because I did the work. I experimented, I explored, I read, I volunteered, I stretched, I observed, I studied. Figuring out your dream job is a process, most of the time.

During this time of transition, invest time in yourself. *Experiment, explore, read, volunteer, stretch, observe, study, and most importantly, do the work.* If you do, you will be blessed with many unexpected benefits during the job search/career transition process.

Throughout the book I have included resources, tools, and information to help you explore and discover your ideal job/career. Be sure to complete all of the discovery activities included; particularly in Chapter 6; and thoroughly review Chapter 7 entitled **Discover Your Passion.**

Completing the work in this book is one very important step toward gaining perspective and clarity in your transition project. One step at a time—be *persistent*, *persevere*, be *patient*, and the pieces of the puzzle will start to fall into place.

CHALLENGE #2 - STAYING FOCUSED

Another challenge is the *ability to stay focused*. A lack of focus usually occurs for one of three reasons:

1. Emotions
2. Not having a plan and/or not working the plan
3. Focusing on the past, not the future

SEEK EMOTIONAL SUPPORT

You will experience highs and lows during your journey to find employment and/or a new career. We all need emotional support to help us move through challenging times. Reaching out to others for emotional support is not a sign of weakness, but of wisdom. In some cases, you may reach out to a family member or close friend. Perhaps you need a professional such as a coach or counselor to help you move through the stages of adjusting to change. Reach out to others as needed. There is no shame, only gain!

(**Note**: See the end of this chapter for a description of the *Stages of Adjusting to Change*.)

HAVE A PLAN AND WORK THE PLAN

Having a plan and working the plan is critical if you are to find success in a reasonable time frame. A *plan* provides direction—and then you must follow the plan to get where you want to go—*action required*! If you need someone to hold you accountable to your plan, then find someone who will help keep you on track. This is where a professional coach may come in handy. In most cases, a family member is not your best choice, as it is too easy to disregard them when you feel lazy and uninspired. If you cannot afford a coach, understandably some of you cannot, then seek out the support of a volunteer from your local job seeker or career transition group. Also see what help is available to you from your local community college.

FOCUS ON MOVING FORWARD

Focusing on the past will do little to move you forward in your career. Draw from your past experiences and lessons learned to help you in your job search. But do not dwell on "What if...?" and "If only...." Getting *stuck* in the past will not serve you at all. Time to move on to **New Opportunities Waiting—NOW!**

In life, you are either moving forward or you are moving backwards,
you will grow or you will decay. There is no standing still.

Take time now to examine the **things that will cause you to lose focus.** What can you do, or whom can you call on, to help you remain focused and productive regarding your job search goals and objectives?

CHALLENGE #3 - NEGATIVE MINDSET

Most of us do not like change and uncertainty. Having to deal with the unplanned and undesirable task of finding new employment can often take a toll on one's attitude and belief system.

During any time of transition, your *mindset* will have a tremendous impact on the results you get. A person's mindset is made up of assumptions, perceptions, and beliefs that they have about themselves and others. Your mindset will impact your attitude, the actions that you take (or don't take), and the possibilities you envision for your future.

Some of the questions, feelings, and attitudes I have heard/observed from job seekers over the years include:

- "Why me?"
- "What if...?"
- Feelings of entitlement
- "I can do it by myself."
- "I can't do it; it's too hard!"
- "Someone else needs to do it for me—not my job!"
- Negative mindset ("I am too old." "I can't learn new things." "I have nothing to offer.")

In the job search process, your mindset is critical. A positive attitude and believing in yourself is necessary if you are to sell yourself to a potential employer. You must have confidence, and confidence does not grow with a negative mindset.

Instead of thinking:

I'm too old/too young

I don't have the experience

I'm not as experienced as...

I don't have the education

I don't have the training

Think and Repeat:

I am knowledgeable

I am competent

I am confident

I have a lot to offer

I can do this—I got this!

MINDSET—your greatest ally or your greatest obstacle!

Action Item # 6

Honestly assess your **mindset toward your job search project**. What, if anything, do you need to do to adjust your attitude, beliefs, and build confidence? Explore your options and the resources available to you and take the necessary steps to move forward. Use the form provided to capture your thoughts and ideas. I have provided some examples to help you understand the intent of this tool. See the **Career Tools** section for a blank template at **www. ProjectCareerQuest.com**.

MINDSET ASSESSMENT

(i.e.: Assumptions, Perceptions, Attitude, Beliefs)

Current Mindset & Date	Specific Example	How to Adjust Mindset/Build Confidence	Resources Needed
Victim mentality (date)	"Why me?"	Seek counseling	Company EAP program/ counselor
Ready to give up (date)	"This is too hard; I'm not making any progress."	Join a job seeker group to learn from the experiences of others, to share ideas and job leads	Career coach; an accountability partner

CHALLENGE #4 - LACK OF SUPPORT

Many of the job seekers I meet have support because they have come looking for it. They show up at job seeker groups. They use services they have been provided by their previous employer. But then there are those who sit at home, alone and isolated. If that's you, or anyone you know, there is help out there. With so many people unemployed and in transition, there are many resources that have sprung up to help those in need of guidance and direction. Go online and search, ask people you know for guidance. Check out your local community college, many offer free courses to the unemployed and under-employed. Reach out to your local Employment Security Commission.[2] There are networking groups and professional organizations—you are not alone! Seek assistance, ask for help, find available resources, and build your transition team.

CHALLENGE #5 - PATIENCE AND SUSTAINABILITY

Finding a job—the right job, a challenging job, a satisfying job—takes time, no doubt about it. Finding a job is work, hard work! Figuring out what you want to do, dealing with your emotions, dealing with the emotions of others, staying focused, dealing with disappointment and rejection can be exhausting. How do you sustain the momentum and keep yourself motivated?

The journey will be different for each of you. Some will find it more challenging than others. As mentioned in Challenge #4, don't try to go it alone. Who you surround yourself with, and the support you seek, will be critical to your ability to carry on.

Some job seekers may give up quickly, while others will never give up. Know where you are on that spectrum and ask for help as needed. Finding a job is a process that requires *persistence, perseverance, patience,* and *hard work.*

"Patience is bitter, but its fruit is sweet."
—*Aristotle*

Action Item #7

I may or may not have hit on your **top five challenges**. Take time now to jot down your challenges, or expected challenges, and brainstorm strategies to overcome them. What resources will you need? Awareness is always the first step. See the **Career Tools** section for a blank template at **www.ProjectCareerQuest.com**.

JOB SEARCH CHALLENGES

Job Search Challenge	Strategy to Overcome	Resources Needed

STAGES OF ADJUSTING TO CHANGE*

Denial	Resistance	Acknow-ledgment	Acceptance	Adaptation
Maintain Status Quo	Anger, Frustration, Apathy	Change is Inevitable	Focus on the Future	Commitment, Executing the Plan

I have found that there are five predictable stages of *adjusting to change*; this would include the loss of a job. It is normal and predictable to go through these stages. I share this model with you so you will know that you are not alone in the feelings and emotions you may be experiencing. The five stages include:

1. **Denial** - When a major change or loss occurs the first stage encountered is denial. In the denial stage people will attempt to avoid the change, pretend it did not happen, and/or maintain the status quo. Occasionally someone who has lost their job will try to hide their loss from others feeling ashamed or embarrassed.

2. **Resistance** - Signs of resistance include anger, frustration, and apathy. This is where the "why me" syndrome may occur. It's natural to feel these emotions but you do not want to get stuck here. Seek help to work through this stage.

3. **Acknowledgment** - Acknowledgment occurs when a person begins to accept that the change is inevitable and starts looking at options to deal with the change. This could include acknowledging the loss of a job or the loss of job satisfaction.

4. **Acceptance** - Focusing on the future and new ways of doing things is a sign that an individual has moved into the acceptance stage. This is the beginning of the *planning phase* to move forward.

5. **Adaptation** - Embracing and supporting the change occurs when the job seeker has developed a *job search strategy* to deal with their current circumstances and is successfully *executing the plan*. Progress is being made.

The amount of time spent in each of these stages will vary significantly depending on a number of factors including a person's resiliency to change and if they have a support system in place. And it is possible to make progress and later regress.

Trying to go through a job loss alone can get one stuck. Stuck in denial perhaps, stuck in resistance very likely. Applying the various strategies addressed in this book, and utilizing the tools and templates provided, will help you move forward towards acceptance and adaptation. Reach out to resources available to help you work through each of these stages appropriately. Doing so will help you gain momentum and eventually find success.

*Adapted from the Kubler-Ross Model[3] on stages of adjusting to grief from Elisabeth Kubler-Ross' book on *Death and Dying*.[4]

CHALLENGES OF WORKING WITH JOB SEEKERS

Before I move off of the topic of job search challenges, I want to share one of my challenges of working with job seekers. It's my biggest frustration, a pet peeve really—call it what you want. These challenges are not unique to me; others working with job seekers have shared similar experiences.

I am a person who likes helping others. I like helping people meet their challenges with confidence. It is so rewarding to see someone move through the stages of adjusting to change after losing their job (or job satisfaction) and see them find success. But not all job seekers find success. Some job seekers get stuck in the denial and resistance stages. Leaders and facilitators of career transition services, myself included, try as we may, cannot help everyone. You see, it is not so much about what we do but about what the job seeker does or does not do. As you will hear me say time and time again throughout this book, the job seeker (*You*, if that's the case) is ultimately responsible for his or her own success. Yes, there are many people who will help along the way, but if the job seeker is not committed to his or her own success, then success will elude them.

Over the years I have determined that job seekers fall into one of two broad categories. There are "job seekers" and then there are, what I call, the "job suckers."

A true job seeker is someone dedicated to completing his or her job search project successfully. They want meaningful employment and will do what it takes to find a job or more satisfying career. There are varying degrees here of dedication and determination, but ultimately, they know they are in charge of their destiny.

Job suckers, on the other hand, are those who say they want success but are not willing to do the work and expect someone else to do the hard stuff for them. These folks will "suck the life right out of you" if you let them. They moan and groan because they are making no progress in their job search, yet they haven't put in the effort. They will take all the free time you are willing to give them but will not follow through and take action on activities necessary to move them forward.

One job seeker to whom I offered help stood me up twice when I agreed to meet her for coffee to review and help revise her resume. She did not call to cancel, she just didn't show up. Amazingly, she did not even apologize for either missed appointment but did reach out to me a third time to reschedule. I told her she would have to find someone else to work on her resume. She was rude, irresponsible, and full of excuses. While I like helping people, I do *not* want to waste my time with someone who is not committed to their own success and not respectful of my time and efforts.

Now, I could go on and on with these types of stories, but I won't. I share this with you only to bring attention to how annoying the job suckers can be. After a while no one wants to help them, not even their own families. They become their own worst enemy.

Job seekers are willing to share and help others. Job suckers rarely help anyone else. They are too focused on their own misery, bad luck, and excuses to help anyone, including themselves. So, will you be a Job Seeker or a Job Sucker? I think I know the answer to that, after all, you are reading this book. Okay, end of rant!

"The important thing in life is to have a great aim and to possess the aptitude and the perseverance to attain it."
—*Johann Wolfgang von Goethe*

☑ CHECKLIST - BEFORE YOU MOVE ON

☐ Have you done an assessment of your top job search challenges?

☐ Have you brainstormed and documented what you will do to meet your challenges?

☐ How's your mindset as you approach your job search project? Are you looking toward the possibilities? Or are you lamenting the loss of your job and the stress of the job search process?

☐ What stage are you in regarding dealing with change? (Awareness is very important to moving forward.)

☐ Are you focused on the **NOW** (**N**ew **O**pportunities **W**aiting) or are you stuck in the past? What can you do to help gain focus and move forward with your job search? What help do you need to enable you to move to accepting and embracing the change?

☐ Do you have clarity as to what you want to do next? If not, what do you need to do or whom do you need to engage to help you gain clarity?

☐ Do you have a support system in place to help guide you through the challenging process of finding meaningful employment? Do you have a strategy to build a support system?

☐ Do you know what resources are available in your community to support your job search/career transition?

Lessons Learned: *You will face many challenges as you approach and carry out your job search project. Identify your challenges and develop a plan to address and overcome them. You can do this, one step at a time. It is natural and inevitable that you will go through the stages of adjusting to change. Take note of where you are on that journey and seek help as needed. Awareness and the right attitude are critical to making progress and ultimately achieving success.*

PART 2

PLAN

Charting the Course

CHAPTER 4

ORGANIZING YOUR JOB SEARCH PROJECT

I will be guiding you through your job search process from a project management perspective. I am a certified Project Management Professional (PMP®)[1] and have been practicing and teaching project management for over two decades. The job search process is a project that can be effectively managed using best practices of project management. Here is a quick lesson in project management.

FOUR CRITERIA OF A PROJECT:

1. Goal-oriented
2. Interrelated activities
3. Time-bound
4. Unique

1. **Projects are goal-oriented** - Each of you has a specific goal as it relates to finding new employment. It may be to find similar work to what you have/had been doing. It may be to start your own business. Or it may be to go in a totally new direction. Whatever your case may be, at some point you will want to determine your goal for your job search project, the sooner the better.

2. **Projects include a set of interrelated activities** - The goal of this book is to teach you the interrelated activities that will help you complete your job search project successfully. If you follow the steps and use the tools and techniques described herein,

you will minimize the amount of time required to complete your project. You will increase your productivity and decrease the frustration factor.

3. **Projects are time-bound** - There is a definite beginning and end to a project. Your job search project started when you were notified that your position was being eliminated or when you decided it was time to move on and do something different. The end of your job search project will depend a lot on how much effort you put into finding a new position or career. If you treat the job search process like a job and work it five days a week for seven and a half to eight hours a day, your end date will come much sooner. If you casually work the job search process and allow many distractions and/or don't do the necessary work, or avoid it all together, this could be a very long and very frustrating project!

4. **Projects are unique** - No two-people reading this book will have the same experience(s) while transitioning from their current situation to another. Your journey will be unique to you. Use this book as a guideline to keep you focused and on track. Also, be sure to reach out to local resources: career transition support groups, local community colleges, and/or to a career coach to help you meet your unique challenges.

—◦◦◦—

Word of CAUTION While you are looking for employment you may hear some of the following:

"Honey, now that you are not working can you do _____?"

"Now that you are unemployed can you serve on _____ committee?"

"Now that you have lots of time on your hands would you mind doing _____ for me?"

REMEMBER—you are working. In fact, you have loads of work to do! Do not allow yourself to get sidetracked. Set *boundaries* and a clear understanding that you are working on a very important project. Learn to say "no" if necessary. "No" is not a bad word, it only means that there are more important things for you to say "yes" to right now. Staying focused is critical if you wish to have a relatively short job search/career transition project.

—◦◦◦—

Now that you have an understanding of what constitutes a project, let's focus on how to organize your project. All projects have processes they go through from the beginning of the project to its completion. The processes include:

Project Initiation
Project Planning
Project Execution
Project Monitor and Control
Project Close Out

(**Note:** This book has been organized to follow the project management process groups as identified by the Project Management Institute (PMI).[2])

PROJECT INITIATION

If you have recently started your job search or career transition project you are in the initiation process. In project initiation, a *need* is recognized—in your case, the need to find a new job or career opportunity. In business projects, a cost/benefit analysis is completed, a go/no-go decision made, a business case is written and submitted for approval, and a project charter developed assigning the project manager.

If your job was eliminated, the go/no-go decision has already been made for you, and it's time to embark on your project! If you are contemplating leaving your current position for something more fulfilling, then some reflection and analysis will be needed as you make your go/no-go decision. You might even want to do a cost/benefit analysis. Assuming you decide it is time to move on, then you are ready to initiate your career transition project and take action to move forward.

In the world of projects, the project manager is named in the initiation process. One very important thing to recognize here is that YOU are the Project Manager of your job search/career transition project. Never been a project manager before? Well you are now! And I want you to be the best project manager you can be. You have a lot at stake here.

Although there is no need here for a business case, I highly recommend you prepare a **project charter**. A project charter will outline your career objectives, high-level deliverables, and other essential information that will bring clarity and an understanding of what needs to be done to achieve the success you desire. I have created a template for you and have also developed a sample project charter to aid in your understanding and use of this document. While this might seem like a lot of work to kick off your job search/career transition project, I promise it will serve you well. *Do not overlook* this document or skip this step. It will provide you focus, direction, and vision. Both the template and sample project charter can be found in the **Career Tools** section at **www.ProjectCareerQuest.com**.

Some of the things you will document in the **project charter** include:

- Project name
- Project manager
- Project objectives
- Key deliverables
- Key stakeholders
- Core team members
- Key milestones
- Core competencies
- Key accomplishments
- High-level list of project activities
- Risk assessment
- Assumptions
- Constraints
- Training needs

To kick-off your project successfully, start by completing your project charter. You may not have all the information available to you initially but do your best to complete and revisit it as you gain more insight.

(**Note**: If you are a project manager seeking PMP® certification, keep track of the time you spend on this project. You may be able to submit the time to qualify for the PMP® exam. If you are already a certified project manager you may be able to submit some of your time working on your career transition project for PDU's, also known as professional development units.)

PROJECT PLANNING

As always, if you hope to be successful, you need to have a good plan in place and then work the plan. "Fail to plan and plan to fail." Or at least plan on a very long job search process filled with mistakes, frustration, and rejection.

Yes, planning how you will go about finding your next job is essential for your success. The majority of this book is about planning: planning your overall approach, planning your communication strategy, knowing what documents you will need to prepare, conducting your market research, planning and preparing for interviews, etc. Once you have your plan developed and documentation prepared, it's on to execution.

PROJECT EXECUTION

If a plan is to succeed it must be executed, and execution is more predictable and controllable with a good plan. They go hand-in-hand. Once you know your strategy and approach and have prepared appropriately, you are ready to take action. You will not be required to have everything planned out and completed in order to start executing part of your plan. In other words, you will not need to complete every document I mention in this book before you start contacting people and taking steps forward on your journey to finding new employment. But be sure you have a plan in place so you don't move forward haphazardly. Good results come from good planning.

PROJECT MONITOR AND CONTROL

In every project there is the need to monitor and control what's happening to ensure you are getting the results you desire. As you start to implement your plan, monitor the results by asking yourself if things are going as *planned* and as *desired*. If they are not, then you will need to adjust your plan to get more desirable results.

For example, perhaps your resume still needs some tweaking to speak to your targeted audience. Ask for feedback from people who review your resume, particularly recruiters and hiring managers. If they say that you did not have enough emphasis on something they were looking for, and you do have that experience, you can go back and revise your resume based on their feedback. It may not help you for that job interview, but it will help you in future interviews.

After each interview, step back and objectively assess your performance. Ask yourself, "What did I do well and what could I have done better?" This type of assessment will help you monitor your performance and get better results moving forward. I have prepared an *interview assessment* tool for you that can be found in the **Career Tools** section at **www.ProjectCareerQuest.com**.

PROJECT CLOSE OUT

Every project has the need to close out certain things for the project to be considered a success. When you finally land a new position, you will want to let people know, especially those who have helped you along the way. It is advisable to wait until you have a signed employment contract and have started your new job before you make major announcements, things are subject to change.

If you have done your job well and engaged people to help you in your job search project, it is appropriate that you thank them for their support and provide an update on your status. In the process of looking for a new job or career, you will likely make many new contacts and build some strong networks. Don't let those networks die. You never know when you will need to call on your contacts again. Also, you should offer your support to them should they need it in the future.

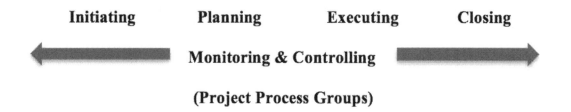

| Initiating | Planning | Executing | Closing |

Monitoring & Controlling

(Project Process Groups)

 Lessons Learned: *Projects have distinct processes with specific activities to be completed in each of the process groups. Initiating is the identification of a need. Project planning is critical to a successful job search project. Planning is defining what to do and how to do it. Executing is implementing according to the plan. Monitoring and Controlling is making sure the plan is working and getting the desired results—adjusting as needed. And a proper project Close Out includes thanking those who help you deliver a successful project and updating them with your current status.*

JOB SEARCH KNOWLEDGE AREAS

The practice of project management is comprised of ten knowledge areas as defined by the Project Management Institute (PMI).[3] For a project to be completed successfully, it should address key issues in each of the knowledge areas. I will briefly go through each of them and let you know how they relate to your job search project.

1. SCOPE MANAGEMENT

Before you can execute a project successfully you must have a complete understanding of requirements and a plan for what needs to be done. Project scope is about defining all of the activities that must be done to complete the project successfully. The biggest part of project scope planning is to create what is called a "work breakdown structure" or WBS. A work breakdown structure is a deliverable-oriented breakdown of a project into smaller project components. It is a detailed list of all the activities of the project. (Think of an outline you wrote in school before writing a term paper.)

WORK BREAKDOWN STRUCTURE (WBS)

To make sure you have a good understanding of what will be required of you in your job search project, I suggest you create a work breakdown structure and list each of the activities you must engage in and/or complete. For example, you can start with the name of your project. I call it "Project Career Quest," but it's your project so call it what you want. Next you will list below the project title the major categories of work to be completed. Then each of those categories will be broken down into smaller, more manageable activities.

Use post-it notes to list out all the activities you need to engage in and complete during your job search project. Write one activity per post-it note, such as:

- Determine career objective

- Complete market research

- Hire a career coach

- Prepare elevator speech

- Attend networking events

- Develop resume

- Develop marketing plan

- Complete LinkedIn profile

- Develop SOAR stories

- Conduct mock interviews

- Interview with prospective employers

- Plan negotiating strategy

- Negotiate and sign employment contract

You might even want to start with the ten Knowledge Areas listed in this section as your main categories and then add your activities under each of those headings. Once you have brainstormed, reviewed, and listed all the activities you must complete, you can then create the hierarchal top-down structure with all the activities defined. Main categories will be at the top of your WBS and then progressively more detailed information will be included as you work down to the lowest level of activities. This will provide you with the "big picture" view of what must be done to successfully execute and complete your job search project.

The WBS is the "heart" of project planning and you will want to create a work breakdown structure to ensure you know what must be done if you are to achieve success. Later you can add timelines, resources needed to complete project activities, people needed to help facilitate or coach you through an activity, risks associated with activities, etc. Instructions for completing a WBS can be found in the **Career Tools** section at **www.ProjectCareerQuest.com**.

SAMPLE WBS

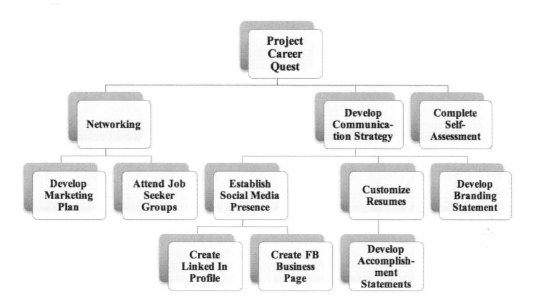

(**Note**: This sample is by no means complete, simply an abbreviated illustration of what a hierarchal work breakdown structure might look like. You would continue to develop this hierarchal structure until you have included all of the activities that need to be completed for a successful career transition project.)

2. SCHEDULE/TIME MANAGEMENT

As stated earlier in the book, my goal is to help you complete your job search project in a timely and efficient manner while achieving the goals you have established. To do so you will need to manage your time effectively.

For starters, plan how much time you want to devote to your job search project on a daily and weekly basis. My suggestion is that you treat it like your job, which was probably a minimum of forty hours a week (assuming you are currently unemployed). Along with the time you spend on your job search, be sure to plan time to exercise, read, spend time with family and friends, and take care of yourself. Your mental, physical, and emotional health are very important to your productivity and ultimately your success.

For a good book on time management read Stephen R. Covey's book entitled *First Things First*.[4] Putting first things first is about focusing on the important things that help us fulfill our purpose and achieve our personal and professional goals. He describes two things that guide us in our daily life, the *compass* and the *clock*. The compass represents where we want to go in life: our mission, our vision, our goals, and our plans to achieve success. The clock represents our schedules and how we spend our time.

Being aware of how and where you spend your time during your job search project will help you use your time more efficiently and effectively, enabling you to achieve your goals. A summary of the quadrant approach discussed in Covey's book follows.

The principles shared in Covey's book were originally established and used by General Dwight D. Eisenhower and are referred to as the *Eisenhower Principle*[5] of time management. The four quadrants are said to be how General Eisenhower organized and prioritized his work; both as an Army General and as the 34th President of the United States; for maximum efficiency and results. Upon reviewing this model, you should begin to understand that to get the results you want and achieve success, you must spend the majority of your time in Quadrant 2, the "quadrant of productivity."

FIRST THINGS FIRST

(Summary)

Quadrant 1 is the *Quadrant of Urgency,* where we put out fires and handle those things that are *important and urgent.* There are two types of activities that occur in this quadrant: those that we could not have foreseen and those that we put off until the last minute. Many of us spend a lot of time in Quadrant 1 because we failed to plan and so we are constantly in reactive mode. If you plan well you should not have to spend much time in Quadrant 1, because through planning you have eliminated much of the urgency.

Quadrant 2 is the *Quadrant of Quality,* where we focus on the *important but not urgent.* Activities performed in Quadrant 2 will help you achieve your personal and professional goals. Examples of things done in this quadrant include planning, organizing, taking care of relationships and our health (such as exercising). This is where we should be spending approximately 80% of our time. The key word here is "should." Unfortunately, many of us spend very little time in Quadrant 2. Spending most of your time in Quadrant 2 during your transition project will enable you to meet your specific project goals and achieve success sooner. **Quadrant 2 is where productivity happens!**

Quadrant 3 is the *Quadrant of Distractions,* where people do what is *urgent but not important.* Focusing on activities in this quadrant will keep you from achieving your goals. An example of this would be racing to answer your phone every time it rings regardless of what you were doing at the moment. Checking emails, Facebook, and other forms of social media constantly detracts from your productivity. If you want to have more time in your day to be productive then you must prioritize your time and stop allowing the unimportant to be urgent! (Using social media as a tool to help you network, research, and get noticed is not wasteful. Remember to stay focused on your business goals during the time you devote to your project each day.)

Quadrant 4 is considered the *Quadrant of Waste,* where time is spent doing things that are *not important and not urgent.* Activities in this quadrant are also distractions and should be avoided as much as possible. Often activities in Quadrant 4 are things others want you to do but do not contribute to you achieving your goals. Establishing boundaries and learning to say "no" is critical if you are to achieve your career goals. Other examples of Quadrant 4 activities include watching hours of mindless television, playing video games, spending time socializing on social media, etc. We all need some down time, but time spent in Quadrant 4 should be limited.

No one, no matter how influential they might be or how much money they may have, has more time in the day than you or me. We all have exactly 1440 minutes in each day. You get to choose how you spend them. If you plan and organize your day, you can spend the majority of your time in Quadrant 2 doing the important things related to your job search and making progress toward your ultimate goal. If you choose to spend a majority of your time in Quadrants 3 and 4 doing the unimportant, you will have a very long, frustrating, and fruitless job search. Also, if you don't plan your day you may end up spending unnecessary time in Quadrant 1, in reactive mode.

Quadrant 1	**Quadrant 2**
Quadrant of Urgency	**Quadrant of Quality**
Important & Urgent	Important & Not Urgent
Putting out fires, handling emergencies, being reactive due mostly to a lack of planning	Planning, organizing, building relationships, being productive

Quadrant 3	**Quadrant 4**
Quadrant of Distractions	**Quadrant of Waste**
Not Important & Urgent	Not Important & Not Urgent
Constantly checking emails, making the unimportant urgent	Watching hours of mindless TV, playing video games, "vegging out," wasting time

(For more detail on the **Quadrant Approach to time management**, see Stephen R. Covey and A. Roger Merrill's book *First Things First*.[6] Also research the *Eisenhower Time Management Matrix*.[7])

"The key is not to prioritize what's on your schedule, but to schedule your priorities."
—*Stephen R. Covey*

In today's business environment one of the biggest challenges and potential time wasters is the addiction to checking email. As one of my mentors, Brendon Burchard would say, "Checking emails first thing in the morning simply allows someone else to set your agenda for the day." Avoid the temptation by scheduling a time, say twice a day, which you will check and respond to email. Perhaps you check emails at 11 a.m. and 4 p.m., allowing yourself thirty minutes to one hour each time to respond to messages. The rest of the day is yours to spend being productive according to *your* plan for the day. (When you are expecting an email from a recruiter or hiring manager you may need to check more frequently. Use your time wisely.)

In the **Career Tools** section (online) I have included a *Productivity Report* that you can use to schedule your time daily if you chose. Be protective of your time and you will get so much more accomplished and you won't find yourself wondering at the end of each day where all the time went. As John Maxwell would say, time cannot be controlled nor managed—you can only manage yourself!

Track your time over the next five to seven days to determine where you are spending your 1440 minutes each day (Quadrant 1, 2, 3, or 4). Are you efficient? Are you productive? How could you better plan your day to use your time more wisely to achieve your career goals?

Keep a calendar; prioritize your activities. Use the *productivity report* provided online, create your own, or check out productivity tools developed by Brendon Burchard, Michael Hyatt, or Franklin Covey. And yes, there are plenty of apps to help you plan your time as well. Use whatever tool you choose to schedule your days for optimum productivity and results. (See *Productivity Report* template in the **Career Tools** section at **www.ProjectCareerQuest.com**.)

3. COST MANAGEMENT

During your time of transition, plan carefully how you will manage your finances. You may have some money coming in from a severance package, but what you don't know is how long your job search will take. Having a monthly budget is a good start, but now you may need to "tighten the belt" and cut expenses to ensure you have enough money to carry you through as long as possible. If you don't have a budget, I suggest setting up one immediately. It is also important, if you have a family, to discuss how your family will be spending money while you are working on your job search project. It will take the support of the entire family to cut expenses and manage your budget effectively. I personally like Dave Ramsey's books on financial management and budgeting.

 Dave Ramsey has numerous books and courses on managing your resources and preparing a budget. Check out *The Total Money Makeover*[8] and *Financial Peace University*.[9]

4. STAKEHOLDER MANAGEMENT

Every project has stakeholders. These are people and organizations that have an interest in your success (or failure). Stakeholders are those who may be impacted by the results of your project and have power and influence to help you be successful in your project. Your family members are stakeholders. Your neighbors and former colleagues potentially have an interest in your success and can be influential in helping you make key contacts and networking. Consider making a list of your key stakeholders and how they can support you in your job search project. (See *Stakeholder Matrix* in the **Career Tools** section at **www.ProjectCareerQuest.com**.)

5. QUALITY MANAGEMENT

Quality, as it relates to your job search project, is doing the right things, at the right time, in the right way. Quality is about having a vision of success and a plan to follow to get the outcome you desire. Quality is about following best practices, keeping track of lessons learned, using the tools and templates provided, and putting in the work required to achieve your career goals. Following the guidelines in this book will help you deliver a quality project!

6. RESOURCE MANAGEMENT

Project managers rarely run successful projects alone, instead they build a team to help them. As the project manager of your job search project, *Project Career Quest,* or whatever you decide to call it, you will want to build your project team. Think about who can help you be successful.

- Who can help you identify job opportunities?

- Who can help you brainstorm, explore ideas, and generate leads?

- Who can help you network with key decision makers?

- Who do you know that knows someone within a company you are interested in pursuing?

- What other resources do you need to be successful in your career transition project?

Most jobs (80-85%) are found through networking, not spending hours online searching the Internet. Start building your team now. Ask people to support you with your project. Be selective with whom you surround yourself. Surrounding yourself with the right people is important!

The right people will help you gain clarity and pull you into your destiny.
The right people will lift you up and fuel your fire.

In the **Career Tools** section, at **www.ProjectCareerQuest.com**, I have provided you with a tool to help you build and engage your project team, it's called a *Marketing Plan*. Check it out and see how you can successfully engage others to help boost your performance and build your network. The personal Marketing Plan is discussed in detail in Chapter 10 on **Networking for Results**.

7. COMMUNICATION MANAGEMENT

Communication management for the job seeker involves creating your overall communication strategy for your career transition project. Chapter 9 is dedicated to your communication strategy and how to get your message out. In fact, most of Part Three of this book, chapters nine through fourteen, are about your communication strategy.

Also, as a job seeker it is critical for you to understand that we do not all communicate the same. The words we choose to use will not resonate with everyone. Effective communication is critical to building the trust and rapport needed to land a position—the coveted job you desire. You may think you are communicating clearly, but your words may fall short of accomplishing your goal.

As you read further in the book you will find a chapter on **Understanding Personality and Communication Styles,** Chapter 13. Preparation is key to success. Prepare yourself for networking opportunities and interviews by reviewing this chapter.

8. RISK MANAGEMENT

All projects have risks, it is the nature of dealing with change. There are positive risks and there are negative risks.

The positive risks are known as *opportunity risks*. Some of the opportunity risks you will encounter along the way include: getting to know yourself better, meeting new people, building new relationships, and hopefully landing a job that's more interesting, exciting, challenging (you choose the adjective) than your previous position.

The negative risks are known as *threats*. Along the way you will encounter many threats to your project's success. You will want to anticipate them and have a plan to avoid them, overcome them, and/or reduce their probability and impact.

If you made a list of your potential potholes in Chapter 2 then you have already identified some of the things that may threaten your success. If you skipped over that exercise, I recommend you go back and do it now. Also, review the top job search challenges you identified in Chapter 3 and make sure you have developed strategies to overcome them. It is to your advantage to take a proactive approach versus reacting to negative things when they occur. Be prepared and your journey will be much smoother.

9. PROCUREMENT MANAGEMENT

Okay, how does procurement fit in here? For starters, you might need to procure some training to fill in skill gaps you may have. Maybe you need a certification to land your ideal job. Maybe you need to sharpen your leadership skills or learn the latest technology. Maybe your career path includes starting your own business and you need some training on topics associated with being an entrepreneur. Some of the questions to explore, as it relates to needed skills include:

- Which of your skills need refining or updating?

- What training will provide the greatest value and impact to achieving your career goals?

- Where do you get the training?

- Can you get the training online?

- Will you take the training in a classroom setting?

- How much will it cost?

- How much time will it take to complete?

- What are the qualifications of the people/organization providing the training?

- What's their success rate?

Make sure you do your homework and select high quality vendors with a proven track record. Spend your time and money wisely when it comes to *brushing up* your skills.

10. INTEGRATION MANAGEMENT

Integration is about tying all the other knowledge areas together. I like to think of the other nine knowledge areas as pieces to the puzzle and integration management as the glue that holds everything together. Throughout your job search project, you will be integrating a number of activities to pull your plan together and accomplish your goals. Leave out one of the nine knowledge areas and your project is incomplete, success will elude you!

I see many training organizations promise great things; "Take our _____ certification course and we guarantee a 98% pass rate on the exam." The reality is most organizations, if not all, have no way of tracking their results accurately. If you don't believe me, call and ask them how they track their results. I have, and the responses are vague at best. Their metrics are most certainly based on people who self-report back to them. Those who are unsuccessful in their pursuit of a certification rarely report back and no one is required to report back. The numbers are not truly reflective of reality. Your best way of validating someone's track record is to talk to others who have used their services.

I am often asked if I can promise if someone takes my PMP® Exam Prep class that they will pass the exam. My response is always "no." Since I am not studying and taking the exam for them, I cannot *guarantee* they will pass *unless* they are willing to do the work. They must do the reading, the study, the preparation, more study, and even more study if they are to pass. I do approximately 20% of the work; they *must* do the rest.

Check multiple references to determine the qualifications of the training provider. Remember, you are ultimately responsible for your own success, whether it is taking a course to obtain a needed certification or landing a position. Put in the effort and you will be successful.

"Anyone can steer the ship but it takes a leader to set the course."
—*John C. Maxwell*

Create a **work breakdown structure** (WBS) for your job search project, including the *total scope* of what needs to be done to successfully land meaningful employment. Complete as much as you can at this point in the process and continue to add to and refine it as you gain more knowledge and insight into what must be done to execute your project successfully. In project management lingo this is known as *rolling wave planning*. Instructions for completing a WBS can be found in the **Career Tools** section at **www.ProjectCareerQuest.com**.

Be sure to review all of the job search knowledge areas above and determine what you must do to have a successful project. Make sure all required activities are included on your WBS.

Create a **list of stakeholders** for your job search project. Who will be impacted during your time of transition? Who has an interest in your success? How can your stakeholders support you in your job search project? Who can help you find job opportunities and connect you with key decision makers and hiring managers? With whom can you network? A template has been included in the **Career Tools** section that you can use to list and analyze your stakeholders. See **www.ProjectCareerQuest.com**.

CHECKLIST - BEFORE YOU MOVE ON

☐ Do you have an understanding of what it's going to take to plan, organize, execute, monitor and control, and close out your job search project?

☐ Have you established appropriate boundaries with friends, family, and others so they understand that you are working and not free to take on unplanned activities at this time? Do they understand that you have a project to complete?

☐ Have you established yourself as the Project Manager of your job search project and do you have a clear understanding of your responsibilities, objectives, and deliverables? Are you committed to your success?

☐ Have you identified your project stakeholders and others who can help you network and identify opportunities?

☐ Have you discussed with your family and other key stakeholders how they can support you in your job search project?

☐ Have you created a work breakdown structure (WBS) outlining all of the activities/ scope, documentation, costs, time, resources, and risk associated with your job search project?

☐ Do you have any skill gaps for which you need training or retraining?

 Lessons Learned: *Effective project managers understand in advance what it takes to bring in a project successfully. Finding a job or new career requires a lot of knowledge and planning. Having a clear vision of what it will take to complete the career transition journey and a detailed roadmap are key to success.*

(**Note:** You will not be able to complete all the action items, checklists, and other activities suggested throughout the book until you have read or at least reviewed most of the chapters. However, it is advisable to get started now and continue to add to your WBS and other tools and templates as you gain clarity and understanding.)

CHAPTER 5

BUILDING YOUR TEAM

If you recall, earlier in the book I stated that *you* are the Project Manager for your career transition project. Although projects require a Project Manager, who is ultimately responsible and accountable for the success of the project, all projects will also include a support team to see things through to conclusion. Team members may come and go but the Project Manager is rarely alone in accomplishing the project's objectives.

Who will be on your team for your career transition project? Your success in this process of transitioning from one job or career to another (or transitioning from college, military duty, family duties, etc.) is dependent on building a team who can support, guide, coach, and mentor you.

In Chapter 4 I talked about creating your list of stakeholders, those who can impact your success or failure. If you completed that activity my suggestion is that you go back and take a look at it now. If you have not completed that activity, this would be a good time to do so.

The purpose of building your team is to have people who will:

PROVIDE EMOTIONAL SUPPORT AND GUIDANCE

- Support you emotionally
- Help you move forward and encourage you to stop looking back

- Guide you throughout the process
- Help you navigate your challenges
- Help you overcome the "what if" and the "why me" syndrome
- Coach and mentor you
- Help build your confidence
- Help you say "no" to lesser things so you can say "yes" to greater things
- Help you avoid your "potholes"
- Help squash the "gremlins"
- Lift you up when you need encouragement
- Be a sounding board
- Help you celebrate your successes
- Love you where you are

HELP YOU "KNOW YOURSELF"

- Help you in the discovery process
- Help you identify your strengths, gifts, and personal characteristics
- Help you articulate your core competencies
- Help you gain clarity

HELP YOU PLAN AND ORGANIZE YOUR JOB SEARCH

- Help you in the planning process
- Help you brainstorm and generate ideas
- Help you identify job opportunities
- Help you develop a WBS
- Help you establish and maintain a budget
- Help you develop a schedule
- Help you with productivity pointers

- Help you prepare your communication strategy and supporting documentation (resume, marketing plan, LinkedIn profile, etc.)

- Teach you tools and strategies for success (mind mapping, Force Field Analysis, vision boards, etc.)

- Help you navigate the unemployment issues

HELP YOU EXECUTE YOUR PLAN AND STAY ON COURSE

- Keep you on track

- Help you overcome roadblocks

- Hold you accountable (creating a plan, executing your plan, meeting your goals, following through, etc.)

- Help you build your network

- Help you identify companies that may need your skill sets

- Help you do market research and generate job leads and contacts

- Help introduce you to hiring managers, recruiters, and other key decision makers

- Be a reference for you

- Help you prep for your job interviews

- Provide feedback

- Help you identify critical resources and training needs

- Teach you new skills

- Prepare you for negotiating your compensation package

Obviously, this is not one or two people but many, including trained professionals, volunteers, friends, and family. Many of those who will support you, you will meet through networking. Be sure to review the *Do's and Don'ts of Networking* in Chapter 10.

"Alone we can do so little, together we can do so much."
—*Helen Keller*

Action Item # 11

Who do you need on your project team? Who do you know that can help you successfully navigate your career transition project? Make a list of your **ideal project team**. Be sure to update your list regularly as you identify new needs. Consider who you need, when you need them, how they can help you, and how you can help them. Your team members are stakeholders. See the **Career Tools** section for the *Project Stakeholder template* at **www.ProjectCareerQuest.com**.

While you want to build a team of people to help you in your job search, remember *finding a job is your responsibility*, not theirs. Far too often I have seen job seekers try to relinquish the responsibility to someone who is trying to help them. Somehow, they think someone else should write their resume (without their input), prepare their marketing plan, and everything short of finding the job for them. Trust me, I see it happen all the time. Finding a job is not fun, and it is a lot of work, but it's not someone else's responsibility—it's the job seeker's responsibility. If you try to relinquish those duties to others you will be seen as a burden and your team members will quickly withdraw and you may become the *solo* Project Manager.

People will help you because they want to, not because they have to. If you are not doing what you are supposed to be doing and you lack follow through, commitment, and execution; your team will crumble (mutiny may be a better word). Your team is there to support your efforts, your hard work, your career transition project—not do the work for you!

Friends, neighbors, family, and former colleagues want to help you, but they do not want to be manipulated or used in the process. Take into consideration how you approach people and what you are asking them to do. Is it appropriate? Do you show appreciation for their help, support, and guidance? Are you open to their suggestions to learn and improve? When you ask to meet with someone do you make it convenient for them? Do you show up on time? When you ask for their time do you respect their time and not exceed the amount of time requested? Engage with your team appropriately.

If you have not had much success building your team then you may want to step back and objectively assess what you are doing or not doing that may be the cause. You will want to seek feedback about your approach; what's working and what's not working.

☑ CHECKLIST - BEFORE YOU MOVE ON

☐ Have you begun building your support team?

☐ Are you asking them to support you appropriately?

☐ When you ask someone to meet you to brainstorm or network, do you make it convenient for the other person?

☐ Do you respect peoples' time?

☐ Do you show gratitude to the people who support you?

☐ Are you reciprocating, providing support and information to others where you can?

Lessons Learned: *Building a team to support your job search efforts is critical to a successful transition. Finding others who can help you navigate the job market and other challenges you will face along the way will keep you on track and productive.*

Chapter 6

Getting to Know Yourself

Okay, now that you know how to set up your project and how to build a team, it's time to dig deep and get to know yourself. Yep, it's time to dig in and start figuring out who you are, where you've been, and what you want to do with your future. It's time to figure out your career objective(s) so you know in which direction to sail! You *must* know yourself and a desired outcome if you are to sell yourself to a prospective employer or establish yourself in your own business.

It seems you, of all people, should know who you are, what you like, what you want to do, and what drives you. But do you? My experience shows that most people do not really know themselves. "Tell me about yourself" stumps a lot of people, if not the majority, when they first embark on this journey.

I was once conducting a training session when one of the participants said she had just been asked that question in her recent job interview. "Tell me about yourself." She expressed her opinion that it was a stupid question (request actually) and could not understand why the interviewer had asked it. Well believe me, it is *not* a stupid question/request and it is one you will be asked over and over again and you need to prepare for it.

As it relates to your job search, hiring managers and others who may ask that question/request are not looking for your entire life story. Where you were born and where you went to elementary school is not important. What they really want to know is, "Tell me about yourself as it relates to the needs I have here at XYZ company." "Tell me about yourself as it relates to satisfying the needs of the job description and meeting the challenges and opportunities this organization faces."

Do you know yourself well enough to make major career decisions and life choices? If not, you've got some work to do. In this chapter, I will outline some of the things you will need to reflect on to have a clearer understanding of who you are, what you want to do moving forward, and what you have to offer an organization, future clients, or to anyone who would seek you out for a business engagement. For tools to help you complete your self-assessment see the **Career Tools** section at **www.ProjectCareerQuest.com**.

ESSENTIAL SELF-KNOWLEDGE

Some of the things you will want to explore and know about yourself include:

- Your career objective
- Personality style/preference
- Core competencies
- Functional and adaptive skills
- Personal traits and characteristics
- Strengths
- Gifts
- Core values
- Priorities
- Roles
- Interests
- Likes
- Dislikes
- Motivators
- Key accomplishments
- Activities that attract you
- Environments that attract you
- Management style (both yours and the style you prefer to work with)
- Career type
- Behavioral/internal barriers

"Whenever you want to achieve something, keep your eyes open,
concentrate and make sure you know exactly what it is you want.
No one can hit their target with their eyes closed."
—*Paulo Coelho*

CAREER OBJECTIVE

While I start here with career objective, some of you may not have a clue what your objective is until you have explored all of the categories listed in this section. Ultimately, the process of exploration will help you define your career objective. It will be hard for others to help you move in a career direction until you have clarity about your career objective(s). Your goal as you move through the list of things to explore is to see how the pieces fit together. Hopefully at some point you will see a pattern or have an "aha moment" that will begin to bring clarity to the direction you wish to proceed. You can start with a broad career objective, but in the end, you want to have a clear vision and be able to articulate your objective moving forward.

My career objective is: (Complete the other activities first, if necessary, and then return here when you have some clarity. I have included this first so that you understand your goal is to eventually be able to articulate your career objective.)

_____

_____

_____

CORE COMPETENCIES

Core competencies are your key areas of knowledge and expertise. Examples of core competencies would include things like computer skills, customer service, project management, business analysis, data management, programming, leadership, accounting, teaching, facilitating, patient care, etc. Your core competencies include your marketable and transferable skills. You must be clear on what your core competencies are as they are your *key selling points* along with your work accomplishments. When it comes to the interview process you will need to not only identify your top four to five core competencies, but also be able to provide specific examples of using your competencies in various business scenarios.

Core competencies can then be further broken down into the skills that comprise that competency. For example, if one of your core competencies is Project Management, under that you might include skills such as: leading projects, building high performing teams, coaching and mentoring others, developing and managing budgets and schedules, risk analysis, implementing risk mitigation strategies, etc.

If your core competency is Data Management, you might include those things required to effectively manage data such as: gathering and analyzing data, data architecture, data modeling, data maintenance, database administration, data integrity, data security, etc.

Perhaps your core competency is Supply Chain Management, then your supporting skills might be source selection, developing and negotiating terms and conditions, contract administration, and managing stakeholder relationships, to name a few.

Be sure to complete the personal *Marketing Plan* when you get to Chapter 10 on **Networking for Results**. It will require a listing of your core competencies and a list of your skills that make up that competency.

MY TOP FIVE CORE COMPETENCIES ARE:

1. _____

2. _____

3. _____

4. _____

5. _____

SKILLS

Associated with core competencies are the skills you possess. Skills include specific talents, abilities, and personal qualities that enable you to accomplish tasks and achieve your goals and objectives. Your skills can be grouped into two major buckets. The two major categories are *functional skills* and *adaptive skills* (may also be referred to as personal characteristics). Let's look at some examples of each.

Functional skills: Functional skills include those areas where you excel at work as it relates to:

1. Solving problems for your organization and customers
2. Creating opportunities for growth and development for the organization, customers, stakeholders, and employees
3. Working with data and ideas
4. Leading and managing people

Some examples of functional skills include, but not limited to: leading others, building high performing teams, strong analytical and problem-solving skills, influencing others, developing accurate budgets and schedules, relating to a diverse audience, designing and developing systems, coaching and mentoring people, facilitating change, conceiving and creating, effective at resolving conflict, and negotiating collaboratively.

Adaptive skills: Describe how you adjust to and prepare for the demands, challenges, and changes you and your organization will face.

If someone were to describe you, what adjectives would they use? Would they use words such as: assertive, confident, diplomatic, persuasive, persistent, patient, competitive, a person of integrity, ethical, hard worker, creative, compassionate, intuitive, detail-oriented, practical, or open-minded? What personal characteristics help you adapt and adjust to the demands and challenges you face at work and at home? Adaptive skills are essentially the same thing as personal characteristics.

See the **Career Tools** section at **www.ProjectCareerQuest.com** for a more comprehensive list of functional and adaptive skills.

FUNCTIONAL SKILLS

My top ten functional skills that help me excel at work include:

1. _____
2. _____
3. _____
4. _____
5. _____

6. _____
7. _____
8. _____
9. _____
10. _____

ADAPTIVE SKILLS

My top ten adaptive skills that help me prepare for demands, challenges, and change include:

1. _____
2. _____
3. _____
4. _____
5. _____

6. _____
7. _____
8. _____
9. _____
10. _____

As you identify your top ten functional and adaptive skills, focus on the skills you possess that will best serve you in your future career or position. Your skills may line up with what you have done in the past. On the other hand, the skills you may need most in the future may be slightly (or significantly) different depending on whether you seek similar work or a whole new career path.

—◦◦◦—

STRENGTHS

Strengths are those things at which you excel; things you do effortlessly. Your strengths may have been developed through your hard work and dedication. However, strengths can also come to you naturally and you may not always recognize them as such. Sometimes it is best to ask other people who know you well what they see as your strengths. If something comes to you easily, you may not recognize it as a strength, where others do.

Your strengths will include functional skills and adaptive skills (personal characteristics). Here you are trying to identify your top five to six strengths. If you refer to the **Career Tools** section at, **www.ProjectCareerQuest.com**, I have provided an exercise that you can use to identify your strengths. The exercise includes emailing trusted friends and colleagues to get their input. Some questions to ask yourself in identifying your strengths include:

- What do I do effortlessly?

- What do I do well that other people find difficult?

- What do others say I do extremely well?

LIST THREE THINGS THAT YOU ARE BRILLIANT AT DOING:

1. _____

2. _____

3. _____

_____

"Success is achieved by developing our strengths, not by eliminating our weaknesses."
— *Marilyn vos Savant*

 A good book that will help you discover your strengths is *Strengths Finder 2.0* by Tom Rath.[5] When you purchase the book, you will be given a unique access code to take an online assessment identifying your top five strengths. For an additional fee, you will receive a report accessing all thirty-four dimensions/most common talents that are a part of the Clifton Strengths Finder assessment.[6]

—◦◦◦—

GIFTS

Gifts come from a divine source, something we are born with, such as the ability to sing like a bird. (Definitely not one of my gifts!) For example, perhaps you have the natural ability to read people or a natural athletic ability. Or maybe you are a talented artist, or you sat down at a piano at age two and played music by ear. There is a fine line between strengths and gifts, but I do see a distinction. It matters little what category you put something in, what matters is that you recognize it is part of what makes you unique.

MY GIFTS INCLUDE:

_____

_____

_____

(Note: Even *gifts* need developing. Sometimes we don't discover our gifts until much later in life.)

CORE VALUES

Your core values are those things that you hold most important. Knowing them can help you make decisions about how you live your life, personally and professionally. Examples of values might be things such as: education, family, integrity, security, relationships, competence, creativity, adventure, kindness, honesty, loyalty, stability, truth, freedom, community, achievement, faith, etc. Having a clear understanding of your core values will help guide you in making important career decisions.

I find the following two questions helpful in determining and articulating one's values. I believe if you examine and reflect on these questions you will have more clarity around what you value most in life and in work.

1. What do you love deeply?

_____

_____

_____

2. What makes you righteously angry?

_____

_____

_____

In the **Career Tools** section at **www.ProjectCareerQuest.com**, I have included
a list of values. However, before you take a look at that list try to identify five to
ten things that you value highly. The list I have included may not include your
values. The list in the Career Tools section is by no means all-inclusive. If you look at the
list first, you may focus on what I have included and miss something that you truly value.

MY TOP FIVE–TEN CORE VALUES INCLUDE:

1. _____   6. _____

2. _____   7. _____

3. _____   8. _____

4. _____   9. _____

5. _____   10. _____

Out of the five to ten that you have identified, select your top three core values. Let
your core values guide you in your decision-making process as you determine your next
steps and your career direction.

—◦◦◦—

PRIORITIES

What is important to you at this point in your life? How do you prioritize things, what's
most important and not so important? What was most important to you in your early
twenty's is probably not the same as what will be important to you in your forty's, fifty's,
or sixty's. Early in your career your priorities might be your family, upward mobility,
and making money. Later in your career those priorities are likely to shift. Knowing
what's most important to you right now will prepare you for making important career
decisions and will provide valuable input into selecting your career path.

MY PRIORITIES INCLUDE:

1. _____

2. _____

3. _____

4. _____

5. _____

—◊◊◊—

ROLES

What roles do you take on in your personal and business life? Are you a mother, father, friend, caretaker, mentor, coach, leader, manager, facilitator, teacher, confidant? Our roles impact our career decisions. For example, mothers and/or fathers may place their careers on hold to spend more time with their young children. If you are a caretaker of elderly parents or a special needs child this may affect the jobs that you are willing to take. Excessive travel may not be something you are willing to do based on your personal circumstances. Your roles should be considered when making career decisions.

MY KEY ROLES INCLUDE:

1. _____

2. _____

3. _____

4. _____

5. _____

—◊◊◊—

INTERESTS

As you are making decisions about your future you will want to explore those things that interest you; it might be a hobby or a volunteer activity. Our interests can often become our vocation. For example, I love taking photographs and would love to be a professional photographer one day (along with many other things). I also love animals and perhaps will combine my love for photography with my love for animals.

MY PRIMARY INTERESTS INCLUDE:

1. _____

2. _____

3. _____

4. _____

5. _____

—◦◦◦—

LIKES AND DISLIKES

Now is a good time to be very clear about those things that you liked in your previous positions and those things you disliked. No need to emphasize on your resume, or during an interview, those things you disliked doing in your last job. Do so and you just might end up doing them again.

On numerous occasions, I have had clients share with me that they keep getting recruiters calling them to do something they are not interested in. Yet when I look at their resume, they have that very activity that they dislike mentioned over and over again.

If you don't like doing something, *don't emphasize it*! Focus on those things you enjoy and want to do in your next career move. Focus on where you want to go, not on where you have been.

For example, I had a client who was a research scientist who managed a lab for his previous employer. He also worked on numerous projects and now wanted to move more in that direction. While he expressed the desire to seek a project management position,

75

his resume emphasized his work as a laboratory scientist with very little emphasis on his project management skills and experience. As a result, all the inquiries he was getting were to work in the laboratory environment, which was not his goal. In other words, his resume (as written) was ineffective and was not moving him in the direction he desired. Be very clear with yourself regarding your likes and put the emphasis on those activities.

THINGS I LIKE	THINGS I DISLIKE
1. _____	1. _____
2. _____	2. _____
3. _____	3. _____
4. _____	4. _____
5. _____	5. _____

MOTIVATORS

Motivation comes from within. It is not something others do to you. Each of us has things that motivates and excites us, that gets us going and keeps us going. Let's explore some possible motivators.

First let me say that money is rarely a long-term motivator. Getting a pay raise may excite us in the short term, but it rarely keeps anyone going. The euphoria we feel when we get the pay raise quickly fades and we are back to "business as usual." A high paying job may sound attractive to you, but if you do not enjoy the work is it worth the sacrifice? A true motivator does not fade within days or weeks. A true motivator will keep you going even through the most challenging of times. As I said before, true motivators are internal, not external.

Think of the student who works incredibly hard to get straight A's, puts in extra effort to get additional credits and to be part of an honors program because she has always wanted to attend a particular university. Or perhaps she has always dreamed of being a veterinarian, a doctor, an engineer, or another profession that she knows is very competitive. Instead of playing video games or chatting on social media with her friends, as many of her classmates are doing, she is putting in the extra effort to ensure she achieves her dream. It is her dream that motivates her.

Maybe you watched your parents or a good friend struggle financially. As a result, you are motivated to work hard to make sure you do not struggle in the same way. Our life's experiences (successes or failures) can be a motivator. Maybe it is the anticipation of being able to do something or go somewhere you have always wanted to visit that motivates you to save your money. Being able to help someone you care about can be a motivator.

We are all different and so our motivators are different. However, there are some basic human needs that motivate us all to achieve and behave in certain ways. Let's take a look at those basic human needs by looking at a model developed by Abraham Maslow. Many of you will be familiar with this model known as *Maslow's Hierarchy of Needs.*[7]

MASLOW'S HIERARCHY OF NEEDS

Physiological needs - To survive we need food, water, and oxygen to meet our physiological needs. This is the lowest level of needs that must be met before we can even begin to address the other needs. People who work for minimum wage, for example, often struggle with the need to put food on the table for their family.

Safety and security needs - We all want to feel safe in our environment, safe in our jobs, safe in our relationships. During any time of transition our safety and security needs are heightened. Uncertainty and ambiguity are not things that most people enjoy. Job seekers are frequently, although not always, motivated to look for jobs to meet their need for security: job security, financial security, health care, and benefits.

Membership and affiliation needs - As human beings, we have a need to know how we fit in and we want to have a "sense of belonging" to something meaningful. We want to feel connected to those around us: to our family, friends, colleagues, to a community, and to an organization where we can add value. Some people prefer to work alone and that need for connection is not as strong, but it still exists. Losing a job, especially with a long-term employer, will certainly have an impact on the human need for belonging and membership. Having lost that sense of belonging leaves many people struggling with a loss of connection, identity, and purpose.

Self-esteem needs - We all like to feel good about ourselves, to have a sense of achievement, and confidence. We tend to feel good about ourselves when we accomplish things such as: bringing in a project on time and on budget, meeting the customer's expectations, getting a certification or completing a college degree, helping others achieve their goals. What makes you feel good about yourself? Knowing what makes you feel good about yourself will help you make career decisions with confidence.

Self-actualization needs - This is the need to achieve a higher purpose, leave a legacy, make a difference in the lives of others. Self-actualization includes things such as personal mastery, reaching one's full potential, discovering and living your purpose—your why, achieving a life-long dream, doing missionary work. Self-actualizing might be serving someone or something bigger than yourself!

"What a man can be, he must be. This need we call self-actualization."
—*Abraham Maslow*

Several years ago I worked with a client at a major pharmaceutical manufacturing plant. He was a senior level manager who had the opportunity to move to another location with his company or stay in his small town and lose his job. He chose the latter. His children were both in high school and he did not want to uproot them. He was very happy living in his relatively small rural community.

His primary goal, at this point in his career and life, was to spend more time with his spouse and his teenage children. His desire was to work at least five more years until his kids graduated from high school and were settled in college. Financially he was fairly well off and so financial security was not his major concern nor motivator. He wanted to be home to attend his kids' sporting events and school activities.

His career with the pharmaceutical company had taken him all over the world and he had spent very little time with his children for many years. He no longer wanted the responsibilities he had before and definitely not the travel schedule. He wanted time with his family and time to do some missionary work for his church.

If you look at the hierarchy of needs, you will recognize his need for membership and affiliation (belonging) and self-actualization (higher purpose). Keeping those things in mind, he was able to articulate his career goals and prepare his communication and job search strategy accordingly.

Action Item # 12

Spend some time assessing where you are as it relates to *Maslow's Hierarchy of Needs*? What are your immediate needs? What are your long-term needs? **What motivates you**? What makes you feel alive and energized? An understanding of your motivators will help you make career decisions that will be more meaningful and satisfying. My motivators are:

_____

_____

_____

———◦◦◦———

KEY ACCOMPLISHMENTS

What are the key things you have accomplished in your career? What are you most proud of? What are you recognized for by your peers, supervisor(s), and business colleagues? Employers will want to know your key accomplishments and *accomplishment statements* are a primary component of your resume.

To help you develop your accomplishment statements I have included some samples in the **Career Tools** section at **www.ProjectCareerQuest.com**. We will discuss accomplishment statements in more detail in Chapter 9. In the meantime, take a few minutes to list out your top five accomplishments from the last five to ten years of your career (or military service). If you are a recent college graduate think about your greatest accomplishments from the past four to five years.

MY KEY ACCOMPLISHMENTS ARE:

1. _____

2. _____

3. _____

4. _____

5. _____

—◈◈◈—

ACTIVITIES THAT ATTRACT YOU

What types of things do you enjoy doing? Are you interested in organizing events, facilitating discussions, negotiating contracts? Do you like extreme sports and new adventures? Or do you prefer activities that are more educational or structured? What activities excite and motivate you? What things do you look forward to in your work or play environment?

ACTIVITIES THAT ATTRACT ME INCLUDE:

1. _____

2. _____

3. _____

4. _____

5. _____

—◈◈◈—

ENVIRONMENTS THAT ATTRACT YOU

What type of work environment energizes you? Do you like structure or flexibility? Do you want the opportunity to work from home, or do you prefer the office setting? An organization's corporate culture will greatly influence the work environment. I have trained for and consulted with companies and organizations that are extremely bureaucratic, some that are at the opposite end of the spectrum (very non-traditional), and everything in between. Do your research and find out as much as you can about different work environments. Where will you flourish? Where will you flounder? This is certainly something you want to take into consideration as you pursue your target companies.

ENVIRONMENTS THAT ATTRACT ME INCLUDE:

1. _____

2. _____

3. _____

4. _____

5. _____

MANAGEMENT STYLES

What is your management style? What management style(s) best fits your personality? Do you like someone who provides a lot of structure or a manager who allows you flexibility? How much direction do you need? When you get to the interview process you will want to take these things into consideration as you evaluate your options. Can you work within the management structure that exists in the organization? How compatible will you be to the existing structure?

MY MANAGEMENT STYLE IS:

_____

_____

_____

MANAGEMENT STYLES THAT I RESPECT AND ENJOY WORKING WITH INCLUDE:

_____

_____

_____

⧼⧽

PREFERENCES

If you want an understanding of how to better communicate and relate to others during your career transition project, then I suggest you complete the *Myers-Briggs Type Indicator®* *(MBTI).*[1] This instrument helps people identify their personality preferences and the preferences of others. You will discover so much about yourself: the way you relate to others, your communication style, how you make decisions and problem solve, how you lead, how you manage, how you like your world structured and organized, where you get your energy, how you manage stress and conflict, and even careers that might attract you and where you might find job satisfaction. The Myers-Briggs is a powerfully insightful tool from which you will learn much about yourself and others with whom you interact. I highly recommend you take the MBTI.

If you have never completed the MBTI, now would be a good time to seek out a professional practitioner and complete the instrument. You can find practitioners online by searching the Association of Psychological Type International (APTi)[2] (you may have a local chapter in your area). Resources for the instrument and associated training include the Center for the Applications for Psychological Type[3] (www.capt.org) and The Myers-Briggs Company[4] (www.themyersbriggs.com).

Local community colleges and universities may also have staff trained to administer the MBTI. If you work at a large company your Human Resources department may have resources available to you. Many career coaches are certified to administer the MBTI. (See Chapter 13 for a brief overview of the MBTI.)

There are numerous instruments on the Internet that call themselves a *free* Myers-Briggs, they are *not* the MBTI. To administer this instrument the practitioner must be certified. I got certified many years ago and it was a four-day certification process with much pre-work to ensure the proper and ethical administration and interpretation of the instrument. It will do you little good to take a free version without a proper interpretation of your results and guidance on how to use the information to make effective career decisions. If you are interested in taking the Myers-Briggs instrument to increase your knowledge and facilitate your career decisions, seek out a certified MBTI practitioner.

The four letters of my **Myers-Briggs personality type** are: ___ ___ ___ ___

CAREER TYPE

After completing the work above, you should now be ready to put some thought into your career type. Are you the corporate type? Do you prefer to be your own boss? Do you prefer jobs that are analytical? Or do you prefer working with more abstract concepts? Do you want a career that requires scientific and mathematical ability? Or are you more people-oriented and would prefer a career leading and developing human capital, or perhaps sales?

 If you take the **Myers-Briggs Type Indicator (MBTI)** you will have resources available to you to help you discover your "career type." I recommend taking the MBTI through a certified practitioner and then referring to books entitled *What's Your Type of Career?*[8] by Donna Dunning and *Do What You Are*[9] by Paul Tieger and Barbara Barron-Tieger.

MY CAREER TYPE WOULD INCLUDE:

_____

_____

_____

"You have to know who you are to grow to your potential.
But you have to grow in order to know who you are."
—*John C. Maxwell*

BEHAVIORAL/INTERNAL BARRIERS

There is one more area I want to explore before we move on, and that is *behavioral/ internal barriers*. Sometimes we seem to be doing the work but not making the progress we would like. Or perhaps, as you reflect back on your previous career(s), you realize there are some things that may have held you back from getting the promotion you wanted, the position you desired, building the trust and relationships you needed. Some of our barriers to success are external, under someone else's control. Some are internal, under our control.

Let's explore a few potential behavioral/internal barriers, and then go to the **Career Tools** section at **www.ProjectCareerQuest.com** where you will find a more complete list of potential barriers. Review them and check off the behavioral/internal barriers that you may be grappling with that might be impeding your progress. After reviewing the list and owning the barriers you have identified, consider the consequences and how you can reduce the impact of those barriers. Your barriers are your *roadblocks*. Remember those from Chapter 2? How can you remove or overcome your roadblocks?

Examples of behavioral/internal barriers include being/experiencing: abrasive, aloof, arrogant, blaming others, confrontational, defensive, domineering, easily discouraged, egotistical, fear of change, fear of taking responsibility, fear of failure, hypersensitive, impatient, inflexible, lack of social skills, negative, overly detached, overly emotional, poor listener, procrastinator, resistant to new ideas, thin-skinned, unrealistic. (These are but a few potential behavioral barriers. Review the **Career Tools** section at **www.ProjectCareerQuest.com** for a more complete list.)

Working through any behavioral/internal barriers that you may identify is not something easily done alone. A career coach, life coach, or professional counselor should be able to help you address your barriers and help you create a course of action to deal with them effectively. Recognition and acceptance are always the first steps if progress is to be made. You may even need to engage the help of a trusted friend or colleague to help you pinpoint some of your barriers.

During your time in transition—whether it is due to a job loss, life transition, or simply the desire to explore other career opportunities—getting to know yourself is critical. If any of us is ever to reach our full potential in life we have to really dig in, do the work, discover who we are and who we can be, determine where we can make the greatest impact, and where we want to go and how to get there.

In Chapter 7 I will discuss the journey to discover your passion. There is a direct connection between discovering your passion and reaching your full potential. The exploration and reflection you do will help you gain insight into your "bigger purpose" and get you headed in the right direction.

"Know thyself."
—*Plato*

Action Item # 13

The list of discovery activities in this chapter is not all-inclusive, but it is a good place to start. I recommend you use the templates in the Career Tools section to summarize the response to the questions asked in this chapter. I also highly recommend you create a **mind map** of these activities. Mind maps are powerful tools that will help you see the bigger picture. You might also find it helpful to create a **vision board**. A vision board is a visual representation of things you want in your life. Creating a vision board will help you gain clarity and vision, as the name implies. An explanation and example of mind maps and vision boards can be found in the **Career Tools** section at **www.ProjectCareerQuest.com**.

A **mind map** is a tool to help you brainstorm, plan, and create an outline for future action. Start with the topics discussed in this section to create your mind map. Once you have captured your thoughts and ideas, I suggest you hang your mind map on a wall in your home office, living room, or wherever works best for you. Then spend some time examining it and reflecting on your journey, both where you have been and where you might like to go. It may take some time but eventually you will begin to see patterns and possibilities. Eventually you will find the clarity you are seeking.

All of the discovery activities in this chapter are to help you pull together the pieces (like pieces of a puzzle) so you will begin to see patterns, possibilities, and the big picture. Completing the activities will help you respond to the request, "Tell me about yourself." You *must* know yourself to be able to make critical career decisions, network and interview successfully, and find career satisfaction.

For some of you, completing these activities will be exactly what you need to gain momentum in your Career Quest. For others reading this book, you may need to dig deeper to find the career that truly engages and energizes you. Read books, hire a career coach, engage others to help you brainstorm and explore opportunities.

Please note that my intentions in providing you a list of reference books throughout *Project Career Quest* are to lead you to other experts and additional information to help you make decisions regarding your journey to meaningful employment. There are many great books out there, and new ones being published every day, that can provide you with the insight and direction needed to make the challenging and difficult decisions you will be faced with on this journey. Ask your friends and colleagues for suggested reading material. Spend your time wisely during your Career Quest project. Reading will help you see possibilities and even open new doors for you!

 CHECKLIST - BEFORE YOU MOVE ON

☐ Have you completed the self-assessment?

☐ Do you have a clear picture of your core competencies, key accomplishments, interests, values, motivators, functional skills, adaptive skills, career type, etc.?

☐ Did you create a mind map to help you see clearly where you have been and where you might proceed in the future?

☐ Do you have any behavioral/internal barriers that you need to work through? If so, who will you reach out to for guidance and coaching?

Lessons Learned: *Knowing yourself and what you want to do next can be one of the most challenging aspects of the job search process. However, if you are to be successful you must dig in and get to know yourself. You will need to gain clarity on your career objectives to be able to sell yourself and your value to others, and most importantly your value to yourself. If you do not value yourself you will be unsuccessful convincing others of your value.*

"The most delightful surprise in life is to suddenly recognize your own worth."
—*Maxwell Maltz*

CHAPTER 7

DISCOVER YOUR PASSION

One of the most difficult aspects of finding meaningful employment is determining what to do next. Do you pursue work similar to what you were doing? If you loved what you were doing, that may be an easy decision. On the other hand, if you did not enjoy your previous work you may find yourself at a crossroads.

What I want to talk about in this chapter is how to discover and pursue your passion. Some of the topics we will explore include:

- What is passion?

- Symptoms of passion-deficit

- Four paths to discovering your passion

- Recognizing obstacles to discovering your passion

- Content vs. context-based passion

- Avenues to discovering your passion

- When passion meets purpose

To be realistic, I cannot help you discover your passion (in only one chapter) if you have no idea what it might be. But what I can do is to get you started on a path of discovery. If you completed the self-assessment activities in the previous chapter you should be that much closer to understanding what your interests are, what motivates you, your priorities, and your values. Now let's dig a little deeper to look into things that you may be passionate about.

WHAT IS PASSION?

Passion, as it relates to what we do to make a living—to create a life for ourselves and our families—can be defined as, "A powerful and compelling emotion or feeling…"[1] It's a driving force.

Passion…

- Something we all possess
- Comes from the heart
- Natural, you do not have to create it
- Heightens performance
- Inspires and uplifts us
- Fills us with energy and excitement
- Enhances day-to-day life
- Can cause you to lose track of time
- Gets you up in the morning
- Keeps you awake at night
- Creates new possibilities
- Enables you to do things you never dreamed possible

God gave us a head (brain) to think and a heart to feel. Too often we allow our head to talk us out of those things we really love, rationalizing why we shouldn't pursue our dreams. Passion comes from the heart; *if you want to discover your passion you must explore that which lies within your heart.*

"What lies behind us and what lies before us are small matters compared to what lies within us. And when we bring what is within us out into the world, miracles happen."
— *Henry Stanley Haskins*

SYMPTOMS OF PASSION DEFICIT

Some of the symptoms of living a life without passion, a life where you have yet to utilize your full potential, include:

- Feeling like something is missing
- Blaming others for your unhappiness
- Deep longing or yearning
- Doubting yourself, your abilities, your direction
- Disillusionment and regret
- Sadness, depression, apathy, feeling out of sync

If this sounds like you, you could have *passion deficit*. I can't imagine anyone who would want to suffer the symptoms of passion deficit yet so many do. Are you one of those people who is filled with doubt and regret, longing for something more?

So why is it that some people discover their passion and others struggle to find something that "charges their batteries" and keeps them engaged? Let's examine that question and explore some of the reasons why you may be stuck and unable to discover your passion.

Some of you reading this book already know what your passion is, but have forgotten. Maybe you have allowed the naysayers, the doubters, the gremlins, and others who are risk averse to talk you out of your dreams. If you fall into this category, this chapter may be more about recovering your dream rather than discovering your passion.

FOUR PATHS TO DISCOVERING YOUR PASSION

According to author Richard Chang, who wrote the book *The Passion Plan*,[2] there are four ways that people discover their passion:

Path #1 - Discovery by Epiphany: "I knew when…"

Path #2 - Discovery through Change: "I figured it out after…"

Path #3 - Discovery through Intuition: "I've always known…"

Path #4 - Discovery through Experience: "I'm not sure exactly when I figured it out, it's come to me over time through my life experiences."

Path #1 - Discovery by epiphany is instantaneous. It can occur as an unexpected life-changing experience where a passion is suddenly revealed. Epiphanies do not occur as a result of planning and cannot be anticipated; they are unexpected and can happen anywhere and anytime—the "aha moment"!

Path #2 - Discovery through change occurs as a result of a major life change such as a marriage or a divorce, a birth or a death, losing a job or starting a new job, or perhaps due to an illness or recovery from an illness. As we learn new things about ourselves due to the change, or perhaps through examining how we've lived our lives up to that point, we may discover our passion. An example of this is when someone suffers a major trauma, such as becoming paralyzed or losing a limb, and then goes on to encourage and inspire others to move beyond their own limitations.

Path #3 - Discovery through intuition generally occurs very early in life, when one senses and understands their passion through the power of intuition and is confident in pursuing it. I think we all know someone who was passionate at a young age whether it was to create (artist, actor, writer, musician), to lead or to serve. People who fall into this category tend to recognize and be guided by their passion throughout life.

Path #4 - Discovery through experience is the category that most of us fall into. We discover our passion not because of a life-changing event or something we have known since childhood but rather as a result of our day-to-day experiences. It took me many years to discover my passion and it was a direct result of my business and life experiences. The signs may be subtle and can be easily dismissed if we listen to our head and not to our heart.

As you read on in this chapter, I will share with you some of the obstacles to discovering your passion, as well as some activities you can engage in that will put you on a path to discovery. Too often we miss out on opportunities to discover our passion because we are set in our ways and unwilling to move outside our comfort zone.

 There are many books written about passion and purpose, and I would recommend researching what's out there. Many years ago, I read Richard Chang's book, *The Passion Plan: A Step-by-Step Guide to Discovering, Developing and Living Your Passion.*[3] I would highly recommend it to help you understand what passion is and how to pursue it.

WHAT'S HOLDING YOU BACK?

Let me share with you what I call "the cheesecake story" and perhaps it will give you some insight into why we often fail to discover our passion. Several years ago, I was teaching a class I developed entitled *Discover Your Passion*. The class was on a Saturday morning at my church. I had told the participants to bring their own coffee and that I would be providing bagels and cream cheese. When the participants arrived, I offered everyone the opportunity to grab a bagel before we got started. At that point, one of the men in the class proclaimed he did not eat cheese and then proceeded to tell us why.

He shared with us that he and his siblings had been raised by his grandmother and that she had never allowed them to eat cheese. As a result, when offered cheese his response was always, "I don't like cheese." When he got married, his wife informed him that her favorite restaurant is the Cheesecake Factory. Thereafter, every visit to the Cheesecake Factory included an invitation to try the cheesecake. Routinely he refused the invitation based on the proclamation, "I do not like cheese." Upon which his wife's response was, "How do you know if you have never tasted it?" After several attempts to get him to try the cheesecake he finally relented to get her "off his back" and prove to her he did not like cheese nor cheesecake. So, he took a bite and (drum roll)—he discovered he loved cheesecake.

The moral of the story is: *If you are going to discover your passion you must be open to trying new things. Try the cheesecake!*

Another story shared in the same class was by a man who had been raised on an island in South Georgia. When his family needed to get to the mainland they simply jumped in their motorboat and raced to shore to do their shopping, go to school, run errands, etc. When he got married, his wife's father had a 35-foot sailboat and one weekend they were invited to go sailing. His first thought was "How boring will this be? Spending the day on a boat with no motor, I can't even ski." His second thought was, "I better go since the invitation came from my new father-in-law." Needless to say, he was not looking forward to the day of sailing. The day, however, did not turn out as he had expected. Instead of being bored he discovered a new passion and is now an avid sailor.

The moral of this story is: *Be open to invitations to try new things.* You will never discover your passion if you are not open to new experiences and possibilities.

Action Item # 14

What's holding you back from trying new things? Fear? Assumptions? Someone else's determination of what you will or will not like? Take some time now to think about the following questions and write down your thoughts, either here in the book or on a separate piece of paper or journal.

What opportunities to try new things have I had in the past that I turned down?

_____

_____

_____

_____

Why will I not try new things? What am I afraid of? What's holding me back?

_____

_____

_____

_____

What do I think will happen if I try something new? (Could be food, could be a new activity such as sailing, a new hairstyle, or a new way of doing something.)

_____

_____

_____

_____

What's the worst thing that could happen if I try _____ **?**
(Fill in the blank)

_____

_____

_____

_____

What benefit might I experience if I try _____ **?** (Fill in the
blank)

_____

_____

_____

_____

**If you are a parent (or a role model) what message might your unwillingness to
try new things convey to children that you raise, mentor, or influence?**

_____

_____

_____

_____

_____

> "Nothing has a stronger influence psychologically on their environment
> and especially on their children than the un-lived life of the parent."
> —*Carl Jung*

OBSTACLES TO DISCOVERING YOUR PASSION

Take a look at the list below and place a check mark next to any of those things that might be your obstacle to discovering your passion.

___ Not in touch with your heart
___ Suppressing your passions as "childish" or "impractical"
___ Buying into what others say
___ Following someone else's dream
___ Doubting yourself, your abilities, your potential
___ Negative self-talk (listening to the gremlins)
___ Low self-esteem
___ Fear of the unknown
___ Fear of change
___ Fear of rejection
___ Fear of failure
___ Fear of success
___ Procrastination
___ Laziness
___ Making excuses
___ Lack of self-awareness
___ Overly cautious
___ Guilt
___ Inability to say *no* (leaving no time to pursue your dreams)
___ Unwilling to engage others to help you discover your passion

---

"Courage is not the absence of fear, but rather the judgment
that something else is more important than fear."
—*Ambrose Red Moon*

**Action
Item
15**

What's keeping you from discovering your passion? Maybe your obstacle(s) isn't on the list above. If not, what is it that's holding you back? Consider enlisting the help of a close friend, family member, trusted business colleague, or a career coach who can add some insight and objectivity.

CONTENT AND CONTEXT-BASED PASSION

Passion can be either "content-based," which is centered around a subject or specialized activity, or "context-based" that resolves around a theme. Some examples might include:

Content-Based Passion	Context-Based Passion
Gardening	Helping others
Cooking	Leading
Computers	Coaching
Architecture	Mentoring
Photography	Teaching
Animal rescue	Learning
Children	Improving organizations
Painting	Managing projects
Sailing	Creating
Sports	Envisioning

AVENUES FOR DISCOVERING YOUR PASSION

Unless you encounter a major epiphany, have a life-changing experience, or you already know your passion through the power of your intuition, let me suggest some ideas to help you discover your passion (or recover your dream).

- Read books
- Take classes
- Try new activities
- Volunteer
- Experiment
- Explore
- Conduct informational interviews
- Shadow someone in a role or career you might find interesting
- Examine your feelings
- Reflect on your childhood (Was there something you loved doing but have shoved aside for more practical pursuits?)
- Take some risks
- Get out of your comfort zone

"The two most important days of your life
are the day you are born and the day you discover why."
—*Mark Twain*

Your "why" might lie within your passion. Don't miss out on the wonderful and exciting things life has to offer because you are afraid to try new things or too comfortable and set in your ways to move out of your comfort zone. If you truly want to discover your passion you have to be open to possibilities and new experiences. If the thing you try is not for you, move on and try something else. Eventually you will find something that excites you. Something at which you excel that you want to share with others. Something that you can turn into a living that you enjoy. Trying new things may even lead to discovering your "why."

"Life begins at the end of your comfort zone."
—*Neale Donald Walsh*

Action Item # 16

Create a **bucket list** of new things you will try and experience. You will want to consider trying new activities; new foods; new ways of doing things; new ways of approaching life; volunteer activities; travel; new physical challenges such as running a marathon or half marathon, scuba diving, mountain climbing, dancing; learning new things by reading books, taking classes, participating in webinars, or hands-on experience; trying new technology; exploring creative activities such as acting, painting, drawing, poetry, writing music, etc. A blank template to create your bucket list can be found in the **Career Tools** section at **www.ProjectCareerQuest.com**.

The possibilities are endless and the rewards are great. Do you want to discover your passion? Then try new things and be guided by your heart.

"Only when people are in touch with their passions do they use their heads to give shape and substance to their dreams. By linking the two in a process of self-evaluation and action, passioneers use their greatest strengths to achieve their greatest goals."
—*Richard Chang*

WHEN PASSION MEETS PURPOSE—THE POWER OF PMP

I have already described passion as a powerful and compelling emotion or feeling, a driving force. Well if that's passion, what is purpose? Purpose is why we exist; why we were created, it's our calling, or as Dr. Tony Colson refers to it in his book, *Unlocking Your Divine DNA,*[4] it's our divine DNA. No one has the exact same calling or purpose in life as you. Your "why" is unique to you. Once you are able to discover your purpose and put passion behind it, you will achieve things you never thought possible. Passion and purpose go hand-in-hand.

Purpose is the "why," but we can't achieve it without passion to get us there. To use a sailing analogy, purpose is our true North—the direction we want to sail, passion is the wind that propels us and keeps us moving in the direction of our purpose. Without the wind, we are dead in the water, stagnant, no movement!

Organizations have a purpose, it's *why* they exist, it's their mission. To achieve that mission, they must have a vision of where they want to go and a map that helps them achieve their vision. But if there is no passion in their employee body, they will become stagnant and eventually cease to exist as an organization.

It is equally true for human beings. If we lack passion, the compelling force to help us fulfill our purpose, our destiny, our "why," our mission in life—call it what you will, then we will live a fruitless life. Without the passion to fulfill your purpose, you too will become stagnant and live a life without real meaning, movement, or excitement. None of us wants to be stuck living the "caged life"[5] as author, speaker, and success coach Brendon Burchard calls it; a life where we feel imprisoned and hopeless. Discovering your passion, and aligning that with your greater purpose, will create a "charged life,"[6] filled with endless opportunities to make a difference.

One of the books that comes to mind here is by Brendon Burchard entitled, *The Charge: Activating the 10 Human Drives That Make You Feel Alive.*[7] This book takes the reader beyond the "caged life"[8] and the "comfortable life"[9] to what he calls the "charged life."[10] People who are living the charged life are actualizing their potential and they look forward to opportunities to learn, to grow, to serve, and contribute to the world in a meaningful way. "Chargers" (as Brendon refers to people living the charged life) are optimistic about the future and they feel empowered to take action necessary to turn their dreams into reality. I highly recommend this book. A perfect read for anyone in transition or wanting more out of life. Do yourself a favor and read this book!

After reading Brendon's book, should you decide to pursue the *charged life* instead of living the *caged life* or settling for the *comfortable life,* you might also want to read Kary Oberbrunner's book entitled *Day Job to Dream Job.*[11] In this book Kary offers practical steps for turning your passion into a full-time gig. He helps you examine self-limiting beliefs that can sabotage your success and shares ideas, strategies, tools, and techniques to help you carve out your niche and gain influence, impact, and income.

If merely existing is not enough for you and you want to bust out of your nine to five job and unlock your potential, read both of these books. They are guaranteed to inspire, motivate, and empower you. Both Brendon and Kary have an engaging online presence; offering free webinars, podcasts, and daily posts to help you learn, grow, develop your potential, and connect with others. Brendon and Kary are mentors of mine and they can mentor and guide you to achieve things you did not think possible. Check them out.

Another highly recommended book, which I mentioned earlier, is by Dr. Tony Colson entitled, *Unlocking Your Divine DNA.*[12] If you want to embrace your true identity; that for which you were uniquely and wonderfully created; if you want to step into your purpose and fulfill your potential; read this book. Tony will lead you on a journey of discovery and transformation to unlocking your divine DNA.

"Your time is limited, so don't waste it living someone else's life.
Don't be trapped by dogma—which is living with the results of other people's
thinking. Don't let the noise of others' opinions drown out your own inner voice.
And most importantly, have the courage to follow your heart and intuition.
They somehow already know what you truly want to become.
Everything else is secondary."
—*Steve Jobs*

CHECKLIST - BEFORE YOU MOVE ON

☐ Have you explored your heart to reveal those things that are most important to you? What do you value? What gets you excited? What keeps you awake at night and gets you up in the morning (and I don't mean coffee)?

☐ Have you begun the process of exploring different activities toward discovering your passion?

☐ Have you examined what might be holding you back from discovering your passion?

☐ Are you willing to try things that may be outside your current comfort zone for the possibility of learning and experiencing new things? Are you willing to try the cheesecake?

☐ Have you created a bucket list of things to try?

Lessons Learned: *If you want to discover your passion you must be willing to move beyond your comfort zone and try new things. You must also look inside your heart to reveal those things that matter most to you, only then will you discover your passion.*

"Your vision will become clear only when you look into your heart.
Who looks outside dreams. Who looks inside awakens."
—*Carl Jung*

CHAPTER 8

NEW OPPORTUNITIES WAITING

So, you lost your job and you are at a crossroads. Maybe you are re-entering the work force after a prolonged absence or entering the job market for the first time. Or maybe you realize it's time for a change and so you are exploring your options. Where do you go from here? What will you do? How will you contribute? How will you make a living? How do you care for your family? What path do you choose? What options do you have? Will your search take you to familiar or unchartered territory?

DO YOUR MARKET RESEARCH

Before making any decisions about where you will stay or where you will go, make sure you have done your market research. How good of an option is staying in your current career field or your field of study? If you work in the call center environment, and you have worked in six different call centers in the past eight years due to outsourcing and layoffs, you might want to start thinking about finding a new career. Some of the questions to consider regarding your current industry include:

- What's the future of my industry?

- What challenges will my industry be facing in the next five, ten, twenty years?

- How is technology changing my industry?

- What skills will I need in the future to be competitive in my industry?

- Do I have the skills needed to remain competitive in my chosen field?

If you are considering exploring jobs in growing markets, Google "hot jobs." Doing so will take you to a number of job search engines that will highlight jobs by industry, location, company, job title, etc.

CHOOSING A CAREER PATH

You will be faced with many decisions on your journey to finding new employment or building a new career for yourself. One of the decisions you must eventually make is which path to take. Will you look for a job similar to what you have/had been doing? Will you work in the same industry? Or perhaps you are ready to try something entirely new, maybe something you dreamed of doing years ago but chose not to for a variety of reasons. Maybe the timing wasn't right before, but it is now. Here are three potential career paths to choose from:

1. Same or similar career path

2. New career path

3. Entrepreneurial path

1. Same or Similar Career Path

Choosing the same or similar career path may not require much retraining. Assuming you have kept your skills up-to-date you should be prepared with many required and transferable skills. However, often when a person has been in a job for a long time some of their skills may need updating. Maybe you became complacent in the old way of doing things and now you need to do a little retuning. If you have kept your skills current you will be ahead of the game and much more marketable.

In Chapter 6 you were coached and encouraged to complete a number of exercises to assess your core competencies and transferable skills. Upon completing those activities, you should be more aware of what new skills you might need to achieve your career goals.

2. New Career Path

Choosing a new career path will typically require a lot of training and/or education to learn new skills that you may not have used in your previous career. Of course, some of your skills are likely transferable. If this is the path you choose, you will have to determine requirements and then how to fill those requirements.

Perhaps you have had a successful career as an accountant and now you want to teach accounting at a local university or community college. You have the knowledge to teach, but delivering training is a lot different than sitting behind a desk crunching numbers. To be successful, and not bore your students, you may need some training on adult learning theories and practices, platform and facilitation skills.

Perhaps you were a mortgage banker and now you want to be an Information Technology professional. With no previous programming experience, you will need to take courses online or in a classroom setting to learn your new chosen career. You are never too old to learn!

Choosing a new career path does not necessarily mean you will need to go back to college and get another degree. Depending on your field of interest you may, however, need to complete a certification program (and perhaps pass an exam) to qualify for an entry-level position or higher.

Many community colleges offer courses specifically for the unemployed and underemployed to retrain them for new careers. There are an abundance of courses online through universities and training organizations. Check out free online courses from edx.org.[1]

3. Entrepreneurial Career Path

If you choose the entrepreneurial path, and you have never run your own business, then I highly recommend you seek out a mentor or business advisor. Owning and running your own business can be very rewarding, but it comes with a new set of risks and challenges. Seek wise guidance and make sure this path is for you. Many people prefer to be their own boss, set their own schedule, choose their own clients, etc.

If this is the right path for you, find organizations and individuals who can help guide you along the way. The Service Corp of Retired Executives (SCORE)[2] is a great resource to help you navigate the entrepreneurial path. They offer free consultation and all sorts of documentation and literature to help you strategize, plan, organize, develop a Business Plan, execute, and launch your business. Look them up online and I bet you will find a local SCORE organization in your area.

Also research the Small Business Development Centers[3] (SBDC) and Small Business and Technology Development Centers[4] (SBTDC). These organizations provide assistance to small businesses and aspiring entrepreneurs throughout the United States and US territories. (See sba.gov)[5]

"When there is clutter, chaos, and transition,
there is a lot of money to be made by the person with clarity."
—*Brendon Burchard*

CULTIVATING AN ENTREPRENEURIAL MIND-SET

Even if you choose to continue on the traditional path, working for an employer, I believe we all need to cultivate an entrepreneurial mindset. I believe we need to put more emphasis on creating our own destinies and stop relying on a company or the government to create stability and security in our lives. The world as we knew it has changed forever. Large corporations have no intentions of providing any of us with a thirty plus year career and a lucrative pension plan. Unless we face reality, whatever that might be, and learn to be adaptive and flexible, we will be forever moving backwards.

Let me share some information with you from the U.S. Bureau of Labor Statistics:[6]

- The average U.S. worker will have 11 jobs between the age of 18-44.

- The average U.S. worker will have 7 or more careers in their lifetime.

- The average job tenure is 4.2 years and 2.8 years for Millennials; those numbers continue to decrease.

- Studies show that nearly half of the American workforce will be made up of independent contractors, consultants, entrepreneurs, freelancers, etc. The *contingent workforce*[7] is growing while full-time employees are decreasing in numbers.

The future does not hold lifetime employment for most, and do you really want to do the same thing forever? Thinking like an entrepreneur will better prepare you for your eleven jobs and seven careers, or better yet, take control of your destiny and plan for the future you desire.

If you don't want to be a victim to every future layoff coming your way, you might want to consider using your skills, knowledge, and experience to create your own business.

What is it that you truly love doing and people would find of value? What service, product, or result could you deliver that people would be willing to pay for? These are questions you can explore in more depth as you complete the exercises in Chapter 7, **Discover Your Passion**. Whether you take the traditional path or the entrepreneurial path, cultivating an entrepreneur's mindset will keep you moving forward and successful.

To move forward we must learn to think like an entrepreneur,
always open and alert to new opportunities, moving beyond our comfort zone—
stretching to achieve things we did not think possible.

Before you decide which path to go down, do your research. There are a number of resources online that can educate you on the job market including information on industry growth, wages, employment trends, job descriptions, characteristics of the job, skills and educational requirements. If you are part of the American job market, the Bureau of Labor Statistics has developed the Standard Occupational Classification (SOC) System[8] that includes over 840 occupations in the United States. You can access that information at www.bls.gov/soc. Another site you may want to visit to find occupational definitions and information including: job titles, job descriptions, tasks, knowledge, skills, abilities, and other related categories, is the Occupational Information Network or O*Net,[9] published by the U.S. Department of Labor at www.onetcenter.org.

Wherever you live, there are likely similar resources available that you can access through an online search. Bottom line—do your homework! Where's the demand? Where's the growth? What are the employment trends? And finally, what skills will you need moving forward to be successful?

 Lessons Learned: *Career transition offers an opportunity to explore a number of different paths. You don't have to be defined by your previous job or career; you have options and can reinvent yourself if desired.*

"There is no security in life, only opportunity."
—*Mark Twain*

CONSIDER YOUR OPTIONS

There are a number of options you might want to consider as you seek employment, a career change, or perhaps even retirement. Let's take a look at some of them.

Find another full-time job in a related career field. Seeking full-time employment in the same or related career field is the route most job seekers seem to explore initially because it is familiar and perhaps it is what they love doing. If you did not love what you were doing before, then you might want to explore some of the other options I have listed in this section. The list of options is not necessarily all-inclusive, you may think of others.

Take one or more part-time jobs. Maybe you do not need full-time work at this point in your career. Or perhaps you would prefer more variety or to try something new. Part time jobs are good filler or survival jobs while you search for your ideal situation or to give you a feel for a new industry without making a full commitment.

Accept a contract position with a company, especially one you would like to get on with as a permanent employee. If you have been out of the workforce for some time, or you are having difficulty finding a full-time position, contract work is a good and viable option. Contract positions can lead to full-time employment.

CONTRACT TO FULL-TIME

If full-time employment is your goal; and you take a contract position with a company you were trying to get on with full-time; make it your mission to create value for the organization and build your reputation so you will be noticed and considered when a full-time position becomes available.

A friend of mine was working a contract position for a company she desired to work for full-time. She had been there several years and was frustrated that she was not getting considered for full-time positions. When I asked her what she was doing to get noticed she said, "Just doing my job." Sometimes just doing your job is not enough.

- What are you doing to network internally?

- Do you know the key decision makers?

- Are you on their "radar screen"?

If you want a full-time job to come out of a contract position you must network internally and get noticed by the key decision makers and hiring managers. If your performance is outstanding and you are adding value to the organization, they would almost always prefer hiring you rather than having to go through the external hiring process.

One of the things my friend finally did to begin networking internally was to start a running group at lunchtime. In doing so, she created an opportunity to network with full-time employees.

WORK FOR A STAFFING OR TEMP AGENCY

Staffing and temp agencies provide resources to employers, everything from administrative staff to executives. This is not the same as contract work. Here you actually work for the staffing agency that will move you from assignment to assignment as needed.

I have a number of friends who have gone this route and enjoy the variety of assignments and the flexibility. And because their performance is good and they have developed a relationship with the agencies from which they get their assignments, they generally stay pretty busy moving regularly from assignment to assignment.

If you are the type of person who likes a routine and does not adapt well to change, this route may not be for you. However, if you like variety and flexibility being part of a contingent workforce might be just what you are looking for.

Staffing agencies need talented and skilled workers to fill temporary positions; maybe an employee is on maternity or family leave, extended absence due to an illness, or for a variety of other reasons. I have a friend who is a Chief Financial Officer (CFO) and he moves from assignment to assignment, some assignments are only a few months, some much longer. He works on special projects or acts as an interim CFO for smaller or mid-sized companies during times of transition.

Agencies need workers for special projects and to handle high workloads during peak seasons. Check out the agencies in your area and who services which industries and clients.

A couple of years ago, on one of my corporate assignments, I met with a man who had just been notified that his entire department was being outsourced. He was the manager of the group and a retired military officer. His wife was gainfully employed by one of the local government agencies. He shared with me that financially he and his wife were comfortable, and he could retire if that was his desire. He also told me retirement was not for him, "I'm a worker," he said. I suggested he might want to consider either contract work or getting on with a staffing agency versus looking for full-time work as an employee. Working this way would give him more flexibility and would allow him time to travel and/or pursue other interests if he desired. At the time of our discussion, he had not even considered anything other than full-time employment, after our session, he considered working for a staffing agency as his primary option.

Working for a temp agency or staffing firm, as well as accepting a contract position, can be an effective way to transition into a new industry and gain new skills. If your ultimate goal is to work for a particular targeted employer, this may be your stepping stone to position you for future opportunities with that employer. Know your goal and keep your eye on the prize.

START YOUR OWN BUSINESS

Start your own company using the skills and knowledge you have acquired from your previous experience. Becoming an entrepreneur can be exciting and lucrative. If you have always wanted to be your own boss, your job loss may be the trigger you needed to get you going. It does, however, take a lot of discipline and willingness to accept ambiguity and uncertainty to go this route. Can you work effectively alone or with a partner? Are you a decision maker and a problem solver? If you think the entrepreneurial route is for you, do your homework and tap into local resources to educate yourself on the challenges and opportunities you will encounter. I know people who have started their own businesses and have been very happy and successful, and others who have decided it's too isolating or challenging to tackle alone. Do your homework—know yourself!

Start your own company based on a passion or interest. You could start from scratch or you could purchase an existing business or franchise. I have my own business and actually do several related things based on my passion to teach, coach, consult, lead others, and speak to groups on a variety of topics. I have what many would refer to as a *portfolio career*.[10] I have some of my own clients and I contract with a number of companies to train, coach, and consult on a variety of topics of which I have expertise. I love the variety and opportunities I have had to travel throughout the U.S., Canada, and internationally.

With the use of technology such as LinkedIn, Twitter, YouTube, Pinterest, Facebook, and other forms of social media, we all have the opportunity to create websites, blogs, vlogs, podcasts, webinars, online businesses, and online communities. We have access to people all around the world like never before. People like Brendon Burchard, Jeff Walker, Michael Hyatt, John Maxwell, Kary Oberbrunner, Marie Forleo, and Amy

Porterfield (among many others) have all created multi-million dollar businesses coaching and mentoring entrepreneurs using social media. The opportunity to learn from these industry experts on how to create, market, and grow successful entrepreneurial businesses, are greater than ever before. Tap into these resources. Also, don't forget to check out the free resources and mentoring for small business owners provided by SCORE.

And if you think you are too old to be an entrepreneur (for those of you in your forty's, fifty's, or sixty's), do an online search about the success of startup companies. Current research indicates that "older" entrepreneurs starting new businesses have a substantially higher success rate. I'll let you do the research.

"Winning careers, like winning start-ups,
are in permanent beta: always a work in progress."
—*Reid Hoffman*

RETIREMENT

Now I know it may sound crazy in a book about your *Career Quest* to discuss retirement, but for some reading this book, retirement is a real option. For some the question is, "Do I continue to work?" Or, "Do I take the package my company is offering and retire?" This is an option many senior workers grapple with, and for most it is not an easy decision. I have had numerous people in my career transition workshops over the years that have come to me and asked how to make that decision. They still want a purpose, they still want to contribute in a meaningful way, but they are not sure what that looks like. Maybe they need benefits and still want to bring in some spending money so they can reserve their retirement savings until they get to a place in life where they are either unable to work or feel fully confident that they are financially secure. It definitely takes some thought and planning.

If you are new in your career the topic of retirement will not apply to you, at least not yet. However, some reading this book may be contemplating retirement (now or in a few short years) but are not sure how they will spend their time not having a routine schedule every day and engaging with others. I know many people are forced into retirement by their organizations or offered attractive packages to retire and reduce the company's headcount. Some of them are enjoying their retirement and finding plenty of activities to fill their time and bring them fulfillment. Others quickly get bored or realize they are not financially ready to retire and begin seeking employment of some sort to satisfy their needs.

There are critical decisions to be made regarding retirement to ensure you are financially and psychologically ready to "hang up your hat" and relax or take on new challenges and responsibilities. As enticing as retirement might sound, it can grow stale very quickly if you have not properly prepared and do not have a new purpose to keep you engaged. It's human nature to need a purpose to keep us motivated, satisfied, and happy. Everyone needs a purpose to get them out of bed in the morning. What will be your purpose when you retire?

There are many free seminars offered on retirement (typically by investment firms and they might even include a free steak dinner) that may be able to address some of your questions and concerns. Maybe you could offer your advice and wisdom to an organization such as SCORE and help others who are much newer and less experienced in their careers.

There are many opportunities that exist to contribute to your community as either a volunteer or perhaps part time employment that will get you out of the house and engaged with others. Retirement can be an exciting and fulfilling time, but it still requires planning.

"Here is the test to find whether your mission on earth is finished: If you're alive, it isn't."
—*Richard Bach*

OPTIONS TO EXPLORE IN RETIREMENT

Retirement may be a long way away for many of you reading this book. If that's the case, skip this section and continue on to the checklist and lessons learned. If you are in a position where you could retire but simply not sure what you would do if you retire, take a look at the information below and see what ideas you can gather. With years of experience, there is so much you could do to add value to others and find fulfillment for yourself.

- **Volunteer.** There are so many worthwhile non-profits out there that would love to benefit from your knowledge, skills, and talents. Check out the volunteer opportunities in your area. Volunteer at your local Red Cross, build houses for Habitat for Humanity, volunteer with a local animal shelter or animal rescue group. Do you like children, animals, building, or creating? Choose a volunteer opportunity based on things you are passionate about. I even sat on a flight overseas one time next to a woman who was retired and now she hops on a plane at a moment's notice to pick up and transport organs that have been donated to save another human being's life on another continent. She has the opportunity to literally make a life or death difference for someone, while also racking up frequent flyer miles for her own personal travel later. There is no shortage of non-profits or volunteer opportunities where you can make a huge difference in your community. See Chapter 10 on **Networking for Results** for more ideas for volunteering.

- **Pursue your passion,** whether it's photography, dancing, sailing, traveling, painting, music, mountain climbing, writing—the things you always wanted to do but did not have time for.

Have you ever thought about writing a book? I happen to know a great publisher who could help you make that dream come true! Author Academy Elite has helped thousands of authors around the world write and publish their books and even create numerous streams of income based on their book(s). Some of the authors I have met are gainfully employed, some are retired, and some have left their day job to pursue their dream job because they were able to create a business based on their book. For more information on Author Academy Elite check out the "Resources" page on my website at www.KerryAhrend.com.

Pursue your passion for yourself, share it with others, teach it to others. Turn your passion into your vocation. See the chapter entitled **Discover Your Passion,** Chapter 7, for more discussion on this topic.

- **Assume a leadership role in a community group or organization.** My father was on numerous boards that kept him busy and engaged over the years. He contributed to his community for many years after his retirement from full-time work and created quite a legacy for himself. Many of the groups he participated in do a lot of fundraising to benefit the community. Through his fundraising efforts, the small community of Singers Glen, Virginia was able to build a very nice facility for the local volunteer fire department.

  Another leadership role my father accepted after he retired, with much pleading and encouragement from others, was to become a County Supervisor. He decided to take on this elected position to help shape the future of Rockingham County, Virginia. He found this work very rewarding as well as challenging. His work as a County Supervisor and other leadership roles kept him sharp, young, and filled with purpose. An added bonus for my parents was that he also got benefits through the county and a small salary. Most importantly, he was actively engaged and contributing in a meaningful and significant way for many years after his official retirement.

- **Teach and mentor others**. This could fall under volunteer activities, but I wanted to highlight this because many of you reading this have tremendous knowledge and wisdom that you can pass onto others. Maybe it's business knowledge, maybe it is a craft such as pottery or furniture making, maybe it's an art such as music or painting or poetry, or maybe it is academic knowledge such as math or science. Whatever your skill, talent, or knowledge, there is an audience out there who would love to learn from you—seek and ye shall find!

  This can be a volunteer activity or your *encore career*.[11] There are a number of companies where you can share your knowledge with others around the world and get paid for doing so. Teachable.com is one such company. If this is something that interests you, do your research and you will find a number of companies you can partner with to develop and share online courses.

- **Learn something new, take an online course, go back to college—fulfill a lifetime dream!** Have you ever wanted to study something but simply couldn't find the time or energy? Retirement might be the perfect time to explore those things you have always wanted to learn more about.

Several years ago, I attended the graduation ceremony of a high school friend's son. He was graduating from the University of North Carolina in Chapel Hill. The ceremony was held in the football stadium and the keynote speaker was Desmond Tutu. Sometime during the ceremony, the oldest graduating undergraduate student was announced. I was blown away when I heard she was ninety-eight years young! WOW!!! All those years this woman probably had a dream to get a college degree and now at ninety-eight years old she had done just that. A dream fulfilled! Imagine having her in your graduating class.

Another example of someone in retirement fulfilling his purpose was a man I met at a networking event. I'm guessing he was in his mid-seventy's and had recently completed his Master of Divinity. He now leads his own church in the area. He said he was in the ministry at age nineteen but then ran from it, scared and feeling unworthy. After decades in a corporate job he retired and decided to follow his calling. This time he didn't run and has found new purpose.

Action Item # 17 — Start thinking about **what path best suits you at this stage in your life and career** and what options you have. Do you want to keep doing what you were doing? Do you want to venture into uncharted territory and try something new? Are you ready to turn a hobby or a passion into a career? Do you want to start your own business and be your own boss? Or perhaps retirement is looking pretty good! Seek out professional counsel as needed. There are many career coaches who can help you work through these decisions.

"There is not one door of opportunity. There is not one door to significance. There is a series of doors."
—*John C. Maxwell*

To assist you in your search for meaningful employment, I have created a list of *job search boards* and have included it in the **Career Tools** section which you can access at **www.ProjectCareerQuest.com.**

CHECKLIST - BEFORE YOU MOVE ON

☐ Have you investigated and determined the appropriate career path for yourself?

☐ Do you need to update some of your skills?

☐ Do you need to develop some new skills? What training is required?

☐ Do you need the assistance of a coach or mentor to explore career opportunities and options available?

☐ Whose assistance do you need to make the career transition you desire?

☐ Based on your circumstances (stage of your career, skill sets, finances, etc.) what option(s) seem most desirable and viable?

☐ What resources are available to help you explore your options?

☐ Who do you need to engage to help you explore your options?

 LessonsLearned: *If you have lost your job, lost your way, or lost your enthusiasm for what you were doing, it does not mean that your options are limited. Start exploring and asking others to help you brainstorm options. Examine your options and eventually you will find an opportunity that's right for you.*

PART 3

EXECUTE

Implementing the Plan

CHAPTER 9

COMMUNICATION STRATEGIES AND TOOLS

Up to this point in the book you have been primarily engaged in exploratory work and the planning phase of your job search project; now it's time to transition into executing your plan. Once you have a clearer vision of what you want to do moving forward, you are ready to create and implement your marketing/sales tools. The communication strategies, tools, and techniques discussed in this chapter will help you get your message out and in front of key decision makers, which is required if you are to land meaningful employment. Specifically, we will address the following:

- Mission statement
- Branding statement
- Elevator speech
- Resume
- Summary statements
- Accomplishment statements
- Cover letters
- Online applications
- Follow up correspondence
- Thank you notes
- Social media

Before you put together a resume and start getting your message out, you still have some work to do. How will you brand yourself? What's your professional identity? What do you want to be known for? What's your value proposition? Let's start with a personal mission statement.

MISSION STATEMENT

In Chapter 7 I talked about discovering your passion and possibly your "why." A mission statement declares your higher purpose, your *why*. Most businesses have a mission statement that represents why they exist as an organization. A well-developed mission statement will help an organization make good business decisions and do the right things. If it's not part of their mission they don't do it.

A personal mission statement will help guide you in your job search, to do the right things and make wise decisions about your future. It will enable you to make decisions about your career with greater ease and confidence. Writing a personal mission statement will make you think about what you want to do moving forward, what you want to accomplish in life, and what you want your legacy to be. It is enlightening and empowering.

My personal **mission statement** is:

"To educate, inspire, and empower people to meet their challenges with confidence and to help them lead more meaningful lives through the development of their special talents and gifts."

I see my *why* as helping people meet their challenges: career challenges, project management challenges, leadership challenges, team building challenges, communication challenges, negotiating challenges, personal growth and performance challenges. My *why* is to help people be successful in college, career, and community. I see my *why* as helping people build their confidence to be successful and to help develop their special talents and gifts so they can reach their full potential and live their purpose. To me, that's a compelling mission that encompasses many opportunities to make a positive impact in the lives of others. Now I challenge you to write your own personal mission statement. Will you do it?

Action Item # 18   Based on the discovery activities you completed in Chapter 6 and Chapter 7, and other things you may have reflected on since initiating your job search project, try to write a **mission statement** that reflects your *higher purpose* in life, your *why*, the legacy you want to leave. My personal mission statement is:

_____

_____

_____

_____

_____

_____

_____

If this is too challenging at this point in your Career Quest project, move on and revisit it later. But do try at some time. It's a powerful and empowering exercise and once you have your personal mission statement you will have a magnet to move you in the right direction. You will have your compass to guide you on your journey.

"There comes a special moment in everyone's life, a moment for which that person was born. That special opportunity, when he seizes it, will fulfill his mission—a mission for which he is uniquely qualified. In that moment, he finds greatness. It is his finest hour."
—*Winston Churchill*

BRANDING STATEMENT

A branding statement is used to communicate what you want to be known for professionally. It should reflect your purpose and what makes you unique and distinctive. Think of your brand as your reputation and how you present yourself consistent with your values. Your branding statement should be written in a way that clearly defines what you do, your areas of expertise, and who you serve. A branding statement provides a snapshot of your attributes, what makes you successful, and how you can add value to others. The components of a personal branding statement include:

- What you want people to say when describing you
- How people benefit from working with you
- Your uniqueness and how you differ from others professionally
- Your "wow factor"

Coca Cola has a brand, Nike has a brand, Apple has a brand. They have created their brands to proactively manage their reputation. What do you want people to say about you? How do you want them to remember you? In one or two sentences, you want to be able to describe yourself to grab the listener's (or reader's) attention.

- What are you best at? (Strength/Value)
- Who do you serve? (Audience)
- What distinguishes you? (Your unique selling proposition and how you help people get results)

"Your personal brand is what people say about you when you are not in the room."
—*Chris Ducker*

EXAMPLES OF BRANDING STATEMENTS:

"The 'Go To' person for solving complex IT problems and delivering successful projects."

"Technical writer who takes the complex and makes it simple; helping audiences ranging from medical doctors to parents of patients."

"A senior project manager with the ability to work effectively to build relationships across all levels of an organization from the production floor to the executive floor."

Your branding statement can be used on your business cards, resume, website, and can be part of a written or spoken introduction. Remember, this is your "wow factor" and why someone would choose to hire you or do business with you.

Write your branding statement. Here is a simple formula to help you get started on your branding statement.

"I help _____ do/understand _____ to achieve _____.
(fill in the blanks)

Your brand is your story and the solution you deliver.

Another activity that may help you is to complete the following:

What three things can I _____ (teach, build, create) that helps my audience/customers most?

1. _____

2. _____

3. _____

Your personal brand should be reflected on your LinkedIn profile, on your website, your e-mail signature, and should be included in your elevator speech (which we will discuss later in this chapter).

SUMMARY STATEMENTS

A summary statement is used on your resume to communicate your unique selling proposition and the value you bring to an organization, generally in three to four sentences. Your branding statement can be embedded in your summary statement. You *must* have a good summary statement to grab the attention of the reader.

I like to think of the summary statement on your resume like a movie trailer—it's a sneak preview, it's a teaser of what's to come. The goal of the movie trailer is to capture the audiences' attention so they will want to see the movie. Your goal, with your summary statement, is to capture the Human Resource manager's attention, the hiring manager's attention, or the attention of anyone reading your resume so they will keep reading. If it is not very good, the reader will put down your resume, never to be seen again!

Your summary statement should include the following components:

1. **Your professional identity** - Who are you in the work force? Are you a Human Resource Manager, a Research Scientist, a Senior IT Executive, a Project Management Professional, a Hospitality Professional, an Executive Chef, a Customer Service Representative, a Financial Advisor? You want to create a vivid image of your professional identity.

2. **Your expertise and core competencies** - What are your specialties, your skills and knowledge? If you are a Human Resource Manager do you specialize in employee relations, benefits and compensation, labor law? As a Research Scientist what are your areas of research; crop and environmental science, oncology research, brain disorders? What's your specialty? "Project Manager specializing in leading and directing complex IT projects from initiation to close out." Where do you excel?

3. **Where and for whom have you worked, types of organizations and environments?** Have you worked in the private sector, public sector, universities, or non-profits? Was the organization a Fortune 500 company, consulting firms, mid-size, entrepreneurial, or start-up? What industry: agriculture, technology, medical, energy, environmental, security, arts and entertainment, broadcasting, financial services, real estate, construction, utilities, retail, telecommunications, transportation? The reader wants to know the types of environments you have worked in and specific industries.

4. **The unique strengths, awards, special knowledge, or technical skills you possess** - You want to share with the reader what differentiates you from others in your field or industry. Have you won any awards for your work? What languages do you speak and level of proficiency? (In today's global market language skills are premium selling points.) Did you serve in the armed forces? Do you possess any special government clearances? Do you have a certification or special knowledge such as a PMP® certification[1] (Project Management Professional); Six Sigma training;[2] Agile;[3] SCRUM,[4] Cisco certification;[5] Microsoft certification,[6] etc.? These things will help distinguish you from others applying for the position you seek.

Examples:

A Senior Professional Human Resource (SPHR) leader with 10 plus years' experience managing and leading all aspects of human capital including recruiting, hiring, training, coaching, and administrating corporate policies and procedures to achieve business objectives. Expertise includes organizational design and development, program management, leadership development, and change management. Certified ICF executive coach and MBTI Master Practitioner. Have worked with companies ranging from startups to Fortune 500; fluent in German and Spanish with basic knowledge of Portuguese.

A Customer Service and Sales professional with a reputation for building long-term relationships, customer loyalty, and increasing market share. Consistently meets and exceeds performance goals and recognized in the top 10% of sales for the past 5 years. Experience in pharmaceutical, biotech, agribusiness, and chemical industries. Executive Board Member for North Carolina Biotech Center.

A certified Project Management Professional (PMP®) with 15 plus years managing and leading complex projects. A proven track record with the ability to coach, mentor, and lead others to accomplish project goals and deliver projects on time, on budget, and within scope. Expertise includes supply chain management, process re-engineering, data management, and stakeholder management. Retired Officer U.S. Air Force.

A senior Information Technology Specialist with the ability to manage complex software and development projects and translate customer requirements into successful project deliverables. Communicates effectively with stakeholders from C-level executives to engineers and technical subject matter experts. Reputation for building high performing teams that meet and exceed performance expectations. Trained in Agile and SCRUM methodologies. Experience spans a wide variety of industries in both the private and public sectors.

Be sure that whatever you put in your summary statement is not so generic that it could also describe a majority of the applicants applying for the position. Stating you have "effective communication skills" without something to back it up will not capture the reader's attention. I imagine they have seen that a few hundred times before. Here are a couple of good examples when stating you have good communication skills that might intrigue the reader, both examples are real from clients I have worked with.

Effective communication skills having produced two PBS Specials.

Effective communication skills, having won three Emmy's as a television news reporter.

Now those have some meat to them! Don't merely insert things in your summary statement that you think a hiring manager wants to see without backing it up with a specific example(s).

So, does your summary statement get a thumbs-up, a thumbs-down, or an "eh, maybe" Even an "eh, maybe" won't get you an interview. Your goal is to peak their attention and keep them reading. If the rest of your resume is as good as your summary statement you may just get that coveted interview you seek.

━━◦◦◦━━

Did you ever think you would have to write so many *statements*? Career transition is a process and as I have been saying all along, it takes a lot of work. Think how much better you are going to know yourself taking the time to reflect on where you've been and where you want to go. All this work and reflection will help you grow during this time of transition and ensure you are on the right track. Remember the old Chinese proverb, "No pain, no gain."

"One that would have the fruit must climb the tree."
—*Thomas Fuller*

━━◦◦◦━━

ELEVATOR SPEECH

Your elevator speech is similar to your summary statement, but instead of being used in the written form, it is used to communicate with others in networking situations. Your elevator speech is used to introduce yourself to others and generally should be no longer than thirty to sixty seconds.

Start with your professional identity and then your areas of expertise, any special skills you may have and the types of environments where you have worked and/or where you would like to work. Your goal, in sixty seconds or less, is to capture your audience's attention so they will want to know more about you.

Write out your elevator speech and then practice, practice, practice, until it becomes comfortable and natural. Many networking groups I have attended allow only thirty seconds for your elevator speech/introduction. Be prepared to deliver your message in thirty to sixty seconds max in any situation.

The name, "elevator speech," is based on the chance that you get on an elevator with someone whose attention you want for a possible job or business opportunity and you have only thirty to sixty seconds to introduce yourself and make a favorable impression. Your goal should be to get a follow up meeting to share more about yourself and explore opportunities. I caution you not to create an elevator speech that sounds like elevator music or you will put your audience to sleep. It should be engaging, informative, concise, and create interest.

Sample Elevator Speech

> *My name is Rebecca Roberts and I am a Sales Professional with experience in a number of industries including manufacturing, transportation, and technology. I recently completed a 5-year contract position where I had the opportunity to work on several new product releases. During that time, I led a total of six project teams and worked with key stakeholders, both internally and externally. I am looking for a position where I can combine my sales experience with the knowledge I have acquired leading project teams. I have an MBA and am currently working on getting my Certified Professional Sales Person (CPSP) certification.*

My name is Tricia Daniels and I am a Human Resource Specialist with over 10 years' experience in employee recruiting, hiring, on-boarding, training, employee relations, with extensive knowledge of state and federal employment laws. Previously I worked as a paralegal in labor law. I have a reputation for working collaboratively with my stakeholders to meet business objectives. I am looking for a senior level position where I can provide guidance, training, and support in all areas of Human Resources.

⚍⚭⚍

RESUMES

Your resume is your key marketing tool to get you in front of hiring managers and recruiters. Its primary purpose is to get you an interview, a foot in the door. If it is not well written and does not contain certain key elements, you probably will not have access to the hiring managers unless you have done a good job networking (which of course you want to do that too). A bad resume will reflect poorly on you and will almost certainly eliminate you immediately.

Most of us will need a resume multiple-times during our career, and crafting an effective resume is no easy feat. A major frustration for many job seekers is developing a resume that will get them in front of a hiring manager. Way too many resumes that I have read are *ho-hum* and generic at best. "I'm a good communicator, hard-worker, fast learner… blah, blah, blah." Why the heck would a recruiter or hiring manager want to keep reading it? Sounds like a broken record—is that expression still used? How many times have they read those exact same words? That's not what they want. Generic wording will not help you stand out and get noticed.

There are so many employable and highly desirable candidates currently looking for work who are not getting interviews. Why? Because they have a poorly written resume (and perhaps they are doing a poor job of networking as well). Time and time again I have worked with job seekers who are frustrated because they are getting no traction from their resume. They have posted them on job boards, applied online, and handed out resumes at job fairs with absolutely no interest. After working with a job seeker to revise their resume, to capture what an employer is looking for, in almost every case the job seeker has immediately started to get inquiries from prospective employers.

Case in point, I worked with a woman seeking an HR position who was frustrated by the lack of traction she was getting from her resume. I met her one Monday morning at a local job seeker group to review and help revise her resume. Bottom line, it was not accomplishment based, instead it included a listing of her former job responsibilities. It told what she had done but not what she had accomplished. With a little tweaking and some other minor revisions her resume was ready to be re-circulated. The following week she got several inquiries and four interviews lined up. Within another two weeks she had two job offers and ultimately accepted one of the positions. Her challenge finding a job was not due to a lack of skills and abilities, but rather a poorly constructed and poorly focused resume.

Make sure your resume is constructed to get you the job that you want, not a rehash of what you've done in the past.

What Recruiters and Hiring Managers Want to Know

The biggest problem many job seekers have is not understanding the purpose of a resume. *An effective resume is not a listing of prior job descriptions.* It's not about what you did in your previous position(s) but rather about *what you accomplished*. What did you do to add value in your previous position(s) that translates into something marketable for the position for which you are applying? The standard off-the-shelf resume will not get you very far.

What a recruiter or a hiring manager wants to know, if they are going to consider you for a position is:

- What makes you unique, what's your value proposition
- How you are going to help their company meet and achieve their business goals, realize opportunities, and overcome challenges
- Why they should hire you

Your resume needs to be clear, concise, and communicate why you are the best fit for the position. Recruiters have little time to read each applicant's resume. They will do an initial scan of your resume (seven to ten seconds tops), *if* it makes it to their desk. This means that the most important part of your resume is the top one-third because that is what the recruiter will see in their initial scan. You better have a good summary statement!

- Have you written your summary statement in a way that captures the reader's attention and inspires them to read further?

- Have you highlighted your unique qualifications as it relates to the specific position?

- Have you included key accomplishments?

Again, if your resume is simply a job description of your previous employment it will not serve you well nor get you an interview. Keep your sentences short and use bullets to list your key accomplishments. Bullets will also make your resume easier to read and easier to find critical information. Imagine if you had to read resumes all day, would you spend the time digging for the information you need? Doubtful—make it easy for the hiring manager!

DO I NEED MORE THAN ONE RESUME?

Another important thing to know about resumes is that you may need more than one, and for sure you will need many versions to reflect the requirements of the position for which you are applying. I myself have four "base resumes,"[7] one for each of my primary areas of expertise. I have a resume for training, one for coaching, another for speaking gigs, and yet another for consulting opportunities. You may not need four base resumes, but you will need more than one base resume if you are considering and searching in more than one career field or industry. Each resume you submit for a position should be customized. Use your base resume as a starting point and then reflect the specific requirements of the position and the appropriate industry terminology.

HOW LONG SHOULD MY RESUME BE?

The standard rule in the private sector is no more than two pages. Some people think the resume should be one page. I use one-page resumes for college students and non-professionals. For most professionals who have been in the workforce for a number of years, a one-page resume does not allow much opportunity to tell their story.

I heard a panel of recruiters recently discuss this topic. The first recruiter said, "One page for every five years of experience, not to exceed five pages." Another recruiter disagreed with him and said he recommended no more than a two-page resume stating recruiters are busy and will not read long resumes. I tend to agree with him and always have my clients develop a resume that is not more than two pages.

On those two pages, which I consider "very expensive real estate," be sure to focus only on what the market is buying. It doesn't matter that you did something you are very proud of. If the market no longer needs that skill, service, or technology, it should not be on your resume. Keep your resume laser focused on what is needed to get your foot in the door for an interview. Focus on your key accomplishments required for the job/position for which you are applying.

CURRICULA VITAE (CV)

If you are a research scientist, or work in the university system, you probably have a very long resume known as a *curricula vitae* or *CV*. I have seen many CVs that go on and on for pages. If you are not familiar with the term, a CV is a longer form of a resume that includes extensive information related to academic background and other career-related activities. A CV will include academic background, teaching experience, degrees, research, awards, patents, publications, presentations, and other achievements. It would be impossible to get all of this on two pages. However, what I tell my clients is if they are applying to a job in the private sector; businesses versus government, research facilities, universities, or non-profits; they should focus on highlighting their key accomplishments on a two-page resume to include some of their academic training. Then they can create a separate document for their awards, patents, publications, and presentations.

I recommend for people who fall into this category to include in their summary statement a phrase similar to the following: "Research scientist with more than a dozen patents and numerous publications on…." "Recipient of the distinguished…award for research in…."

The summary statement allows the scientist or researcher to give a preview, and then they can follow up with additional pages listing all of their awards, patents, and publications. By creating two separate documents they won't lose the reader's interest but will still have a listing of all their academic credentials that can be provided later.

Bottom line on the number of pages—I tell my clients it's their resume and they can do whatever they want. However, if they want it read, I recommend no more than two pages. Your goal is to get someone to read your resume and get an interview!

How Far Back Do I Go?

This question comes up all the time; "How far back should I go with my resume?" The general rule of thumb today is to go back ten to fifteen years. Certainly, you can go back further if you wish and it may be advisable to do so depending on your experience and how relevant it is to the position for which you are applying. If you do not want to put dates that far back you might call it "Other Relevant Experience" and list the knowledge, skills, and abilities (KSA) you used in those previous positions. For example, when I started my career I was a Paralegal with a major telecommunications company. My legal experience has always been a plus in the eyes of a hiring manager and so I still include it on my resume despite the fact that I did that a very long time ago. The skills I learned, and was trained for, have not been forgotten and still have a lot of relevance, so I include them under "other relevant experience." If you did something a long time ago and it adds no value and is no longer relevant, do *not* include.

Types of Resumes

There are several different resume formats you could use for your career transition project. I will discuss three of your options. Which format you use will depend on your specific situation and, to some extent, your industry. Since your resume is your key sales tool, it is important that you choose wisely the most effective format for your circumstances. Your resume needs to be constructed in a way that reflects your unique selling points, your value to an organization, your accomplishments, and results—anything less will not contribute to your success.

I highly recommend you invest in an experienced career coach and/or resume writer to help you develop an effective resume. Too often I see job searches stall because of a poorly written, poorly focused resume. What you will pay for resume/coaching services are minor compared to the income you will lose in the meantime as you limp along with an ineffective resume—seek professional help as needed to move forward. Make sure if you hire a resume writer and/or career coach that you get recommendations regarding their services and the results they have delivered for others.

There are companies out there who will prepare a resume for you, with little or none of your time invested in the process. They do it all for you and charge you a steep price to do so. Be careful of using those services. You will end up with an off-the-shelf resume that you paid way too much for and does not represent you well.

It will take a time investment on your part to work in collaboration with your resume writer or career coach to develop a resume that reflects accurately your experience and accomplishments. Invest your time and money wisely so you can get the results you want and need to be successful.

The three resume formats most widely used include:

1. Chronological Resumes

2. Skill-Based Resumes

3. Project-Based Resumes

I will briefly provide a description of all three with my focus on the chronological resume, which is still the traditional format and most widely used. Skill-based, also known as "functional resumes," are most commonly used for people re-entering the work force after a long absence or someone changing fields/industry and their previous position(s) are not relevant (although their skills may be). People with large gaps in their employment history also tend to use skill-based/functional resumes. As a result, recruiters and hiring managers are often suspicious of this style of resume. Use one if it is appropriate to your circumstances. Project-based resumes are becoming more popular in technology fields and particularly for contractors who move from project to project.

Regardless of which format you use, it is essential that you focus on your knowledge, skills, and abilities (core competencies), your accomplishments, and results. Your core competencies are the strengths you bring to an organization; they help you excel at accomplishing your work objectives.

CHRONOLOGICAL RESUMES

A chronological resume is the most frequently used resume format and highlights, in reverse chronological order, the work history of an individual. This is the conventional resume format and should include the following:

- **Name and Contact Information** - Include your name, along with any professional designation you might have such as Ph.D., MBA, PMP, P.E., J.D., etc.; one phone number (usually a mobile number, the one you have most control over); email address (nothing cutesy or offensive, typically including your name); and your LinkedIn address.

You might even want to consider setting up an email address specifically for your job search. Then be sure to check it first every day before your personal email. Be selective as to whom you give this address. I don't know about you, but I get so many emails that information can occasionally get lost. Having an email designated for your job search can reduce the probability of that happening. Also, one advantage of having an email address specifically for your job search is that you can delete it later if desired.

LinkedIn is the social media tool that most recruiters and hiring managers use, so be sure to include your LinkedIn address in the header. (See more on LinkedIn in Chapter 12.) You can also include your city and state, but *do not* include your home address. If needed you can provide later; for now, keep your home address private.

- **Summary Statement** - A summary statement highlights your expertise, personal characteristics, types of organizations you have worked for, special honors or certifications, language skills, and military experience. The summary statement should be three to four sentences and describe you in a way that captures the reader's attention. If the summary statement is vague and generic it is unlikely to inspire the reader to read on and you are likely to go no further in the hiring process. Your goal with the summary statement is to *CAPTURE THEIR ATTENTION!* (As discussed earlier in this section with sample summary statements.)

- **Professional Experience** - Here you will list, in reverse chronological order, the jobs you have had. You will start with the name of the company you worked for, the years you worked for them, and a job title that reflects what you did. I generally put the job title before the company name because I think it is more relevant, it's a matter of preference.

The job title you use on your resume does not have to be the exact title you held at your previous employer. It is more important to reflect the job that you did so it will translate well for those reviewing your resume. For example, one of my job titles in my corporate career was Warehouse Engineer. A job title that better reflects what I actually did is Project Manager. It is more descriptive and far more marketable, and therefore, it's what I use on my resume. Only if you are applying to a job internally do you need to use the exact job title you held. Understand that different companies use different titles. It's not about the title but rather about the work you did. Choose a job title for your resume that is descriptive, relevant, current, and marketable.

Make your job title descriptive of your responsibilities. For example, if your job title was Lead Scientist II, that will not translate as well as perhaps Senior Research Scientist. Another example: perhaps your job title years ago was Vice President Human Resources Recruiting and today that same job is being called Vice President Talent Acquisition. Essentially the job is the same but the titles have changed. Using the old title may not get you noticed or picked up by the applicant tracking systems (ATS) if you apply online. It also dates you.

- **Responsibility Statement** - After your job title and the name of the company you worked for, you will include a one to two sentence responsibility statement. This sentence or sentences should describe, in a nutshell, your overall responsibility in the position you held. It should be short and concise. For example:

Led and managed a manufacturing facility with over 200 employees. Responsible for overseeing day-to-day operations, customer service fulfillment, and production requirements.

- **Accomplishment Statements** - These are the bulleted statements that follow your responsibility statement and highlight your major accomplishments, those accomplishments most relevant to the position for which you are applying. Again, employers are not interested in all the tasks and activities you did in your previous job; they want to know what you accomplished, what value you can bring to their organization, and how you can help them solve problems and realize opportunities?

Write your accomplishment statements with the potential employer in mind. Your bullet points should not read like your old job description. I call that an "obituary resume." Keep your sentences short, concise, and quantify your accomplishments whenever you can. "Exceeded sale's goals by 50%" and "Reduced error rate by 40%" are both examples of accomplishment statements.

You will use only five or six accomplishment statements for your most recent position and then progressively fewer bullets as you move backwards in your work history. Yes, it is tempting to put ten or twelve of your accomplishments for your last position, but don't do it—too many. Stick to the top five to six accomplishments most relevant to the position.

Like your summary statement, you will need to customize your accomplishment statements for each employer, always sharing your most relevant accomplishments. See more details on accomplishment statements later in this chapter.

- **Education and Professional Development** - These two categories can be separate but I usually combine them since they are related and space is usually at a premium on the resume. Include your highest level of education first and then additional education and training/professional development. So, if you have a master's degree that will go first, and then your bachelor's degree and where you attended college. If you graduated from college within the past five years include your GPA, if impressive, otherwise you may want to avoid including. If you got a 4.0 in 1992 it won't get you much mileage today so leave it off. At this point, your experience and accomplishments are what you will be evaluated on, not your GPA.

  If education isn't your strong point, then include any training that you may have received from your previous employer(s) such as computer skills, safety training, conflict resolution, supervisory training, leadership development, etc. If it is a professional position, do not include your high school education (as I often see people do who have no college). Doing so only highlights your lack of advanced education. Focus on training you have received instead.

- **Other relevant information** that you might provide at the bottom of your resume, if you still have space, includes:

  Professional organizations to which you belong

  Technology and/or software of which you are proficient

  Certifications

  Language skills (fluency or proficient knowledge of)

  Military experience

  Volunteer activities

Note that any language skills you have (fluency), job-specific certifications, and prior military experience, should also be included in your *summary statement* at the beginning of your resume. Don't leave it to the reader to get to the bottom of the second page to find these things. The reader may never get there!

I worked with one client who spoke multiple languages. He was fluent in Czech with a working knowledge of Russian, Arabic, French, and several other languages. Pretty impressive for an American! The problem was he listed this information on the bottom of the second page of his resume. His resume was not well written when I met him, and understandably he wasn't getting any traction. It was unlikely his extensive language skills ever got noticed. I doubt many recruiters or hiring managers ever made it past the first page. Some information absolutely belongs on the first page under the Summary Statement. In his case, his language skills should have been included in his summary because they were part of his value proposition.

(Sample resumes and templates can be found under the **Career Tool** section. See **www.ProjectCareerQuest.com**. You can also find many examples of resumes and resume formats online.)

SAMPLE CHRONOLOGICAL RESUME

NAME, PMP
Email

City, State   **LinkedIn Address**   **Cell Phone**

SUMMARY

A results-driven leader with over 15 years in the mortgage industry. Proven strategic expertise in leading programs, projects, and process improvement initiatives to increase productivity, revenue, and operational efficiencies. Strong record of leading, coaching, and developing team members and working effectively with senior leadership. Designed and implemented enterprise-wide compliance, regulatory, process improvement, and technology solutions for several financial institutions. Certified Project Management Professional (PMP®) and Lean Six Sigma Black Belt certified. Fluent in Spanish.

PROFESSIONAL EXPERIENCE

XYZ HOME LENDING, Phoenix, Arizona
Vice President/Process Engineer   **20XX–Present**
Provide direct consultation and lead initiatives across the organization.
- Analyze current state processes and design future state processes to increase efficiency, improve quality control, and enhance customer and team member experience.
- Identify risk and opportunities associated with redesign/improvement approach and ensure alignment with business objectives.
- Work closely with senior leadership on customer complaints and regulatory initiatives, including action plan responses to the Consumer Financial Protection Bureau (CFPB), ensuring customer satisfaction and corporate compliance.
- Track and evaluate initiatives that have been implemented ensuring performance criteria are met. Maintain lessons learned database for improvements on future initiatives.
- Provide onboarding, coaching, and mentoring for new team members resulting in less turn over, higher productivity, and greater employee satisfaction.

Assistant Vice President/Senior Project Manager   **20XX–20XX**
Project Management Office (PMO)
Managed matrix resources in the development of project plans, business process mapping, design solutions, and implementation plans. Served as liaison between business and technical stakeholders for large and complex efforts.
- Reviewed initiatives and determined size, scope, risk, budget, impacts, and strategy on all assigned initiatives.
- Completed all project management artifacts, including the presentation and approval process of business cases to senior leadership.

- Managed change requests assessing impact on project constraints and worked closely with technology partners and mortgage leaders on prioritization and implementation of approved changes.
- Mentored team members on career development and process to obtain PMP credentials, with a 60% increase in certifications in a 3-year period.

ABC MORTGAGE, Tempe, Arizona

Assistant Vice President/Business Systems Consultant   20XX–20XX

Project Team Lead and Business System Consultant on the design and implementation of technology solutions for sales and fulfillment teams.

- Managed business requirements and user test plans ensuring project timelines were met.
- Facilitated and supported production validation testing resulting in a 67% increase in user acceptance.
- Increased productivity and reduced the amount of help desk calls by implementing and leading monthly technology sales forum calls.

ACACIA MORTGAGE GROUP, Tempe, Arizona   20XX–20XX

Director of Retail Mortgage Sales and Operations Support

Led sales and fulfillment team members on all mortgage fulfillment functionalities.

- Increased customer satisfaction ratings and reduced mortgage cycle times by 30%.
- Implemented new processes and procedures to improve quality and regulatory compliance audits by 43%.
- Redesigned manual and automated processes to increase efficiencies and cost savings for the division.

ACACIA MORTGAGE GROUP, Mesa, Arizona   20XX – 20XX

Executive Mortgage Manager

Led and restructured a mortgage company and implemented a governance program, technology solutions, underwriting, and quality standards.

- Managed regional office and 5 branches increasing volume by 48% and reducing expenses by 22%.
- Ensured all state and federal policies and procedures were documented and implemented throughout the company.

EDUCATION AND PROFESSIONAL DEVELOPMENT

BA in Business Administration, Arizona State University
Project Management Professional (PMP) certification, PMP #XXXXX
Lean Six Sigma Black Belt certified
DE Certified Underwriter

NO "OBJECTIVE STATEMENT" REQUIRED

Notice I *do not* include objective statements on the chronological resume. While some people will tell you to include one, I believe it is a waste of valuable space and the reader's time. Prospective employers are not concerned about your objective at this point. They want to know what you have to offer them. How can you solve their problems, help them create new opportunities, find new business, increase revenue, cut costs, build something bigger and better? It's about them, not you. Besides, every objective statement I have ever read says exactly the same thing. "I want a good job, with a good company, that pays me good money, and treats me well, blah, blah, blah." Objective statements offer little to no value to the hiring manager or recruiter. Your focus on your resume should be what you can do for the company, not what they can do for you.

SKILL-BASED RESUMES

Skill-based resumes, aka "functional resumes," highlight an individual's skills and expertise versus work history. They are typically used for people who:

- Are making a major shift in careers and the chronological resume highlighting work experience and job titles does not offer much value.

- Have been out of the job market for many years due to family obligations.

- Have recently embarked on their career without a lot of work experience (recent high school or college graduate).

- Want to turn their hobby, passion, or volunteer work into a full-time paying job and their relevant experience comes from unpaid positions.

- Have sketchy work history, prolonged gaps in employment.

While skill-based resumes serve their purpose, many recruiters view them with suspicion assuming gaps in employment. However, if you have been out of the job market for a number of years raising a family, taking care of an elderly parent, or caring for a sick relative, a skill-based resume can be used to highlight your core competencies and accomplishments. Also, those of you who want to make a major career change may find this format more applicable than the chronological resume. Your accomplishments and results will be associated with your core competencies and related skills versus with a specific employer.

A skill-based resume should include:

- **Name and contact information** - See chronological resume section.

- **Career objective** - Optional (Only use if it adds value and understanding).

- **Summary statement** - See chronological resume section.

- **Listing of core competencies and associated accomplishments** - Stated with bullets highlighting key accomplishments including the actions you took and results.

- **Relevant experience** - Here you will include the name of the company you worked or volunteered for, associated job title, dates of employment, and city and state. Experience can be non-paid experience including volunteer activities.

- **Education and professional development** – See chronological resume section.

- **Other relevant information** – I.e., military experience, language skills, technical and computer skills.

The skill-based resume sample I have included highlights core competencies and accomplishments followed by work and volunteer experience. Again, core competencies include the knowledge, skills, and abilities that help you be successful; they are your strengths and your competitive edge.

I would recommend using one similar to the one I have included if a chronological resume does not make sense for you. If you are to get any interest however, you must highlight your core competencies in a way that demonstrates value to an employer and emphasizes specific accomplishments in line with the available or advertised position.

Note that on the sample skill-based resume I have included, an objective statement has been used. Only include an objective statement if it adds value and understanding to the employer. Otherwise, a well-written summary statement will suffice. Do not omit the summary statement.

SAMPLE SKILL-BASED RESUME

NAME, CAPM
Email

City, State   **LinkedIn Address**   **Cell Phone**

CAREER OBJECTIVE: After taking a career sabbatical to provide a high-quality education for four children, seeking a position as a project manager where I can use my skills as a trained and educated design engineer and project management professional.

SUMMARY

Certified Associate Project Manager (CAPM®) and proactive, detail-oriented professional with the proven ability to plan and execute projects and coordinate business operations in a variety of settings. An analytical and process-oriented thinker who leverages strong interpersonal skills to engage stakeholders, build customer loyalty, and improve operational/process efficiencies. Competencies include:

• Project Management	• Process Improvement	• Team Development
• Stakeholder Engagement	• Analytical Problem Solving	• Conflict Resolution
• Scheduling and Logistics	• Organizing and Planning	• Customer Relations

CORE COMPETENCIES AND RESULTS

Project Management

- Collaboratively develop procedures to streamline business processes and create a memorable and seamless experience for local restaurant guests.

- Plan and organize large gatherings and a variety of projects for busy start-up restaurant in downtown business district directly increasing profitability.

- Assist head brewer with project management support to increase production and distribution of beverages at local microbrew.

- Participated in a two-year pilot program for new curriculum design for home school program; provided vital feedback used to improve curriculum effectiveness.

- Coordinated innovative design projects working collaboratively with Quality Engineers, Quality Control Specialists, Suppliers, and a Manufacturer.

Process Improvement

- Refine internal best practices to improve efficiencies and service levels for a better customer experience.

- Resolved design issues, streamlined processes, and trained engineers on best manufacturing processes to increase efficiency.

Planning and Organizing/Operational Support/Customer Relations

- Manage all incoming reservations for a busy start-up restaurant achieving high customer satisfaction ratings.

- Coordinate supply shipments and field questions from suppliers ensuring accuracy and timeliness of delivery for start-up restaurant.

- During opening months of restaurant, liaised among multiple teams supporting management and providing operational stability.

- Developed and manage website for start-up restaurant increasing visibility, traffic, and popularity of establishment.

- Researched and coordinated state-specific curricula for home schooling coop; organized academic and extracurricular activities that engaged students and improved learning outcome.

- Collaboratively developed, organized, and taught classes for home school coop with students consistently achieving high levels of academic success.

- Created and delivered original curriculum for home school students based on local art exhibits. Curriculum used to develop skills such as critical and creative thinking, complex analysis, problem solving, risk-taking, and inventiveness. Also prepared students to be more well-rounded learners and leaders.

WORK EXPERIENCE

Brewery Nirvana, Chicago, IL   20XX–Present
Reservation Coordinator/Project Manager

Home Educator, Oak Park IL   20XX–20XX

Caterpillar, Lafayette, IN   19XX–20XX
Design Engineer

EDUCATION AND PROFESSIONAL DEVELOPMENT

- B.S. in Mechanical Engineering, Michigan Technological University

- Master's Certificate in Project Management, George Washington University, 20XX

- Certified Associate in Project Management (CAPM®), Project Management Institute, 20XX

TECHNICAL SKILLS

- 3D CAD

- Graphic Design

- MS Office Suite (Word, Excel, PowerPoint, Outlook)

PROJECT-BASED RESUMES

Instead of a resume organized by companies worked for, a project-based resume is organized by projects completed, technology used, and accomplishments. A project-based resume will highlight selected projects that are most similar to an upcoming project offering. This type of resume is particularly effective and applicable for contract technology project managers.

I have a friend who is a recruiter for technology companies and she prefers this resume format. What she is looking for is the experience someone has, if they have worked on similar projects, and the technology used.

The primary sections of the project-based resume include:

1. Name and contact information
2. Qualifications
3. Project Portfolio
4. Education and Professional Development

Under the section Project Portfolio, you will highlight the following:

1. The title of the project, company you worked for, job title
2. Duration of the project
3. Technology used
4. Description of project accomplishments

Review the sample/template on the following page and you can find additional examples online with a simple Google search. Remember, for a project-based resume you are selecting those projects that are most relevant and similar to the project to which you are trying to get assigned.

SAMPLE PROJECT-BASED RESUME

NAME, PMP
Email

City, State   **LinkedIn Address**   **Cell Phone**

QUALIFICATIONS

Project management professional delivering best-in-class hardware and software solutions that exceed quality standards and customer expectations. Creative problem- solver and team-oriented leader, leveraging expertise in proactive risk management. Have managed cross-functional teams of 100+ onshore and offshore staff to develop and deliver complex projects. Clearly deliver complex project information regarding scope, schedule, budget, risk, and technologies to clients, senior management, and other key stakeholders ensuring on time execution of project deliverables.

Core Competencies: Leading and managing complex projects, technical project management, change management, stakeholder management, collaborative team building, and excellent communication and presentation skills.

Technical Proficiencies and Programming Languages: MS Project, Project Server, Jira, Sharepoint, C/C++, Java, Javascript, Perl

Agile Methodologies: Scrum, Test Driven Development, Kanban, Agile software development

PROJECT PORTFOLIO

Project 1: Project Name, Company Name, Job Title
Duration: 4 months
Technologies Used: (List technologies)
- Accomplishment statement
- Accomplishment statement
- Accomplishment statement

Project 2: Project Name, Company Name, Job Title
Duration: 12 months
Technologies Used: (List technologies)
- Accomplishment statement
- Accomplishment statement
- Accomplishment statement

Project 3: Project Name, Company Name, Job Title
Duration: 60 days
Technologies Used: (List technologies)
- Accomplishment statement
- Accomplishment statement
- Accomplishment statement

Project 4: Project Name, Company Name, Job Title
Duration: 3 months
Technologies Used: (List technologies)
* Accomplishment statement
* Accomplishment statement
* Accomplishment statement

EDUCATION AND PROFESSIONAL DEVELOPMENT
* B.S. Electrical Engineering, Stanford University (date graduated if within 5 years)
* PMP Certification #00000
* Scrum Certification
* Tableau essentials
* Agile Product Owner Role
* Hadoop Fundamentals
* JavaScript

ACCOMPLISHMENT STATEMENTS

Whether you use a chronological resume, a skill-based resume, or a project-based resume, you will need to include relevant accomplishment statements. Accomplishment statements are used to inform recruiters and hiring managers what you accomplished in your previous job that can translate into value for them. They will not hire you because of your old job description, they will hire you because you made a significant impact to the success of your previous employer and they want you to do the same for them. Employers hire people to solve problems, overcome their challenges, excel over the competition, acquire new markets, build their reputation, and achieve success. Some of the things you will potentially want to include in your accomplishment statements include, but not limited to:

- How you helped your employer(s) be more efficient; streamline processes.

- How you increased effectiveness; provided greater customer or employee satisfaction.

- How you helped reduce something such as: costs, cycle time, number of errors, number of safety issues, number of customer complaints, etc.

- How you helped increase something such as: productivity, number of projects completed on time, return on investment, market share, sales, number of contracts awarded, etc.

- How you helped your previous employer comply with relevant laws, regulations, and codes, thereby reducing risk to the organization.

- How you helped solve complex problems or issues facing your previous employer(s).

- How you built relationships with customers, senior management, employees, and other key stakeholders.

Quantify as much as you can. If you have numbers and percentages, that is good information to include. If that information is no longer available to you or it has been a very long time and you simply do not remember, use words like "significantly increased the number of on time deliveries," "achieved significant cost savings for the organization," etc. Sample accomplishments statements can be found in the **Career Tools** section at **www.ProjectCareerQuest.com**; several are included below.

Successfully led established 501(c)(3) organization in strategic planning and tactical execution of donor cultivation and various community events to secure $2.3M in major gift solicitations.

Implemented new platform delivering revenue of $900M on a goal of $500M.

Optimized capital budget saving $250K annually.

EFFECTIVE SENTENCE OPENERS (FOR ACCOMPLISHMENT STATEMENTS)

When developing your accomplishment statements, you will want to use strong action verbs to describe your specific accomplishments. Do not start an accomplishment statement with the words "Responsible for." Responsible for does not mean that you actually did it. Are you responsible for taking out the garbage at home? Do you do it? Maybe, but then again, maybe not! Let's stick to things you actually did, not just responsible for.

Strong verbs include words such as: acquired, automated, consolidated, collaborated, cultivated, enabled, equipped, implemented, led, negotiated, streamlined, etc. An alphabetical list of suggested sentence starters can be found in the **Career Tools** section at **www.ProjectCareerQuest.com**. Also, to help you with your accomplishment statements I have included a list of strong action verbs grouped by specific skill sets on the pages that follow.

"It is through accomplishment that man makes his contribution
and contribution is life's greatest reward."
—*John Portman*

Action Item # 19

Develop **accomplishment statements** to be used on your resume. Be sure to start each of them with strong action verbs. Describe the actions you took and the results you got adding value to your employer/ organization. See the charts to follow for a list of strong action verbs.

STRONG ACTION VERBS

Worked on a Project	Managed/ Led Others	Supported Customers	Research & Analysis	Communica-tions	Personal Development
Approved	Coached	Advised	Analyzed	Advised	Achieved
Budgeted	Coordinated	Advocated	Assembled	Appraised	Advised
Chaired	Corrected	Arbitrated	Assessed	Authored	Attended
Collaborated	Counseled	Assisted	Audited	Clarified	Coached
Consolidated	Cultivated	Attended	Calculated	Coached	Collaborated
Converted	Delegated	Checked	Critiqued	Collaborated	Completed
Coordinated	Developed	Clarified	Discovered	Communicated	Corrected
Created	Empowered	Coached	Evaluated	Composed	Counseled
Delivered	Enabled	Collaborated	Examined	Convinced	Delivered
Executed	Fostered	Consulted	Experimented	Corresponded	Empowered
Finalized	Guided	Corrected	Explored	Counseled	Encouraged
Implemented	Handled	Corresponded	Forecasted	Edited	Equipped
Initiated	Headed	Delivered	Identified	Encouraged	Facilitated
Launched	Hired	Diagnosed	Interpreted	Facilitated	Guided
Led	Inspired	Educated	Interviewed	Guided	Identified
Merged	Interviewed	Evaluated	Investigated	Illustrated	Influenced
Monitored	Mentored	Fielded	Mapped	Influenced	Instituted
Motivated	Mobilized	Fostered	Measured	Interviewed	Introduced
Orchestrated	Oversaw	Furnished	Modified	Lectured	Invested
Organized	Recruited	Guaranteed	Observed	Persuaded	Learned
Oversaw	Shaped	Handled	Qualified	Questioned	Modified
Planned	Supervised	Influenced	Quantified	Recognized	Motivated
Produced	Taught	Informed	Surveyed	Reported	Obtained
Programmed	Trained	Investigated	Tested	Updated	Positioned
Scheduled	Unified	Maintained	Tracked	Verbalized	Strengthened
Summarized	United	Resolved	Uncovered	Wrote	Qualified

Note: Use the additional spaces to add words that may apply.

STRONG ACTION VERBS CONT.

Developed/ Created Something	Improved/ Changed Something	Increased Productivity	Saved Time/Money	Brought in Funding or Resources	Oversaw or Regulated
Analyzed	Achieved	Achieved	Absorbed	Acquired	Appraised
Built	Approved	Analyzed	Balanced	Engaged	Authorized
Charted	Automated	Converted	Centralized	Enlisted	Blocked
Chartered	Balanced	Designed	Condensed	Evaluated	Controlled
Composed	Centralized	Developed	Conserved	Forged	Corrected
Conceived	Corrected	Diagnosed	Decreased	Increased	Delegated
Created	Decentralized	Duplicated	Deducted	Initiated	Dispatched
Designed	Established	Established	Diagnosed	Investigated	Enforced
Developed	Facilitated	Experimented	Expedited	Leveraged	Ensured
Engineered	Implemented	Generated	Instituted	Lobbied	Evaluated
Envisioned	Innovated	Implemented	Lessened	Merged	Governed
Established	Invented	Improved	Liquidated	Motivated	Influenced
Formed	Invested	Innovated	Lowered	Navigated	Informed
Formalized	Launched	Installed	Managed	Negotiated	Inspected
Formulated	Merged	Integrated	Merged	Partnered	Instituted
Founded	Modernized	Leveraged	Negotiated	Positioned	Interpreted
Guided	Modified	Maximized	Overhauled	Promoted	Investigated
Implemented	Overhauled	Measured	Realized	Publicized	Itemized
Incorporated	Persuaded	Minimized	Reconciled	Qualified	Monitored
Initiated	Positioned	Optimized	Reduced	Raised	Reported
Introduced	Refined	Reconfigured	Reorganized	Recruited	Restricted
Launched	Reorganized	Refined	Revamped	Researched	Reviewed
Modernized	Revamped	Reorganized	Standardized	Secured	Screened
Pioneered	Revised	Restored	Streamlined	Solicited	Scrutinized
Spearheaded	Simplified	Standardized	Tracked	Strengthened	Standardized
Tailored	Updated	Upgraded	Updated	Wrote	Verified

Note: Use the additional spaces to add words that may apply. An alphabetized list of strong action verbs can be found in the **Career Tools** section.

SUMMARY OF KEY DO'S AND DON'TS FOR YOUR RESUME

Do's	Don'ts
Write your resume to reflect where you want to go in your career, emphasizing the core competencies and experience you have to get you there.	Do not emphasize things on your resume that you have no desire to do moving forward.
Customize your resume for the job and industry for which you are applying. Be sure to use key words relevant to the position that will get you noticed. Many companies use Applicant Tracking Systems (ATS) that scan for key words. If those words are not on your resume the computer will not select it.	Do not use a standard resume for all jobs. Create a base resume and then customize for each position for which you apply.
Ensure that your resume reflects how your knowledge and experience correlates with the job requirements and include specific accomplishment statements to communicate your value to the employer.	Do not use the words "responsible for" with bulleted items. What's important is not what you were responsible for but rather what you actually accomplished. The bullet points you use should be written as accomplishment statements.
Include a compelling summary statement that will grab the reader's attention so they will want to read your entire resume. If your summary statement does not express clearly your value proposition the reader will stop reading!	Do not include an objective statement on a chronological resume. Companies are not interested in your objective. Use instead a summary statement that highlights your expertise and skills the employer is looking for.
Back up what you say on your resume with examples and results. Your resume is a starting point for interview questions. Be sure to reflect your experience accurately.	Do not exaggerate or misrepresent your experience. Doing so is dishonest and will set you up for failure. A good interviewer will be able to uncover inconsistencies and statements that are inaccurate or untrue.
Make sure your resume is without spelling errors and with proper use of grammar and punctuation.	Do not include references or the statement, "References provided upon request." You will need to provide references as a separate document when you get called for an interview.

COVER LETTERS

"Do I need a cover letter?" This is a question I hear all the time. My answer is "no," but I definitely recommend you send one along with your resume. Don't get lazy in the process. Your goal is to stand out and differentiate yourself in your job search. Yes, you are creating a lot of documentation and the cover letter gives you another opportunity to highlight some of your accomplishments and why you are the best candidate for the position. The two formats for cover letters that I recommend are: 1) AIDA format or 2) "T" format. Both are described below with a sample to follow.

AIDA is an acronym for *Attention, Interest, Desire,* and *Action.* AIDA is a model or tool designed for sales, and of course your goal here is to influence the hiring manager to look at your resume and ultimately get an interview.

Before you start the body of the letter you will include the *date and salutation* at the top of the page. You should include the hiring manager's or recruiter's name if possible. Do your homework. Who does the hiring for this company? If you do not know the person's name to whom you are writing, or cannot discover the name, you can use something like "Dear Hiring Manager." Again, make sure you do your homework first.

If a friend referred you to the job, you should be able to get the manager's name and title. Make sure the spelling is correct. In some cases, you can call the company and ask for the hiring manager's name.

Paragraph # 1 - Attention

In the first paragraph of your cover letter you want to **grab the hiring manager's attention** by letting him or her know why you are writing. Let the reader know what position you are applying for and where you found the position advertised or who recommended that you apply for the position. If there is a job or position number include that as well. Companies like to know where their jobs are being found, such as a publication, job board, their company site, or through social media. Also, let them know why you are applying for the position; give them a reason to read your resume.

I am applying for the position of Customer Service Manager that I found on Indeed.com, Position #3456.

Sarah Swenson, a former colleague of mine who now works for your company, recommended that I reach out to you regarding the position of...

Paragraph #2 - Interest

In the second paragraph, you want to **peak their interest** by briefly describing your qualifications for the position and highlighting some of your relevant accomplishments. I typically list accomplishments using bullets to give them special focus. Highlight those three to five things that are most relevant to the job.

- *I am a project management professional (PMP) with experience that closely aligns with the position of Senior Project Lead. My experience includes…*

- *Expertise in Agile project management; reputation for delivering high-quality IT projects using a value-driven approach.*

- *Ten plus years' experience leading, directing, and executing complex IT projects.*

- *Effectively manages stakeholder relationships from the production floor to the executive suite.*

Paragraph #3 - Desire

In this paragraph let them know **why they should hire you** and create the desire for them to meet with you. What makes you the best fit for the position? How can you help them meet their challenges, solve their problems, and create new opportunities for them?

Having worked on similar projects in both the private and public sectors, I have the ability to…

Paragraph #4 - Action

Thank them for considering you for the position and **take the initiative to ask for a time to meet or speak** to discuss how your qualifications and experience align with their job requirements. *If you want action, request action!* You might even let them know you will reach out to them to schedule a time to meet. Is this pushy? No, you are simply being proactive for a job you are interested in pursuing. If you sit back and wait, the call may never come. How you word this last paragraph should express your enthusiasm to meet with the recruiter or hiring manager.

I look forward to the opportunity to meet with you to explore how my knowledge, skills, and experience can help your company achieve your business objectives. You can reach me via email at…or by phone at…. I will reach out to you in the next couple of days to see when we might meet.

Your cover letter should be no more than one page, keep it brief and focused. If you are emailing your cover letter and resume be sure to include the job title, position number, and hiring manager's name in the subject field. You do not want your resume and cover letter to end up in someone's junk file. Unless the employer tells you otherwise, copy and paste your cover letter into the body of your email and include your resume as an attached PDF file. See the **Career Tools** section for *sample cover letters* at **www.ProjectCareerQuest.com**.

T-COVER LETTER

An alternative to the AIDA format is one referred to as the T-cover letter. This format demonstrates the applicant's ability to meet the job requirements by listing side-by-side the company's requirements and the applicant's skills and accomplishments. This can be a very effective way to quickly capture the reader's attention and illustrate how the applicant's experience and qualifications align with the organization's business needs. Many people prefer this format because of its simplicity.

In creating a T-cover letter select three to five of the job requirements and highlight your ability to meet those requirements. Keep it short and concise, and as always, do not exceed one page with your cover letter.

SAMPLE COVER LETTER
(AIDA FORMAT)

September 21, 20XX

Re: Project Manager Position #3712

Dear (Hiring Manager's Name):

Attached is a copy of my resume for the Project Manager position #3712 which I found on Indeed.com. I have a degree in mechanical engineering and am a certified Professional Engineer (PE). I am also currently working on a certification in Risk Management. **(Paragraph 1-Attention)**

Most recently I worked in the automotive industry designing and engineering electric and solar vehicles and would bring great experience to your organization. My background closely aligns with the requirements of the position. My expertise includes:

- Lean manufacturing

- Background in statistical analysis

- Ability to work effectively with others in a fast-paced environment

- Known for developing strong stakeholder relationships and effectively gathering requirements **(Paragraph 2 - Interest)**

Having led a number of multimillion dollar complex projects, I have the skills and competencies to get results and meet your project deliverables. I have a reputation for building high performing teams that deliver and I would bring my expertise and leadership skills to your organization. **(Paragraph 3 - Desire)**

I look forward to meeting with you to explore how my background and qualifications can help you meet your business goals. I appreciate your consideration and will reach out to you next week to see when we might meet. I can be reached via email at…and by phone at….**(Paragraph 4 - Action)**

Sincerely,

T-Cover Letter Format

January 13, 20XX

RE: Position #4019

Dear (Hiring Manager's Name):

I am responding to your job entitled *Supply Chain Management Architect*, Reference #4019, which I found on Glassdoor.com. I have extensive experience leading complex Supply Chain projects and developing high performing teams to meet project goals and customer expectations. I have included a copy of my resume for your review.

Below is a comparison of your job requirements and my qualifications as they align with your needs:

Your Job Requirements	My Qualifications
Plan, lead, and facilitate architecture workshops for complex business processes.	3+ years leading 6 project teams designing lean business processes; eliminating non-value-added activities; streamlining for greater efficiency and effectiveness
Anticipate customers' needs and identify appropriate solutions leveraging best practice experience.	Extensive experience in gathering and prioritizing stakeholder requirements and effectively engaging stakeholders to ensure solutions meet customer's needs and expectations.
Help scope project, develop cost and schedule estimates, and identify project risks.	Certified CPSM who utilizes best practices to execute, monitor, control, and close out projects successfully. Develops total scope of a project using a work break down structure (WBS) to plan; estimate time and cost; identify risk, resources, and procurement needs; and ensure quality results.

I am confident that my knowledge, skills, and extensive project management experience; combined with my training as a Supply Chain professional; can help you achieve your business goals and add value to your organization. I look forward to the opportunity to meet with you and will contact you in a couple of days to follow up. In the meantime, feel free to reach out to me via email at…or you can call me at…. Thank you for your consideration.

Sincerely,

ONLINE APPLICATIONS

You need to become familiar with the online application process. While the majority of your job opportunities will come through your networking contacts, you will still want to search for jobs online and apply for those you are interested in and for which you qualify.

Different companies have their own process. The best advice I can give you here is to *read and follow their process carefully*. If they ask you to do something, do it. If you cannot follow simple instructions then you will likely disqualify yourself. Many of the online sites will allow you to provide a cover letter and may refer to it as optional. As I have said before, don't get lazy in the process. Do it—send one!

Online applications will ask all kinds of questions including your salary requirements. In most cases you will not be able to complete the online application without providing that information. I know this is uncomfortable, especially when you don't even know all the requirements of the position. This may seem somewhat unfair, but we don't make the rules, the employer does. The employer wants to ensure they do not spend their valuable time on a candidate with unrealistic salary expectations. Never give an exact amount if you can provide a range. Do your homework and determine a reasonable range for the position. Make sure you have a good feel for your minimum acceptable compensation when providing a range.

I have included some websites where you can research salary in Chapter 16, **Negotiating Your Compensation Package,** under the heading *Where do I find salary information?*

FOLLOW UP CORRESPONDENCE

Follow up correspondence is anything you need to send the interviewer(s) so they can make a decision about you moving further in the hiring process. This might include things such as a list of references, recommendation letters, licenses, proof of certifications, proof of citizenship, green card information, etc.

THANK YOU NOTES

I was brought up in a generation, and by a mother, that valued and expected thank you notes. Even if you have never written a thank you note in your life, now is the time to start. Send a thank you note to everyone you meet with during your interview. An email thank-you is a good start and should be sent immediately after your interview. I recommend following up with a handwritten note. Ask for business cards from the people you meet so you have their contact information. If they do not have a business card you may be able to get their contact information from an administrative assistant or other internal contact. Handwritten notes should be in the mail within twenty-four hours of your interview. Use your thank you email and handwritten note as an opportunity to:

- Thank them for their time and interest in you.

- Recap your key selling points.

- Include any critical information you may have forgotten during the interview.

- Answer again the question "Why should we hire you?"

- Express your interest in the position and seek a next interview.

Vary your message slightly between your email and handwritten note so you are not repeating yourself. Your follow-up email might include all the bullet points above and your handwritten note might simply say something like:

I want to thank you again for the opportunity to interview for the position of (job title*). I am excited about the possibilities of working with* (name of company/ organization/team*). I look forward to hearing from you regarding next steps.*

Even if you realize at this point that you are not interested in the position, still send a thank you email. It is the polite thing to do since they took time to meet with you and you never know when another position with the same company may open up that you are interested in.

"Gratitude is not only the greatest of virtues, but the parent of all others."
—*Cicero*

REFERENCES

You will need to provide at least three references to the prospective employer. Generally acceptable are two business references and one personal. However, some companies will want three business references. Remember that a list of references is provided to an employer when they invite you to interview, not when you submit a resume.

Be selective in whom you choose as your references. If you choose the wrong person this can be a liability for you. Some people can be great friends and colleagues but not represent you well even with their best attempt. Some questions to consider when selecting your references:

- Do they know me well and can they speak to my strengths as it relates to the job and industry I am pursuing?

- Can they be clear and concise and focused on what I need them to share to help me get an offer?

Be sure to ask for permission to use someone as a reference and provide them with a copy of your resume and a copy of your personal marketing plan. Your references will not need the list of companies you are targeting, which is one of the elements of a personal marketing plan. The marketing plan will be covered in detail in the next chapter.

I recommend that you prepare your references with some bullet points of information you would like for them to share with a prospective employer who might call them. You will be doing them a favor as well as yourself. Don't leave it up to your references to decide what to share about you and your experience. I promise, they will appreciate your guidance.

A sample **List of References** can be found in the **Career Tools** section at **www.ProjectCareerQuest.com**.

⟨⟨⟨⟨⟩⟩⟩

SOCIAL MEDIA

The use of social media is an important part of your overall communication strategy. Recruiters and hiring managers are using social media to find qualified candidates for positions they are trying to fill. If you want them to find you, you must have a presence on social media. Currently, LinkedIn is the primary tool used by recruiters. Twitter is also very popular with recruiters for posting positions. (See Chapter 12 for more detailed information on social media.)

"I'm a great believer in luck, and I find the harder I work, the more of it I have."
—*Thomas Jefferson*

✅ CHECKLIST - BEFORE YOU MOVE ON

☐ Do you have a communication strategy and plan? Is your message consistent throughout?

☐ Do you have a mission statement that declares your higher purpose and will help you make wise career decisions?

☐ Do you have a branding statement that clearly states what you do, your areas of expertise, and who you help?

☐ Have you created all of the documents you need to get your message out? Resume, cover letters, list of references, etc.?

☐ Is your resume clear, concise, focused, error-free, and accomplishment-based?

☐ Is your summary statement written in a way that it will capture the reader's attention and inspire him to keep reading your resume?

☐ Are your accomplishment statements written using "strong" action verbs? Have you quantified when possible? Are your accomplishment statements relevant to the job for which you are applying?

☐ Have you selected references who can speak to your strengths and qualifications? Have you provided your references with guidance and support so they can speak to the things you wish to emphasize with a prospective employer?

☐ Do you have an effective social media presence? Are you capturing the attention of recruiters, search firms, and hiring managers?

Lessons Learned: *Getting your message out effectively requires a communication strategy and a plan that is consistent with your overall career goals. You must have a thorough understanding of your market and be able to articulate your accomplishments and value to a prospective employer.*

CHAPTER 10

NETWORKING FOR RESULTS

Network, network, network! One of the greatest tools in your job search toolbox is *networking*. The research shows that somewhere between 80-85% of jobs are found through networking. Sitting at home on the Internet all day will rarely find you the kind of meaningful work you desire. It's who you know and who they know that will enable you to find success and land quicker than trying to find a job on your own. This is not to say you should not use the Internet and various job boards to explore employment opportunities, just don't spend all day on your computer searching for a job. Get out there and do some face-to-face networking!

You can and should create a profile on Indeed.com and other search engines so you will be sent relevant jobs on a daily basis automatically. Doing so will free up time for you to engage in essential networking activities.

One very important thing to consider, when looking for a job, is the fact that a majority of jobs are never advertised. Especially those positions that are commonly referred to as the "attractive jobs." Reports I have seen indicate that somewhere between 70-80% of jobs are not advertised. Those unadvertised jobs are known as the "hidden job market."[1] The only way you will access the attractive jobs that are part of the hidden job market is through effective networking.

Yes, that's right, finding the ideal candidate is most often through word of mouth. Posting highly desirable jobs on a job board will likely result in a landslide of resumes.

What companies end up getting is a quantity of resumes but not always the quality of candidates they are seeking. Companies and organizations would rather interview potential candidates that have been referred to them by their own employees or other trusted sources. Wouldn't you?

It is critical to get your resume in front of a hiring manager if you are to get an interview and land the position you desire. To do so is becoming more and more challenging. There are fewer available jobs as companies continue to downsize and outsource and the market is flooded with eligible candidates. The use of technology is making it harder and harder for your resume to even get in the hands of a human being. If you don't have the right key words and phrases on your resume you will not make the cut. Your greatest opportunity is not through online applications but rather through networking; finding a "side door" or "back door" to gain access to hiring managers and key decision makers.

WHAT IS NETWORKING?

The Merriam-Webster's dictionary defines networking as, "The exchange of information or services among individuals, groups, or institutions; specifically: the cultivation of productive relationships for employment or business."

Networking, for the job seeker, is the process of connecting with people and cultivating relationships to gain a competitive edge in the job market. Networking can help the job seeker to:

- Discover unadvertised job openings.

- Gain access to the "hidden job market."

- Get introductions to key decision makers.

- Identify hiring managers.

- Find business opportunities.

- Gather industry specific and market information.

- Gather company specific information.

- Gather job specific information.

- Exchange information and ideas.

- Learn from the experiences of others and gain valuable advice.

- Get their resume into the hands of an influencer.

- Get their resume seen by a decision-maker.

- Get an interview.

POWER OF NETWORKING

Networking effectively is critical to your success because:

- 80–85% of jobs are found through networking.

- 70–80% of jobs are never advertised.

- Who you know can help you gain access to the hidden job market.

- Who you know can help you gain access to hiring managers, influencers, and decision makers.

- Who you know can help you uncover critical information.

- Who you know can help you land your next position.

BENEFITS OF YOUR EXISTING NETWORK

Your existing network, as I use it here, are those people with whom you regularly engage or people you have known in the past; versus new contacts you have recently made as you network in your job search. Your existing network consists of friends, colleagues, and acquaintances that are either "active" or "dormant."

Active contacts are those people you are in touch with on a fairly regular basis. Dormant contacts are those people you have not been in touch with in some time, perhaps a school friend, or former colleague. Some of the benefits of tapping into your existing network include:

- Their previous knowledge of your character, strengths, and skills.

- Their general willingness to help; they can connect and promote you to others.

- They can provide advice and recommendations to help you in your job search.

- They can help you build your network.

- They can open doors and expose new opportunities.

- They can be a referral and recommend you to others.

WHY AREN'T YOU TAPPING INTO YOUR EXISTING NETWORK?

Tapping into your existing network can generate leads, introductions, and get you in front of hiring managers. Let's take a look at are some of the reasons people give for *not* reaching out to their existing network of friends, relatives, neighbors, classmates, previous co-workers, business contacts, etc.

- Don't want to bother them.

- Haven't been in touch in a long time; feels awkward to reach out to them now.

- Embarrassment; don't want people to know I lost my job.

- They won't be able to help me.

- _____ (What's your excuse?)

If your reason for not tapping into your existing network is any of the above, then you are listening to your *gremlins* and creating obstacles for yourself. Stop it! Do not make assumptions about what people will or won't do or will or won't think about you. Ask yourself these two questions: If I tap into my 'old acquaintances'…

1. What's the worst thing that can happen?

2. What potential benefits might the contact produce?

I am absolutely certain that the benefits will far outweigh any negative consequences.

"When one door closes, another opens. But we often look so long and so regretfully upon the closed door that we do not see the one which has opened for us."
—*Alexander Graham Bell*

MYTHS ABOUT NETWORKING

"Networking is only for extroverts; introverts are not good at networking!"

Not so! While an extrovert, as a rule, may be more comfortable speaking with people they have just met, they might spend more time working the room, meeting as many people as possible, but not connecting at a deeper level. An introvert, on the other hand, will typically meet and focus on only one or two people during a networking function. At the end of the event they may have gathered more information (while not as many business cards) and perhaps made a contact or two that will yield a lead, a potential interview, or a next meeting.

To say that an introvert is not good at networking simply is not true. It is not so much about the number of contacts you make while networking—it is about the *quality* of the contacts you have made. Taking time with an individual to build rapport is critical to effective networking. (If you are an introvert, stop using that as your excuse for not networking—you can effectively network!)

Introverts also tend to focus more on the other person rather than talking about themselves. They typically do a lot more listening and a lot less talking. This tends to make a favorable impression on others who appreciate someone who will listen to them. *Listening is a great strategy for building relationships.*

(Disclaimer: By no means am I saying that extroverts cannot and do not engage in meaningful conversation during networking events. But for me personally, it means that when I network, I need to go in with a goal in mind and not simply meet everyone in the room. I also need to listen more and talk less.)

(**Note:** For more information on *extroverts* and *introverts*, see Chapter 13 entitled **Understanding Personalities and Communication Styles**.)

"I do not know anyone to network with."

I have heard that many times before, but I don't buy it. Everyone knows someone to network with. Do an inventory of whom you worked with in the past, went to school with, go to church with, your kids play soccer with, and where you get your services (doctor, dentist, accountant, etc.). Networking can occur at the grocery store, standing in line to purchase a cup of coffee, on an airplane—anywhere there are people. Unless you live out in the woods, totally isolated from society, you know someone with whom you can network.

When I was looking for my first professional job out of college I flew to Atlanta, Georgia for a job interview. On my flight home through Dulles Airport in Northern Virginia, I sat next to a man who inquired why I had been in Atlanta. Did I live there or was I just visiting? I told him I had interviewed for a job as a paralegal. He then proceeded to hand me his business card and tell me he was an attorney with the tenth largest law firm in Washington, DC and they were currently hiring paralegals. He asked me to call his office on Monday and set up an appointment for an interview. Wow, that was a nice surprise I wasn't expecting. Networking can happen anywhere, anytime.

 Lessons Learned: *Networking can happen anywhere and anytime; sometimes when you least expect it a job opportunity can present itself.*

"I have to know someone well to network with them."

Again, not true. Sometimes your best networking can come from people you have just met, barely know, or only know through social media. For the most part, people love to share information and love to let you know how well connected they are!

"Networking is about who you know and knowing lots of people."

Actually, networking is about building relationships. Even if you don't know anyone, which is highly unlikely, you can still build relationships. Three questions to keep in mind when seeking to build relationships—here is what the other person wants to know (will be thinking) about you:

- Can I trust you?

- Can you help me?

- Do you care about me?

To build a successful relationship with another person you will want them to be able to answer, "yes" to all three of those questions. Building trust and having a caring and helpful attitude and approach will enable you to build relationships with others.

"People may find it annoying if I reach out to network."

That's usually not the case, especially if done correctly. There is a right way and a wrong way to connect with people. Be sure that your intentions are sincere and genuine and that you show appreciation for someone's time and their willingness to connect with you, either face-to-face or online. When you reach out to someone, asking for their advice, people are generally flattered and willing to share what they can.

"Online networking does not work."

Again, not true. In fact, most organizations are using social media now as one of their primary tools for recruiting and finding quality candidates for job vacancies. Recruiters and hiring managers are trying to find creative ways to identify potential candidates at the least cost to their organizations. LinkedIn is currently the number one tool that many organizations are using. Twitter, Facebook, Instagram, and other social media platforms are also widely used. Your opportunities to network online and create an online presence will give you exposure you would not otherwise have. (Refer to Chapter 12, **Social Media**, for more information about how to network online.)

"Networking costs money."

Yes, it can, but there are lots of networking opportunities that are free. Networking can happen at social events, school activities, alumni events, church, soccer games, meet up groups, and a plethora of other places. Why not start your own networking group? Another great place to network is at job seeker groups that may meet in your local area, and those are always free. You can find professional meet up groups in your area at www.meetup.com.

Also, you don't have to go anywhere to network; you can network from the comfort of your home if you chose. (But don't do it exclusively.) It is not always about face-to-face interaction. Participating in online communities can increase your networking power exponentially. LinkedIn and Facebook offer groups where you can connect with people of similar interests and professional backgrounds. However, be aware of your potholes and stick to business networking. Don't waste time on social networking sites during your "business hours." Remember you have a project to complete!

Another effective way to network is to create a blog on a topic on which you have expertise and ask others to comment on your blog. This gives you exposure and an opportunity to network with people with similar interests and/or expertise. You can also create a video blog known as a *vlog*.

"Networking with other job seekers will not help me."

Absolutely *not* true! In fact, other job seekers in many ways will be your best allies. Who knows better how to find a job or whose hiring than other job seekers. Trust me, your friends who are gainfully employed and have not looked for a job in a decade or more have no idea where to start or what to do.

Those job seekers who have been looking for a while can help direct you to many useful resources, networking groups, free educational opportunities, free services for those unemployed, and answer many of the question that you will have as a new job seeker. In other words, they can shorten your learning curve. Because they are also unemployed does not mean they don't know anyone that may be helpful to you in your job search. Other job seekers will understand what you are going through and most will be willing to support you in your search if you are willing to reciprocate.

My advice to job seekers is to always offer help to other job seekers first. Don't make it all about you. Ask them how you can help them. Offer leads, contacts, and ideas. Generally, people will reciprocate if you take that approach. If, however, you attend a networking event or job seeker group and focus only on your own needs, you may find little help from others. Those who help get helped.

"You should attend as many networking events as possible."

Like everything you do in your job search project you should plan your time strategically. Do not attend a networking event simply to make an appearance. Do your research. What is the purpose of the event? Who will be attending? What value will you get from attending the event? All networking events are not equal. Do your homework and spend your time wisely. Ask others who may have attended a similar event in the past for their feedback. Was it worth their time? Would they recommend this event?

"Don't spend too much time with any one person."

Networking is about building relationships, and relationships take time to develop. Generally, your goal at a networking event is not to meet as many people as possible, it's about making quality contacts. Think about the time you spend with a person as time invested in that relationship. Making one or two quality contacts *is* successful networking!

———✑———

DO'S AND DON'TS OF NETWORKING

Okay, now that we have debunked some of the myths about networking, let's talk about the do's and don'ts of networking.

Do's	Don'ts
Show up authentically; be yourself.	Do not put on airs or try to impress.
Be prepared to share a concise "elevator speech" in 30–60 seconds and engage your listener.	Do not show up unprepared and unable to articulate your professional identity, expertise, and value proposition.
Ask open-ended questions, listen actively, and seek to understand.	Do not talk too much, especially about yourself.
Show a genuine interest in the other person; build rapport.	Do not be afraid to approach new people, they probably won't bite!
Focus on the person you are speaking with; give them your undivided attention.	Do not interrupt or seem distracted.
Engage in meaningful conversation; focusing first on the other party and then sharing your interests.	Do not speak negatively about others; always keep your conversations positive.
Follow up; seek another meeting if desirable. Ask for leads, referrals, and introductions. Offer leads, referrals, and introductions.	Do not attempt to meet as many people as possible at a networking event; effective networking is about quality, not quantity.
Share your business cards and ask others for theirs so you have the opportunity to follow up with those you meet.	Do not flit around the room like a hummingbird to get as many business cards as you can; focus on building relationships.
Be a giver; create value for others helping them with suggestions, ideas, and contacts as you can.	Do not focus on yourself, coming across as demanding or needy.

"The successful networkers I know, the ones receiving tons of referrals and feeling truly happy about themselves, continually put the other person's needs ahead of their own."
—*Bob Burg*

WHO DO YOU KNOW?

Do an inventory of whom you know. Don't rule anyone out because you think they can't help you; assumptions can become your obstacles. The list below should give you a good start on identifying your existing network.

- Friends, relatives, neighbors

- Former colleagues

- High school and college alumni

- Professional organizations

- Community organizations (Lion's Club, Elk's Club, Rotary International, Ruritan National, etc.)[2]

- Social activities (tennis league, garden club, book club, dancing, dinner club, etc.)

- Volunteer activities

- Church family

- Professional business connections (lawyer, doctor, banker, broker, accountant, etc.)

- Spouse's network

- Children's network (soccer, lacrosse, football, baseball, basketball, swimming, tennis, ballet, etc.)

Included in the **Career Tools** section, at **www.ProjectCareerQuest.com**, is a template you can use to create a list of your network. Once you have compiled a list of your contacts, examine your relationship with each of them. Do you actively engage with them (**Active**)? Is it someone you knew well in the past but have had very little interaction with recently (**Dormant**)? Or are they a new contact, someone you have yet to build a relationship with (**Passive**)? All of your contacts; whether active, dormant, or passive; can potentially provide you with job leads and **N**ew **O**pportunities **W**aiting!

"AAA" RATING

How well do you know your network? How well do they know you? Some people you know well and they can speak to your skills and core competencies. Others may know you by name and face, but know very little about you otherwise. You may want to get better acquainted with the people in your network that you do not know well in order to build a business or personal relationship that is mutually beneficial. Your network will consist of:

- **Acquaintances** can include neighbors, colleagues, and others you have met or spoken with, but whom you may know very little about personally or professionally. Nor would they know you well either. Acquaintances may be willing to make an introduction and share information about available resources that would be valuable to you in your job search project.

- **Allies** are people who know you professionally (and perhaps personally) and would be willing to speak to others on your behalf. They know your competencies, skills, abilities, character, and would be willing to help you gain access to others as needed in your job search project.

- **Advocates** are people who know you well and have confidence in your abilities and will actively approach others on your behalf. They are willing to put their reputation on the line because they believe in you.

Action Item #20

Review your **existing network**. Who do you know and how well do you know them? Are they 1) **Acquaintances**, 2) **Allies** or, 3) **Advocates**? Regarding your interaction with your contacts, is your relationship active, dormant, or passive? Of your existing network, which of the relationships do you want to broaden or deepen? What gaps do you have in your existing network? Complete the template provided in the **Career Tools** section (online) to assess your network and how you can best leverage your contacts to help you meet your career transition goals?

See sample template that follows. A blank template has been provided for you in the **Career Tools** section at **www.ProjectCareerQuest.com**.

Name	How	Interaction with them	Role/Title	AQ	AL	AD	Contribution/ Action Required
Marty Richards	NG	Active	Career Coach		X		Helped develop resume
Sandra Marks	FR	Dormant	Training Industry		X		Similar net-work; Need to reconnect
Robert Couch	BC	Active	Former Manager/ Mentor			X	Follow up for networking opportunities and brain-storming
Jennifer Peele	PO	Passive	IT/PMP Professional	X			Met at PMI meeting, works for targeted com-pany; need to arrange informational meeting

(Note: NG = Networking Group, FR = Friend, BC = Business Colleague, PO = Professional Organization; make up your own abbreviations. AQ = Acquaintance, AL = Ally, AD =Advocate)

―◦◦◦―

MARKETING PLAN

A personal Marketing Plan is one of the best-kept secrets and most under-utilized tool in the job search process. Many of you have no clue what I am talking about and have never heard of such a tool. Well, I am going to tell you about it and the benefits of having one. I recommend a personal Marketing Plan for all of my clients. It will add momentum and exposure to your job search project!

Resumes are for hiring managers and recruiters. A personal Marketing Plan is for everyone else. Let me tell you why.

Have you ever had a friend, neighbor, or acquaintance that was looking for a job and you agreed to look at their resume to see if you could help, only to find out that their resume looked like Greek to you? Oh my, whatever their job was before you can't relate to, and have no idea how to help them. It's like reading a foreign language. Gosh, now you feel bad, after all you said you would help, if you could. Or maybe you looked at their resume and you do understand what it says but still you're not sure how to help them even after reading their well-written accomplishment statements. Or perhaps you asked someone to take a look at your resume after they agreed to help you with your job search. After a quick scan, they apologized to you and told you they don't know your industry and probably can't help you.

Resumes can be terribly intimidating to someone not familiar with your industry and specialty. People want to help but they often feel helpless and unable to provide the support needed. Feeling inadequate and unable to help, they may withdraw from any further assistance—not what you want or need. This is where the marketing plan comes in.

The marketing plan is a simple, straightforward document that contains information about the job seeker in a very concise format. The biggest takeaways will be:

- Your career objective
- An understanding of your core competencies and related skills
- Companies you are interested in pursuing

Now others can help you by suggesting companies you might want to consider based on your core competencies and names of people they know who work for the companies you are targeting.

The components of a personal Marketing Plan include:

- A **header** that will include your name, email address, phone number, and your LinkedIn address. (Looks like the header on your resume.)

- An **objective statement** - I do not recommend objective statements on your resume but I do recommend you include one on your marketing plan. Your family, friends, business acquaintances, neighbors, and others you will share your marketing plan with want to know what your career objective is so they can help you achieve your goal.

- A **summary statement** - Here you can use the same summary statement you used on your resume. Your summary statement will provide a snapshot of your areas of expertise, special skills, environments you have worked in, and personal characteristics including any awards, language skills you possess, or other key information of interest.

- **Your top three to five core competencies** that you will use as headers for columns you create. Below each of the core competencies you will include a short description of the functional skills that support that competency.

- **Location, company size requirements,** and **industry requirements**. For example: Large to mid-size companies within a 40-mile radius of Houston, Texas; public or private sector including energy and environmental industries.

- List of **targeted companies** generally grouped by industry or type of organization. For example: Financial, engineering, consulting firms, or private, public, non-profit organizations.

- You may also want to include a list of **preferred job titles** or **positions** you are seeking.

- Additionally, you could include bullet points stating the **three most important things you are looking for in your next career opportunity.**

Try to limit your marketing plan to no more than two pages. You don't want to overwhelm people with too much information. You do want to give them enough information so they can point you in the right direction to help you achieve your career goals. The following is a sample Marketing Plan, and you can find additional examples in the **Career Tools** section at **www.ProjectCareerQuest.com**.

SAMPLE MARKETING PLAN

Cyndee Hughes
Houston, Texas
713-000-0000
clhughes713@me.com
www.linkedin.com/in/cyndeehughes

Objective: To obtain an executive administrative assistant position where I can use my expertise in planning, organizing, and managing small to mid-sized projects to add value and achieve results for the organization.

Summary of Qualifications: Detail-oriented, highly adaptable executive administrative support professional with 15+ years experience; ability to work in fast-paced team environment. Strong planning, organizing, and interpersonal skills. Effectively manage multiple priorities to achieve deadlines. Excellent Microsoft Office skills (Word, Excel, PowerPoint, Outlook); Notary Public.

Core competencies include:

Administration	Planning/Coordinating/ Organizing	Customer Service
Maintain calendars/ schedules	Event planning & coordination	Stakeholder management
Prepare and distribute documentation & reports	Coordinate projects; plan & coordinate workshops & conferences	Coordinate client visits & schedule customer appointments
Receive & screen calls, mail, & other correspondence	Coordinate travel itineraries; secure passports & visas	Resolve issues as required to ensure a satisfied customer
Prepare purchase orders & invoices; reconcile discrepancies	Logistics planning; secure conference space, hotels, etc. Conduct negotiations	Establish & build relationships with third party suppliers & vendors
Write, edit & proofread correspondence	Plan and coordinate meetings; prepare agendas, minutes, & action items	Work collaboratively across organizations to achieve results

Demographics: (size, location, industry)
Market includes private and public sectors, large corporations and small to mid-size companies within a 40-mile radius of Houston, Texas. Willing to travel.

Target Companies:

Oil/Gas/Energy	For Profit	Not-For-Profit	Public Sector
Exxon-Mobile	AT&T	Teach for America	Texas DOT
Phillips 66	Sysco Corp.	Ronald McDonald House of Houston	Lone Star College System
ConocoPhillips	Fluor Corp.	Lighthouse of Houston	Dept. of Veterans Affairs
Valero Energy Corp.	American Airlines	United Way	University of Houston
Halliburton Company	Kimberly-Clark Corp.	AARP Foundation	Rice University
Baker Hughes Inc.	Southwest Airlines	Arthritis Foundation	Texas Association of Counties
Marathon Petroleum	Celanese Corp.	Heaven Scent Paws	Department of Homeland Security
Spectra Energy Corp.	Quanta Services Inc.	Hope International Industries	Port of Houston Authority

Other categories you might include on your Marketing Plan:

- Target position; target job title

- Three most important things you are looking for in your next career opportunity

⟞⟋⟋⟋⟞

As you can see, the Marketing Plan is simple, straightforward, and user friendly. This marketing tool will greatly help you by providing your network contacts the information they need to help you network effectively. The more you share your marketing plan with others, the wider your span of possible contacts, leads, and referrals becomes. This is a powerful tool *if* used. It will increase your momentum, create possibilities, and open doors to **N**ew **O**pportunities **W**aiting!

Your marketing plan will help you to secure job leads and make contact with hiring managers at your targeted companies. Remember to keep it fresh by updating your list of targeted companies. As your network contacts help you identify other potential opportunities and employers, you can eliminate companies (based on your research) that you no longer wish to pursue and add those you do.

Your goal should be to identify between thirty to fifty companies where you might pursue career opportunities. This may sound like a daunting number at this point in the process, but as you share your marketing plan, and do your own research, you should be able to identify a large number of potential employers. After identifying companies, you will then research each of them online and through your network contacts to determine if they are a good fit for you based on your experience, qualifications, and career goals.

Ultimately you want to identify your top ten to fifteen companies. After you have done that, the next step is to take action to locate key contacts within your network and hiring managers with those companies. Locating the ideal position requires having a strategy and taking action. Your personal marketing plan is the tool to help you do that.

Who do you send it to? Everyone and anyone who can help you identify job leads, get an introduction to hiring managers, help you network with connectors and decision-makers, help you brainstorm new opportunities, find companies that align with your career goals, and find companies that may need someone with your expertise. Send your marketing plan to your active, dormant, and passive contacts. You can start by sending your marketing plan to the list of network contacts you prepare using tools discussed in this chapter. Again, your resume is for hiring managers and recruiters, your marketing plan is for everyone else.

—◦◦◦—

Informational Interviews – Once you have identified the top ten to fifteen companies you want to target in your job search, you will need to dig deeper to find out as much as you can about those companies/organizations. My suggestion is that you set up informational interviews/meetings with internal contacts to find out more about: a specific role or position, to get job leads and referrals, and to gather other information relevant to the targeted company.

You can also set up informational interviews with people in the industry you are targeting. An industry lead may then be able to point you in the direction of an internal contact at one of your targeted companies and possibly make a personal introduction.

Your goal in an informational interview; with a contact within one of your target companies; is to find out as much as you can about the industry, company, its reputation, the culture, the people who work there, the senior leadership, and the challenges and opportunities the company or organization faces. Being informed about a company you hope to interview with is critical to your success. An informational interview will enable you to gather information about the company that may not be available through external resources, i.e., print media and online searches. It is a great way to get referrals to other key internal contacts and ultimately a hiring manager.

How do you set up an informational interview and with whom do you meet? Your personal Marketing Plan, as well as LinkedIn, is exactly what you need to identify key internal/industry resources. Once identified, reach out to them and request an informational interview. Better yet, ask people in your network to make an introduction. Your best chance of getting someone to say "yes" to an informational interview is through a mutual friend, friend of a friend, or business acquaintance.

The fact that a company is not currently hiring for a position you might desire should not stop you from reaching out and requesting an informational interview. At this point, you are merely gathering information and preparing for the day when that "door of opportunity" opens. Your informational meeting may create new connections and opportunities for you previously not identified.

When asking to meet with someone to gather information about their organization or industry, be specific regarding:

- Why you would like to meet; your purpose for getting together.
- Who referred you or how you found them.
- Establishing a date and time for the meeting.
- Establishing time expectations.
- Establishing a venue for the meeting.
- How they might benefit from meeting with you.

That last bullet listed will require some research on your part. If you have some information that would be helpful to them, you can include that in your request to meet to peak their interest and desire to schedule time with you.

Some of the things you should do when conducting an informational interview include:

- Make the time and location convenient for the other person, after all, you are asking for their personal time and help. Better yet, go to their location if it is a business location.

- If you invite someone for coffee, you should offer to pay. If you invite someone to lunch you might offer to pay for that as well. Again, you are asking for their help and their time. I personally recommend you conduct informational interviews over coffee, it will cost you a lot less!

Have a plan for conducting your informational interview. Have questions prepared in advance. An effective way of structuring your meeting is as follows:

- Begin by introducing yourself and the **purpose** for the meeting. Next you will share your **summary statement** (from your marketing plan and resume) so that the person you are meeting with can begin to focus on how they might help you. This step should take no more than two to three minutes and will lay the groundwork for your informational meeting. Remember, you are there to gather information, not sell your qualifications or get hired. Keep that in mind as you plan your script for the meeting. You are there to ask questions and listen actively to gather the information you will need in the future when you do get a job interview. (2–3 minutes)

- Share your personal **marketing plan** that outlines your career objective, core competencies, and targeted companies. (Do not share your list of targeted companies with a person whose company you are interested in working for.) Leave them a copy of your marketing plan so they can review in more detail after your meeting and perhaps it will generate future discussions and/or leads. (4–5 minutes)

- **Ask questions** appropriate to the individual with whom you are meeting. Is it his industry you want to learn more about, the company he works for, are you looking for leads? The majority of your time should be spent here to gather information, explore possibilities, identify key decision makers and hiring managers, and other relevant contacts. When asking questions, be sure they are open-ended to encourage your contact to share information. Listen attentively and take notes as appropriate. (15 minutes)

- **Ask for referrals**. "Do you know of anyone else with whom I could meet to gather information about…?" If they can offer any leads, ask them if they would consider making an introduction. If they cannot think of anyone at the time of your meeting, ask them if you can reach out to them again in the near future to see if anyone has come to mind. Leaving them your personal marketing plan may trigger some thoughts and lead to additional contacts. (3–5 minutes)

- **Close your meeting** by thanking them for their time and for sharing information with you. Let them know you will follow up with them as you progress in your job search. Also, as you conclude your informational interview, if there is a lead, a referral, or some industry knowledge you could share with the person you interviewed, that would be an added bonus for both of you. Not only would both of you walk away feeling like your time was well spent, it may also create a door of opportunity for future engagement. (3–5 minutes)

Be respectful of time. If you ask for a thirty-minute meeting, start wrapping it up in twenty-five minutes. The majority of your time should be spent asking questions to gain knowledge and insight.

After concluding your informational interview, be sure to follow up with a thank you email or note. I suggest a handwritten note, it is more personal. Your email (or hand-written note) might read something like this:

> *Thank you so much for your time today. I appreciate the information you have shared with me regarding.… I will keep you posted as to my progress. If there is anything I can do for you, please don't hesitate to reach out to me.*

If you really want to thank the person with whom you conducted the informational meeting, and leave a lasting impression, you might want to do something special for them. On more than one occasion I have received a hand-written thank you note with a $5.00 Starbucks gift card inside. It is a small investment to make. It will leave a positive impression and convey your sincere gratitude for the time the person invested in you.

—⚬⚬⚬—

NETWORKING OPPORTUNITIES

Now that we have examined some of the myths about networking and explored some of the do's and don'ts, it is time to talk about where to network and with whom. Establishing relationships and building bridges are essential to locating coveted positions and career opportunities. Some potential networking opportunities include:

Job Seeker Groups - Groups established specifically for those in transition can be found in almost every major city and even in small towns. They can be held anywhere, but my experience is that they are primarily organized through local churches. You should be able to find job seeker groups in your area through an online search. Fellow job seekers are some of your best allies and resources for your job search project. Do not overlook fellow job seekers just because they are unemployed. They know people; they have connections and resources available to them. Most will be willing to share information and leads with you if you reciprocate and have the right attitude and approach. Job seeker groups typically provide seminars and speakers on topics that will help guide you in your transition and help you locate critical resources for your success.

Professional and industry organizations - Many professional organizations have monthly meetings to promote the profession and to serve as continuing education for their members. Some of the professional organizations that come to mind for me include the Project Management Institute (PMI), Women in Bio (WIB), the Society for Human Resource Management (SHRM), and the Association of Training and Development (ATD). There are professional organizations for IT professionals, health care professionals, engineers, lawyers, teachers, chemists, and journalists. From A to Z, Accountants to Zoo Keepers—there is something for everyone! Professional groups are a great place to network and to learn more about the current trends in your industry or chosen career field.

Service organizations - Rotary International, Ruritan National, Lion's Club, and other similar organizations that bring together business and professional leaders for fellowship, goodwill, and community service are great places to meet influencers in your community. Do an online search of service organizations in your local area and you are likely to find one where you can network as well as add value to your community.

Meetup groups - Meetup groups are not all about socializing. While some are, some are more focused on a particular profession, common interests, or hobbies. An online search will help you locate more Meetup groups than you can even imagine. And if there isn't one that suits you, start your own. A few years back I started a Meetup group called "Dining with the Dogs." My goal was primarily to socialize and dine with other dog lovers. The group lasted for about two years, but then I found it was too hard to keep going with my travel schedule. It was fun while it lasted, and I met some very interesting people, mostly with small dogs. I had a Lab and a golden retriever. I guess I should have called it "Dining with the Big Dogs." Point being, if there isn't a Meetup group that satisfies your interests, create one and network on! To locate a Meetup group, go to www.meetup.com.

Business networking groups - Business Network International (BNI's) are also plentiful these days. BNI's mission is to provide business and professional networking opportunities and referral services. If your chosen career path is the entrepreneurial route you will definitely want to check out a BNI in your area. You can find a BNI in your local area at www.bni.com.

Business acquaintances - Who have you worked with and who has used your services in the past? Meet with people one-on-one or in a group setting to network and get job leads. A true networker is networking all the time, not only when they are looking for a job.

Several years ago, a guy I know was laid off from his job in sales; let's call him Nick for the purpose of this example. Fortunately, Nick was the sort of person who networked constantly (that's what makes successful sales people). Every Wednesday night he met a group of guys at a local restaurant for "seafood and suds." One of the regular attendees worked for a company that Nick saw a huge sales opportunity with that he felt they were missing out on. Nick was constantly encouraging the other guy to tap into that market. When Nick got laid off from his job, he called his Wednesday night networking buddy and declared, "I'm a free agent now, how about I come over to your company and help you break into that market we've been talking about?" Within three weeks the company created a director level position for him, and he was on their payroll to expand their business and create new opportunities for the company—now his employer.

Internships - A good way to get your foot in the door, learn some skills, and network with employees and hiring managers internally is to seek out internship opportunities. If you are in college and looking to start your career, this is one of the best things you can do to gain experience and network inside an organization. If you are new to an industry, you may want to consider taking on a short-term internship to get some experience under your belt. Also, if you are re-entering the job market after an extended absence, taking a paid or unpaid (as many are) internship can be exactly what you need to start or restart your career.

Several years ago, on a flight to Chicago, I met a North Carolina State University student on his way to Melbourne, Australia. He was on his way to begin a summer internship with a startup automobile manufacturer specializing in hybrid and electric vehicles. While his internship was unpaid, he learned so much about the automobile industry. He reports that he made some great contacts and has several exceptional mentors whom he intends to keep in touch with and continue to learn from about his chosen career field.

The most interesting aspect of his story to me was how he secured the internship. Determined someday to design and engineer electric cars for the automotive industry, he began by researching conferences in the U.S. for professionals in his targeted field. His next step was to find out what companies were attending the conference as presenters and vendors. He then proceeded to write twenty of the companies he identified expressing his interest to intern for them for the summer—even though none of the companies had posted any student internships. Out of the twenty companies he sent letters to, one responded to his request and offered him an internship in Australia. Hey, who wouldn't want to go to Australia for the summer!

His ultimate goal is to someday work as a design engineer to help the world transition from gasoline powered vehicles to electric and solar cars. With determination and drive like his I know he will be successful at whatever he chooses to do. This college student knows exactly what he wants and has taken a very proactive approach to achieve his goals. He is wise beyond his years—I hope there is a lesson for you in his success.

Another example of the benefits of networking is about a woman in my Women in Bio (WIB)[3] mentoring group. She had been out of the job market for many years raising her children and was finding it difficult to get employers to look at her resume due to her prolonged absence. Determined to get back into her chosen field, through persistent networking she found an opportunity to work in a lab at Duke University for the summer to get some much-needed experience and exposure. It was an unpaid position, but she saw it as a stepping-stone to get her career back on track. It gave her the opportunity to network at one of the premier private research universities in the country.

⟨⟩⟨⟩⟨⟩

Volunteer organizations - A great place to network is by volunteering either with a professional organization and/or with a non-profit. The benefits are three-fold. 1) You will meet people who can help you in your job search. 2) You can include your volunteer work on your resume. 3) You will be helping others!

Choose a volunteer organization that aligns with your career objectives and will help you maintain and/or update your skills. For example, let's say you are a project manager and you decide to join your local Project Management Institute (PMI) chapter. During your time of transition, get involved, sign up for a committee such as membership or programs. If you are already involved in a professional organization, reach out to folks and leverage your contacts. Perhaps you are an administrative assistant looking for similar work. Non-profits and other organizations can always use someone with good administrative, organizational, and computer skills. You will be able to maintain your skills and perhaps learn some new skill, the latest software, or new technology.

I want to share with you some of my favorite volunteer activities in the hopes that I might inspire you to find a non-profit organization to share your knowledge, skills, and talents. By volunteering you will have the opportunity to refresh your skills, develop some new skills, and to network and connect with some pretty awesome people. **Recommended volunteer opportunities** (including skills that can be developed through these activities):

- **Habitat for Humanity** - This international non-profit builds affordable housing for low-income households. This may not be consistent with your career objective or current skill sets but you will meet a lot of interesting and well-connected people to begin building relationships and networking. I worked Habitat for Humanity in Atlanta, Georgia for many years through my church. We built more Habitat homes per year than any of the large corporations in the greater Atlanta metropolitan area. I coordinated volunteers to build on Saturdays and was responsible for getting family sponsors for the new homeowners. It was a very rewarding experience and I met so many amazing people during the years I was building and coordinating volunteers. The wife of the CEO of Delta (at the time) was part of our volunteer team, as were the wife and daughter of the CEO of BellSouth Telecommunications, which is where I worked at the time. A side benefit of working for Habitat was learning basic building skills that come in very handy at home. (**Skills**: Leadership, team building, planning, organizing, project management, volunteer coordination, construction, carpentry, roofing, landscaping, and many others.)

- **Special Olympics** - This international non-profit provides year-round sports training and competition for people with intellectual disabilities around the world. I have volunteered with Special Olympics of North Carolina (SONC) for over 18 years now. I am a certified Alpine Skiing Coach for Winter Games and have participated also in Summer and Fall Games. At one time, I was the golf coach for Johnston County, North Carolina athletes until one of my athletes told me "Ms. Kerry, I think you better stick with skiing." (Ouch!) In reality, the team folded because all of my athletes moved on to cheerleading that met on the same night of the week. Probably for the best. (**Skills**: Coaching, leadership, event planning, organizing, team building, mentoring, and many others.)

- **Animal Rescue Groups** - I personally have been fostering dogs, and one cat, since 2005. I have fostered with a variety of rescue groups in my area including Neuse River Golden Retriever Rescue, Triangle Beagle Rescue, and Love Mutts Rescue. I have met some of the most wonderful and interesting people and get to save lives and bring joy to families when they adopt dogs and cats through the rescues. I have made many great business connections through the rescues and along the way I get lots of unconditional love. (What could be better than that!) There are so many great animal rescue groups (throughout the world) that need volunteers to foster, transport, do intake, write grants, fundraise, develop and maintain websites, etc. Save a dog, build your skills, and find a job. (**Skills**: Leadership, fundraising, grant writing, event planning, organizing, event management, project management, volunteer coordination, developing newsletters and websites, and many others.)

- **Work with "at risk" youth.** Locally I volunteer with an organization called Corral Riding Academy. Corral ministers to and mentors at risk girls ages eleven to eighteen that have been referred to them from the court systems, school systems, and a variety of other sources. Corral provides equine assisted therapy, tutoring, mentoring, and leadership development. The program gives the girls a "leg up in life" and is transformational in their development socially, emotionally, and academically. As a volunteer, I have helped with their college prep, administered instruments such as the Myers-Briggs Type Indicator[4] and the DiSC,[5] helped with planning and executing events, and fundraising. I am also a part of their public engagement team who shares their message with other organizations to raise awareness and gain much needed sponsorship and funding. (**Skills:** Fundraising, project management, organizing, planning, executing events, team building, public speaking, mentoring, grant writing, volunteer coordination, and many more.)

Some of the potential **benefits to job seekers from volunteering** include: building relationships, learning or enhancing skills such as leadership and team building, mentoring others, planning, organizing, leading and managing projects and special events, facilitating, public speaking, fundraising, computer skills, website development, and social media marketing to name a few. All are critical business skills.

While you may not get paid for volunteer work, you can and should include it on your resume. If you are out of work for a significant amount of time, companies will want to know what you have been doing since you left your previous employer. If you volunteer a couple of hours a week, you have the opportunity to keep your skills fresh or even learn new skills. Through volunteer work you might even discover your passion. Volunteering helps others, helps the community, and helps you get closer to finding a job. And who knows, a volunteer opportunity might even turn into full-time employment. It has for many that I know. Remember, the majority of jobs are found through networking.

Volunteering, in my experience, *helps people maintain perspective*. Losing a job is minor (and "this too shall pass") compared to what some of the people, or animals, you might serve have had to endure. Volunteer for your mental and emotional health. Make a difference in your community and in the world. If everyone gave a few hours a month to a cause they believe in, think what a different world we would live in!

To help you find some volunteer opportunities in your community, or on an international basis, I have provided a few websites for you to begin your search. Google "volunteer opportunities" and you will find many websites that can match your interests with an organization or nonprofit.

- VolunteerMatch.org – connecting people with causes they love and care about including issues relating to children, education and literacy, animals, health, and senior care. Nearly 100,000 nonprofits use this site to recruit volunteers.

- DoSomething.org – was established to help people interested in starting their own volunteer project or find an existing campaign. It is considered one of the most popular giving platforms for millennials.

- Volunteer.gov – provides a listing of natural and cultural resource service projects with government agencies including the National Park Service, Army Corps of Engineers, U.S. Geological Survey, and the Forest Services. (U.S. based)

- Unv.org – offers volunteer opportunities through the United Nations with focus in two specific areas: 1) human development assistance and humanitarian efforts and 2) peace keeping operations.

- Onlinevolunteering.org – is a database to find online volunteering opportunities with organizations that serve communities in developing countries. This is a United Nation's program that contributes to peace and development through volunteerism.

- Idealist.org – helps people find volunteer opportunities as well as internships and jobs in the non-profit sector.

- Allhandsandhearts.org – is a volunteered-powered relief organization dedicated to responding to families and communities when natural disasters happen.

- Operationhope.org – looks for volunteers with experience in financial industries (such as bankers, brokers, mortgage lenders, tax consultants, etc.) to provide free financial literacy empowerment programs. Their goal is to help low and moderate-income youth and adults to achieve financial independence and create a more secure future.

- BoardnetUSA.org – helps to match individuals interested in serving on the board of a non-profit, with a non-profit seeking leadership, to assist in overseeing the activities of the organization.

Volunteering knows no boundaries, there is something for everyone and there is always a need to fill. No matter how much you give, of yourself and your time, you will always receive more in return.

"We make a living by what we get, but we make a life by what we give."
—*Winston Churchill*

While you are networking, do not forget to have your personal Marketing Plan available to share with people you meet along your journey. Your marketing plan is your *best* tool to help you engage others in your job search/career transition project. With the help of your marketing plan, those you meet while volunteering or at networking events will be able to understand your career objective, your core competencies, and the companies you are targeting. Your marketing plan provides them something to work with and can position them to provide you with ideas, suggestions, leads, and potential opportunities.

Resumes are for hiring managers and recruiters. Share your marketing plan with everyone else!

To wrap up this chapter on networking, I want to share one of my favorite quotes that I think offers wise counsel and will serve you well when networking.

> "No one ever learned anything by speaking."
> —*Eleanor Roosevelt*

When you network your goal is to gather information and build relationships. Both are best served through more listening and less speaking. Learn to ask open-ended probing questions and then listen actively. Be genuinely interested in what the other person has to say and the ideas, leads, and opportunities they may share. Also, as always in the process, ask how you can help them. Give, don't just take!

BUSINESS CARDS

Be sure to invest in some professional business cards to use when networking (as well as when you are interviewing). Your name and contact information, including your LinkedIn address, should be on the front side of your business card. I recommend you include three to six bullets on the backside of your card stating your core competencies. My business card also includes my mission statement as well as a photograph. Since I am an author, trainer, coach, and public speaker, I like having the photo for recognition purposes. Whether you include a photograph or not depends on what you do as well as personal preference. You can get business cards printed very inexpensively through a number of companies you can find online.

✅ CHECKLIST - BEFORE YOU MOVE ON

☐ Do you have a networking strategy in place?

☐ Are you networking on a regular basis to find job leads?

☐ Are you building relationships, establishing trust, and rapport?

☐ Have you done an assessment of your current network: your acquaintances, allies, and advocates?

☐ Is the networking you do effective? Do you need to look for other places to network that will yield better results?

☐ Have you explored volunteer opportunities where you can network, build skills, and contribute?

☐ Have you completed your personal Marketing Plan? Are you sharing it with your network contacts to find leads, referrals, contacts within targeted companies, and to open doors?

 Lessons Learned: *Networking is about building quality relationships and is one of your most valuable tools in career transition. Networking can be face-to-face or online and opportunities to network present themselves daily. Anyone can network successfully, especially if they focus on the other person and practice active listening.*

CHAPTER 11

WORKING WITH RECRUITERS
AND SEARCH FIRMS

Should I work with a recruiter? What are the advantages? What are the disadvantages? Should I work with more than one recruiter or search firm? Can I apply directly to a company if I am working with a recruiter? What are recruiters and hiring managers looking for? What do they want to see on my resume?

I will briefly touch on this topic and give you some food for thought. My suggestion is that you do your research and talk to others who have worked with recruiters and executive search firms for their perspective as well. Find out who's in your area and what reputation they have for helping job seekers.

More and more companies are using recruiters and search firms to fill their vacancies. Some organizations have eliminated or outsourced their Human Resources department and have built relationships with search firms to meet their human resource needs. Recruiters and search firms work hard to build trusting relationships with the companies they represent. You may want to tap into those relationships to get in front of your targeted company. As I heard one recruiter say to a group of job seekers, "We have more relationships with more companies than you do, so you should tap into that."

ADVANTAGES OF WORKING WITH RECRUITERS

Working with recruiters can help:

- Improve your chances of getting in front of the company you want to work for; they can be your advocate.

- Get your resume to the top of the pile, if you are the right candidate.

- Locate contract positions for you until full-time work can be found.

Disadvantages—none really; but please do understand that recruiters work for and represent the companies that hire them, not you. I have known job seekers who try to relinquish their job search responsibilities to a recruiter. Again, the recruiters work for the companies who contract with and pay them, not you.

If you are the right candidate for a position, the recruiter will want to get you hired. That's how they make their money. Recruiters have influence with their clients, and therefore; you have a better chance of getting in front of a hiring manager of a company you want to work for. This can give you a strategic advantage.

HOW TO FIND A SEARCH FIRM THAT SPECIALIZES IN YOUR AREA OF EXPERTISE/INDUSTRY

Do your research online, attend networking events, search job boards, see who's recruiting on LinkedIn, Twitter, and other social media sites. Ask other job seekers for their recommendations. Often, they can provide a lot of insight in this area. Who have they worked with in the past? What company and recruiters would they recommend and why? Most importantly, do your homework and find out which recruiters the companies you are targeting are using and then seek them out.

Recruiters search for potential candidates online so having a strong online presence can get you noticed. Make sure you use key words that match job postings in which you have an interest, both on your LinkedIn profile and resumes you post online. Blogging, vlogging, and posting comments on relevant LinkedIn discussion groups are good places to showcase your industry knowledge and get noticed by recruiters.

HOW TO WORK WITH RECRUITERS

Working with a recruiter requires building a relationship. Behaviors that build strong relationships include:

- Honesty
- Integrity
- Persistence
- Perseverance
- Patience
- Follow-up
- Attention to detail
- Willingness to listen actively and take advice

Recruiters are looking for top-tier candidates to present to their clients. They are looking for candidates that have distinctive qualities and distinctive qualifications. You should treat your encounters with recruiters just like a job interview. Be knowledgeable about the company and prepared to share your accomplishments and provide clear evidence of why you would be an ideal candidate for the position under consideration. If you have a strong relationship with a recruiter, and you are a good match for the position they are looking to fill, it is likely your resume will get in front of the company's hiring manager.

Most recruiters use an applicant tracking system[1] (ATS) to pull candidates' resumes from online searches based on key words. If your resume makes it through an initial screening, the recruiter will then turn to social media to see if you would be a good fit for the position. (See Chapter 12, **Social Media** for tips on how to attract recruiters to your LinkedIn profile.)

SHOULD YOU WORK WITH MORE THAN ONE RECRUITER/ SEARCH FIRM?

There is no apparent stigma for working with more than one search firm. If you are looking at more than one industry it might be appropriate to work with more than one firm/recruiter. Search firms and recruiters specialize in different industries and represent different clients. Do your research and find the firm or firms that work with the companies you are targeting. Know their reputation and ethical standards.

When selecting a recruiter to work with, one of the questions you may want to ask them is, "How many people have you placed with my area of expertise in the past 6 months?" Ask other job seekers and your local career transition volunteers what recruiters or firms they recommend.

More and more companies are using recruiters to fill key vacancies—and they are looking for top-tier candidates to fill those vacancies. Tap into that network.

Make sure you understand the nuances of the relationship you will have with the search firm or recruiter and *review carefully* any paperwork or contracts before signing anything. Also, make sure you know to whom the recruiter is submitting your resume. If you submit a resume to a company directly and the recruiting firm also submits your resume unbeknownst to you, your resume may not be considered. This situation would be considered a conflict of interest and the targeted company may not be able to consider you as a candidate for the position.

CHECKLIST - BEFORE YOU MOVE ON

☐ Have you looked at the advantages of working with a recruiter or search firm?

☐ Have you identified a recruiter(s) that specialize in your industry?

☐ Do you know the reputation of the recruiters in your area?

☐ Will it benefit you to work with more than one recruiter?

☐ If you choose to work with a recruiter or search firm, have you read their contract and do you understand their expectations? What are your obligations? What are theirs?

 Lessons Learned: *Working with a recruiter or search firm has many advantages. They have built relationships with employers and you will want to tap into that. Be sure that you understand the dynamics of the relationship, expectations, and any paperwork that you sign.*

CHAPTER 12

SOCIAL MEDIA

For some people, using social media to network, attract recruiters, and assist in their job search can be a scary prospect. It doesn't have to be if you know what you are doing and understand the value of using social media. Let's delve into that now.

More and more recruiters and hiring managers are looking to social media for potential candidates. LinkedIn, Twitter, Facebook, Pinterest, You Tube, you name it. Recruiters and others are searching these sites to help fill their needs. If recruiters and hiring managers are using social media and you are not, then you will not be found!

Other reasons you will want to use social media include: to reinforce your brand, support your career objectives, emphasize your accomplishments, and network. Network not only with recruiters and hiring managers, but also with others who can help you identify opportunities, companies, and key decision makers.

To be successful using social media, be strategic and consider the following:

- What's my overall approach in using social media to communicate, research, and network?

- How can I best attract recruiters using social media?

- How do I network using social media?

- What are the best sites for networking?

SOCIAL MEDIA APPROACH

Social media offers you opportunities to network, conduct research, and communicate with people you would otherwise not find accessible. Your overall approach to using social media should be to get on the radar screen and get noticed by recruiters, hiring managers, influencers, and others with whom you may want to network.

You need to know: 1) How to use social media effectively, and 2) how to create a positive and consistent online presence. Hiring managers and recruiters are likely to Google you when a resume is submitted, or they have identified you online. They will look you up on LinkedIn and Facebook for starters (if your resume appears to be a good fit).

HOW DO I NETWORK USING SOCIAL MEDIA?

Since the majority of jobs are found through a network contact, networking is key to your success. Face-to-face networking is great when you can do it, but social media expands your world exponentially. Social media allows you to establish new connections and re-establish connections with people whom you may have lost contact. Social media is an effective tool that can help you identify and land your dream job. It's a two-way street, you can reach out to others and they can reach out to you.

I personally have had a number of people find me, mostly through LinkedIn, to request my services as a trainer, speaker, and coach. I have trained for companies located in Switzerland, Germany, and India who hired me to train for clients in the U.S.

Networking online can help you:

- Get on the "radar screen" so others are aware of who you are and what services, skills, and knowledge you have to offer.

- Secure key contacts to help you gain access to the hidden job market— those jobs that are not advertised.

- Get introductions to recruiters, hiring managers, and others within your targeted companies.

- Research companies and gather information-rich data.

- Help you explore possible career fields and industries.

- Get offers for contract work and temporary positions.

- Land your dream job!

With all the benefits listed, and others you may think of, there is no reason why you should be reluctant to utilize social media as part of your job search strategy. In fact, not doing so will almost certainly result in a much longer career transition project and you missing out on greater possibilities and perhaps the job of your dreams.

When you get an invitation, or offer to connect on LinkedIn (for example), my suggestion is that you review the person's profile to see what or who you have in common and determine if you wish to accept the invitation. If there are any red flags or anything that makes you feel uncomfortable, go with your gut and delete. When accepting a LinkedIn invite, I will look for a common connection such as a mutual friend, a professional organization we both belong to, a LinkedIn group we share, or a common skill or profession. I do not accept LinkedIn invitations if there is no photo and no common link. Use your best judgment.

Facebook professional/business pages are one way to connect with others and create a social media presence. If you have a personal Facebook page, I caution you to only post things that you would not mind a prospective employer seeing. Be sure to create privacy settings for your personal Facebook page.

The daughter of a friend and colleague was hired by a company to support their social media efforts. Apparently, there were several applicants being considered but my friend's daughter was offered the position because she had a very large following on Pinterest. Depending on the field or industry you are in, social media will play a larger or smaller role. In my friend's case, her daughter's large following on Pinterest gave her the competitive advantage she needed to land the job.

If you are a research scientist, for example, then social media may not be as important to your day-to-day responsibilities, but don't let that steer you away. Most of the Ph.D. research scientists I have worked with/coached spend a majority of their time in a laboratory and tend not to be too well networked/connected. They have often expressed skepticism to using social media and sometimes get freaked out when someone unknown reaches out to them with an invite. The reaction is understandable, but do not be afraid to reach out to others. There are **N**ew **O**pportunities **W**aiting but it may require getting out of your comfort zone to reap the benefits of networking on social media. LinkedIn offers opportunities to connect with fellow alumni, former colleagues, influencers, and others in your field of specialty.

How to Attract Recruiters and Hiring Managers to Your LinkedIn Profile

Currently, LinkedIn is the number one tool recruiters and hiring managers use to find candidates for positions they are working to fill for their clients or employer. Recruiters and hiring managers are on LinkedIn every day searching for and reaching out to candidates for new job opportunities. A number I saw recently indicated that 97% of recruiters currently use LinkedIn to source and review potential job candidates.

The primary reasons given for using LinkedIn in the hiring process include:

- To verify candidates' qualifications.

- To evaluate an individual's fit to a company's culture.

- To assess the professionalism of a potential candidate.

The important message to job seekers here is: *Get your LinkedIn profile up-to-date and consistent with the overall message you want recruiters to know about you.* If you want to attract recruiters and hiring managers to your LinkedIn page, you *must* have a complete and consistent profile. Your profile must speak to the job and industry you are targeting.

There are many free resources out there to help you create an effective LinkedIn profile. Seek them out. If nothing else, you can always find information on YouTube. I created my own LinkedIn page years ago and I found it to be very intuitive to set up. However, if you want the best results from your profile, I suggest taking a course, a webinar, or researching online tips, techniques, and best practices for using LinkedIn. Many community colleges offer free LinkedIn training for job seekers, those unemployed, and underemployed. Here are some quick tips that will help you attract recruiters to your LinkedIn page:

- **Your profile needs to be professional and complete.** LinkedIn gives you the opportunity to showcase your experience, education, accomplishments, skills, certifications, publications, presentations, and other information that illustrates your expertise. You will be overlooked by recruiters and hiring managers if your profile is incomplete. Be sure to include your unique selling points and write your summary in a way that grabs the reader's attention. Be interesting!

- **Conduct preliminary research before crafting your profile**. I suggest you first look at other peoples' profiles in your industry to see what captures your interest and catches your eye. Looking at other LinkedIn profiles can help you be more efficient and effective in creating your own profile. Find profiles that look professional and present a clear and concise message. Once you look at a few profiles you will see some that clearly stand out above the rest. Use those as your model to construct your own personal profile that will clearly and concisely represent who you are and the value you have to offer others.

- **Create an appealing and targeted headline that points to the job you are seeking.** Leverage the title field with the 120 characters available. For example, if you are seeking a project management position then your headline should reflect that.

- **A complete profile includes having a photograph of yourself**. Your photograph does not have to be taken by a professional photographer, but make sure it looks professional. It should be a "head shot" with you dressed in business professional attire that is appropriate to your industry. Some job seekers are reluctant to include a photograph of themselves but I have heard many recruiters and hiring managers say they will not even consider a candidate from LinkedIn without a photo. Some people, including myself, will not accept LinkedIn invitations without a photo.

- **Your profile must be consistent with your resume.** LinkedIn offers you the opportunity to expand on your resume, but it must be consistent with your message and key selling points. Inconsistencies will confuse recruiters and hiring managers who will ultimately lose interest in you as a potential candidate.

- **Communicate and quantify your value and accomplishments** to management, your team, your clients, and other key stakeholders. How have you improved the bottom-line, reduced costs, met deadlines, delivered successful projects, built strong customer and stakeholder relationships, improved processes, created and designed solutions? Recruiters and hiring managers will want to read about your accomplishments.

- **Load up key words throughout your profile.** Research words that are likely to get you noticed and incorporate them into your profile as they relate to your experience and expertise. Be sure to use relevant key words to your industry.

- **Share your expertise.** Get involved in discussion groups, add a blog under publications, and share a presentation. Recruiters and hiring managers like candidates who are engaged.

- **Ask for and post recommendations**. Recommendations give people an opportunity to hear from those who have worked with you, for you, or have hired you to help them solve their problems and attain their goals. Recommendations can only be given from your 1st connections. You can be recommended as a colleague, service provider, business partner, or student. You are in control of what recommendations you decide to add to your profile. You can display them or hide them if they do not reflect the message you are trying to create.

- **Add relevant skills so you can get endorsements from others**. While recommendations carry more influence with recruiters and hiring managers, they will often look to see the number of endorsements you have for a particular skill.

Your LinkedIn profile can be written in either the first or the third person, but be consistent throughout. LinkedIn offers many great features for the job seeker so do your research. Take a class and seek the advice of others on how to get the most from this very powerful networking tool.

WHAT'S ALREADY OUT THERE ABOUT ME?

Besides creating your online presence, you will also want to do an online search to discover what might be out there about you. In many cases, there may be more than you think. When I Googled myself, I found an article about me in Polish. I could not read it without a translation service, but I could tell from the headlines it had to do with a project management leadership conference where I spoke at the Warsaw School of Economics several years past. I found other articles where I was mentioned, but all positive and nothing I needed to be concerned with. You will want to do the same for yourself. See what others are seeing when they search your name.

If you have a common name there may be information on the web about you, or at least about someone with the same name. This is good information to know, as it could be a liability and affect your reputation.

Many recruiters report that they have found information online that influenced their decision *not* to hire someone. Do your due diligence and see if you have any reason for concern (even if it's not really you).

WHAT ARE THE BEST SITES FOR NETWORKING?

As stated previously, currently LinkedIn is considered the #1 site for business networking. While Facebook was established for social networking, LinkedIn's purpose has always been to help business people network. That being said, there are many sites you may want to consider for networking, I will name a few and by the time you read this book there will undoubtedly be many others!

- **LinkedIn** - Business-oriented social networking service; considered the #1 social media site for business networking. Used by recruiters and hiring managers to source and vet quality candidates for positions they are trying to fill. (Launched 2002)

- **Twitter** - Online social networking service that enables users to send and read short 140 character messages called "tweets." Many recruiters use Twitter to advertise positions they are seeking to fill. (Launched 2006)

- **Facebook Social** - A popular free social networking site to connect with friends, family, and business associates. Great place to network but be careful what you post. Always keep your image and reputation in mind when posting and responding to others. (Founded in 2004, originally for Harvard students to connect with each other.)

- **Facebook for Business** - Used by many small and large businesses as a way to grow their business by advertising and marketing online, often with the goal of driving traffic to a company website. Since already over a billion people use Facebook to connect with friends and family, Facebook for Business capitalizes on that market to increase brand awareness and sales. Facebook is a popular site to set up *private online communities* for entrepreneurs. These online communities are a great place for people to connect to share their ideas, questions, and successes.

- **Instagram** - An online mobile photo sharing, video sharing, and social networking service. Instagram allows individual users and businesses to deliver high quality visual content and build a brand online or create a portfolio. (Launched 2010)

- **Pinterest** - A web and mobile application that allows users to share photos, videos, songs, inspirational quotes, recipes, projects, and creative ideas known as *pins*. Users create *boards* to share their pins. The largest percentage of users are women. It's a free website that requires registration to use. (Launched 2010)

- **YouTube** - A global video sharing website that allows users to upload, view, rate, and share videos. YouTube offers the job seeker many opportunities to showcase their knowledge and expertise. (Launched 2005)

- **Meetup** - An online social media portal that allows members to find, form, and join various Meetup groups for face-to-face networking. Meetup Inc. helps individuals find or form groups that meet their particular interests. You can find a Meetup group by entering your zip/postal code and then selecting a topic of interest. If you don't find a Meetup group that meets your interest, then start one. (Launched 2002)

- **Quora** - This is a question-and-answer (Q&A) platform that allows its users to share knowledge by asking and answering questions and collaborating with others. This site attracts executives, industry leaders, journalists, and entrepreneurs. Quora is a site where you can follow thought-leaders in your industry. You can also contribute by answering questions using your expertise. You can build relationships on Quora by sharing questions and answers with people of similar interests. (Launched 2009)

Look online, there are many more social media networking apps. I recommend finding the format that works best for your career goals and your key audience. You most definitely need a LinkedIn page. Make sure it is complete ("All Star" level) and consistent with your other communication tools such as your resume and marketing plan. Networking on social media will serve you well in your job search or career transition if used appropriately and consistently.

Social media offers you the opportunity to connect with hiring managers, recruiters, and others in your field of interest. It will help you get on the "radar screen" and find opportunities to advance your career. Use it wisely to build your network. Use it to navigate your journey to **N**ew **O**pportunities **W**aiting!

 # CHECKLIST - BEFORE YOU MOVE ON

☐ Do you have a social media presence that will help you get noticed by hiring managers and recruiters?

☐ Are you using social media effectively as a networking tool?

☐ Is your social media presence professional and does it present a clear and consistent message of your personal brand?

☐ Do you have a LinkedIn profile that communicates and quantifies your value and accomplishments? Does it convey a consistent message with your overall communication plan for your job search?

☐ Do you know what is out there about you on social media? Have you done an online search to see what others can find about you?

 Lessons Learned: *Social media is a powerful tool for networking, marketing your personal brand, and communicating your value to others.*

CHAPTER 13

UNDERSTANDING PERSONALITIES AND COMMUNICATION STYLES

As we have discussed throughout the book, finding that next career opportunity requires connecting with others. The more you understand about personalities and communication styles, the more likely you are to connect with others and achieve your career objectives. Also, understanding personality preferences will help you understand yourself better, which is critical to your success.

You've seen the job descriptions, "Effective written and oral communication skills required." Landing your ideal job will entail a lot of written and oral communication skills. If you are not communicating effectively, you won't get the job.

But what exactly is effective communication? That's a tough one because it depends in part with whom you are communicating and in what ways that person is different from you. The more you know about the person or persons with whom you will be communicating, especially face-to-face, the better prepared you will be. Let me attempt to prepare you for your face-to-face interview; or anytime you will be communicating with others during your job search project; using my knowledge of an instrument called the **Myers-Briggs Type Indicator® (MBTI).**[1]

HISTORY AND APPLICATION

The Myers-Briggs Type Indicator® (or **MBTI** as I will hereafter refer to it) is the most widely used personality inventory in the world. It was originally developed as a tool to help people understand themselves better and understand how to communicate more effectively with people who have different preferences.

The MBTI is a psychological instrument developed by Katherine Briggs and Isabel Briggs Myers.[2] It is based on the theory of psychological type, as developed by Swiss psychologist Carl Jung.[3] The instrument has been revised over the years by a team of Ph.D. psychologists and translated into over twenty languages.

Some of the **applications** and **benefits of the MBTI** include:

- Career planning/career choices
- Better problem solving and decision making
- Effective communication
- Leadership development
- Team building
- Conflict resolution
- Stress management

For the purpose of this book, we will look at the MBTI to explore how you can better communicate with and relate to potential employers, recruiters, hiring managers, and others during the job search process.

WHAT DOES THE MBTI MEASURE?

The MBTI is a measure of psychological preferences and identifies four separate dichotomies: Extroversion versus Introversion, Sensing versus Intuition, Thinking versus Feeling, and Judging versus Perceiving. The personality profiles of the MBTI are based on sound theory and empirical observation of human behavior.

Preferences are different from competencies and skills. For example, are you left-handed or are you right-handed? Did you make a conscious decision to be left-handed or right-handed? Probably not! Personally, I have been right-handed since I was a baby. It was not a choice I made nor one my parents made for me. They did not teach me to be right-handed, I simply was. And although I am clearly right-handed, I still use my left hand (non-preferred) every day to complete tasks such as eating, dressing, washing, picking up things, etc. In fact, it would be very difficult for me to get through the day without using both my preferred hand and my non-preferred hand.

Since core preferences come naturally, we rarely give much thought to them or how they influence our behavior and how we process things. An awareness of our preferences and the preferences of others can help us modify our behavior when needed to get the results we desire and to communicate more effectively with others.

The MBTI measures your preferences on four distinct bi-polar scales as follows:

1. Your attitude or orientation to *energy* (Extroversion versus Introversion)

2. Your preference on *how you collect information* (Sensing versus Intuition)

3. Your preference on *how you make decisions* based on information you have collected(Thinking versus Feeling)

4. Your attitude or orientation to *how you prefer your world to be structured and organized* (Judging versus Perceiving)

The MBTI does not measure skills, ability, nor intelligence, and all preferences are regarded as equally valuable and important. Also, there is no *better than* or *worse than* type. All sixteen personality types are assumed to have equal value. In a home or business environment each of us brings unique strengths and we each have our own unique challenges.

HOW CAN THE MBTI HELP ME IN MY JOB SEARCH?

We all have natural preferences in how we approach things, communicate, and relate to others. Sometimes we are effective, sometimes not so much. Being aware of our natural preferences and the preferences of others can help us develop an approach to achieve our career objectives and get desired results.

After reviewing the four scales of the MBTI, I will introduce you to a communication strategy, based on the MBTI, that will help you communicate more effectively with your audience during your job search project.

WHO CAN ADMINISTER THE MBTI?

Many career coaches are certified in the MBTI or could recommend a resource to you. You can find certified MBTI practitioners through the Association of Psychological

Type International[4] itself, or a local APTi Chapter. There are a number of organizations specializing in the MBTI including The Myers-Briggs Company (instrument publisher),[5] the Center for the Application of Psychological Type (CAPT),[6] and the Association of Psychological Type (APTi),[7] a non-profit organization for both type professionals and type enthusiasts. Also, many universities and community colleges have trained, certified professionals who can administer and interpret the instrument for you.

OVERVIEW OF MBTI PREFERENCES

Let's start with a very quick personality overview using the four scales of the MBTI. I do not expect that by the end of this chapter that you will be well-versed on the preferences the MBTI measures. I do, however, want to introduce the instrument to you, or perhaps remind you of its value if you have taken it before (as many of you have).

I have included some charts to help you identify the characteristics of each of the preferences so you can begin to identify your type. Notice I used the word "begin." To accurately assess your personality preferences, you will need to complete the MBTI instrument and meet with a certified MBTI practitioner for analysis and insight. They can help you understand how to utilize this information in your search for a new job, new career, professional development, or whatever your objective is for completing the instrument.

The MBTI contains four separate scales designed to determine a person's preferences on four dichotomies, E-I, S-N, T-F, and J-P. The object of the instrument is to ascertain, as accurately as possible, the four categories to which the respondent naturally belongs.

(E) Extroversion vs. **Introversion (I)**
(S) Sensing vs. **Intuition (N)**
(T) Thinking vs. **Feeling (F)**
(J) Judging vs. **Perceiving (P)**

WHAT'S YOUR TYPE - A QUICK ASSESSMENT

The MBTI seeks to identify a respondent's preference on one of two opposite personality categories (E-I, S-N, T-F, and J-P), both of which are regarded as neutral in relation to emotional health, intellectual functioning, and psychological adaptation. Take a look at the charts that follow and select one of the preferences in each scale that most resonates with you. After reviewing all four scales, write your four-letter type, as you determine from this exercise, at the end of this section. (You can use this information as a "working hypothesis." This is not a substitute for completing the actual instrument!)

EXTROVERSION/INTROVERSION SCALE
(Orientation/Attitude toward Energy)

E: Extroversion "Let's talk this through."	I: Introversion "Let me think this through."
Energized by people and external experiences	Energized by time alone, through reflection and internal experiences
Expressive, energetic, and active	Reflective, calm, and quiet
Has a breadth of interests; likes experiencing many things	Has a depth of interests; requires concentration and focus
At social gatherings likes to engage with many people; likes to be where the action is	At social gatherings will gravitate to one or two people preferring to stay out of the crowd
Asks questions and thinks out loud while working through a decision	Thinks things through before sharing thoughts and ideas with others
Expresses thoughts and emotions freely; may be at risk of saying too much	Keeps thoughts and emotions private; may be at risk of saying too little
Needs relationships	Needs privacy
Generally approachable and easily engages with others; a stranger can quickly become a friend	Generally reserved and can be hard to get to know; tends to have a small group of close friends
Learns and works best when able to share, discuss, and process information with others	Learns and works best when able to process and understand information on own
Attracted to careers and work activities with high people contact; lots of action and interaction	Attracted to careers and work that require a depth of concentration and tasks that can be performed alone

Everyone uses both Extraversion and Introversion to carry out day-to-day activities. However, one of the two will be more natural and comfortable. The preference that best describes me is:

Extroversion _____   **Introversion** _____

SENSING/INTUITION SCALE

(Mental Function of Data Gathering)

S: Sensing "Let's start with the facts."	N: iNtuition "Let's start with the big picture."
Uses their five senses; can I see it, touch it, taste it, smell it, hear it? Have I experienced this before?	Uses their sixth sense; intuition or gut-feel
Focuses on facts, data, and historical information; keeps things grounded	Focuses on patterns and relationships; the big picture; vision and theoretical ideas
Draws from the past to understand the present; focuses on the here-and-now	Focuses on the future possibilities; what might be
Starts at the beginning; takes things step by step	Jumps in anywhere; leaps over steps
Uses and interprets words literally	Uses analogies and metaphors
Solves problems using a practical approach	Solves problems using ingenuity and creativity
May prefer activities that are repetitive and familiar; resists change	Needs variety; challenges ideas for wide-scale change
Reads instructions to complete a task or assemble something	What instructions? Reads instructions as last resort
Wants the details and back ground information	Wants the executive summary
Relies on their perspiration	Relies on their inspiration

Everyone uses both Sensing and iNtuition to take in information and gather data. However, one of the two will be more natural and comfortable. The preference that best describes me is:

Sensing _____   **Intuition** _____

THINKING/FEELING SCALE

(Mental Function of Decision-Making)

T: Thinking "What are the logical implications?"	F: Feeling "Will anyone get hurt?"
Focuses on analysis and logical implications	Focuses on beliefs and values
Decisions from the head; may appear impersonal and uncaring	Decisions from the heart; appears personal, empathetic, and caring
Emphasis on objective data and logical frameworks	Emphasis on subjective decision-making, reflecting the needs of individuals
Looks at the impact on measureable things such as return on investment, market share, bottom line	Looks at the impact on people such as family, employees, stakeholders, the community at large
Offers frank and honest feedback	Offers feedback gently; may "sugar-coat"
Tends to be blunt and to the point	Chooses words carefully to avoid hurting anyone's feelings
Finds it uncomfortable to deal with the emotions and feelings of others	Emphasizes the importance of addressing peoples' feelings
Initially views conflict as a normal part of work and an opportunity to problem-solve; will tend to withdraw as conflict and emotions escalate	Initially views conflict as negative, disruptive, and something to avoid; will later address conflict to ensure no one gets hurt
Values principles, fairness, justice, and industry standards	Values relationships, harmony, empathy, and a positive environment
Addresses the pros and cons of information, ideas, and opinions; naturally skeptical	Addresses areas of agreement; naturally supportive

Everyone uses both Thinking and Feeling preferences to make decisions. However, one of the two will be more natural and comfortable. The preference that best describes me is:

Thinking _____   **Feeling** _____

JUDGING/PERCEIVING SCALE

(Orientation/Attitude to the External World)

J: Judging "Just make a decision!"	P: Perceiving "Let me consider all the options."
Likes their world structured and organized; methodical and systematic	Likes their world flexible and adaptable; comfortable proceeding without a definite plan
Motto: "Have a plan and work the plan"	Motto: "Go with the flow"
Likes to have life under control; driven by schedules	Likes to experience life as it happens; the schedule is subject to change
Makes decisions as soon as possible; Joy of Closure	Keeps options open as long as possible; Joy of Processing
Likes to complete a project before moving onto the next	May have many projects open and that's okay
J's may seem demanding, inflexible, and rigid to a P	P's may seem disorganized, messy, and unable to make a decision to a J
Deliberate; sticks to commitments, plans and schedules even when it gets boring	Spontaneous; willing to adapt to the moment and likes to have fun
Typical do not like change; messes up their plan(s)	Natural change agents; change is seen as an opportunity to learn something new
Makes lists for things to be completed; if something is done that was not on the list, it will be added to the list so the box can be checked as completed. Lists are meant to be completed!	Makes lists primarily as a reminder or memory jogger; if not completed, will transfer to new list.
Sees work and play as distinct aspects of life; "I can play when all my work is done."	Sees work and play as intertwined; "I can play anytime."
What's the deadline?	What deadline?

Everyone uses both Judging and Perceiving to structure and carry out day-to-day activities. However, one of the two will be more natural and comfortable. The preference that best describes me is:

Judging _____   **Perceiving** _____

After selecting the preferences that best describe you, fill in the letters below to determine your personality type. (working hypothesis)

Extroversion or Introversion? (Fill in E or I) _____

Sensing or Intuition? (Fill in S or N) _____

Thinking or Feeling? (Fill in T or F) _____

Judging or Perceiving? (Fill in J or P) _____

My four-letter type is: _____ _____ _____ _____

Using the combination of the eight letters, there are a total of sixteen personality types. Following is a chart showing each of the four-letter types.

ISTJ	**ISFJ**	**INFJ**	**INTJ**
ISTP	**ISFP**	**INFP**	**INTP**
ESTP	**ESFP**	**ENFP**	**ENTP**
ESTJ	**ESFJ**	**ENFJ**	**ENTJ**

(A more detailed chart of the sixteen personality types can be found in the **Career Tools** section at **www.ProjectCareerQuest.com**. I have recommended a book at the end of this chapter that will help you go deeper into the study of personality preferences, entitled *Type Talk at Work*. In that book, you can find detailed information about each of the sixteen personality types. There is also an abundance of information available online regarding the MBTI.)

COMMUNICATION TIPS

The communication tips below summarize communication strengths and characteristics, communication preferences, observable behavior, and things to keep in mind when you are communicating with others. The more you read and learn about the MBTI, the more you will pick up on the clues people give you about their preferences. Observing the behavior of others to understand preferences is known as "Typewatching."

E: EXTROVERTS

Communication strengths/characteristics: Extroverts are energized through active involvement in events and activities. Their communication style tends to be energetic and enthusiastic. They can be good networkers as they like to connect with others. They have a breadth of interest which generally means they are good at small talk and building rapport. An extrovert will provide extensive information, sometimes *too* much, and immediate feedback.

People who prefer extroversion:

- Prefer to communicate by talking.
- Tend to speak first and reflect later.
- Think out loud in order to process information. (referred to as verbal brainstorming)
- Share their thoughts freely.
- Change topics and opinions as dialogue progresses.
- Share ideas and information immediately.
- Tend to be animated and use more exaggerated body language.
- Talk more than listen.
- Uncomfortable with silence.
- Will interrupt. (as they share their thoughts freely)

When Communicating with an E:

- Provide immediate feedback and verbal acknowledgment.
- Express enthusiasm.
- Maintain eye contact.

- Allow them to talk things through, understanding their ideas may be random and not well thought out.
- If it enhances your understanding and ability to communicate more effectively, ask them to list out their ideas and then focus on one at a time.

I: INTROVERTS

Communication strengths/characteristics: Introverts generally have a quiet and calming presence. They prefer to think things through and will respond carefully and thoughtfully. In a networking situation, they will get to know a few people well and tend to listen to others without interrupting. Introverts are private and guarded with their thoughts, comments, and how much they are willing to share with others, especially in a public setting.

People who prefer introversion:

- Prefer one-on-one interaction versus group setting.
- Need quiet time to reflect and process information before discussing or changing perspectives.
- Prefer to communicate in writing.
- Like to understand topics in depth before offering ideas or solutions.
- Prefer to have information ahead of time for a thorough review before discussing.
- Will wait for a pause before speaking.
- Listen more than they talk.
- Will tune you out if you talk too much.
- Are comfortable with silence.
- Sometimes spend too much time reflecting and may fail to act quickly enough.

When Communicating with an I:

- Practice active listening skills; do not interrupt.
- Think before speaking or let others know you are thinking out loud (E's).
- Speak slowly and calmly.

- Pause and wait for a response; create space for them to speak.
- Focus on one topic at a time; don't jump around.
- Select a quiet environment with limited distractions for important discussions.

S: SENSORS

Communication strengths/characteristics: Sensors perceive a situation using their five senses (hear it, see it, smell it, taste it, touch it), and will gather information from their experiences. For a sensor, experience speaks louder than words or theory. Sensors are grounded in the past and present. They approach a situation with a focus on the details and the practical application of ideas and things.

People who prefer sensing:

- Seek facts and detail; background and historical information.
- Work from the facts to understand the bigger picture.
- Allow their experiences to guide their decision making.
- Want specific plans and procedures.
- Like step-by-step explanations.
- Prefer plain literal language to metaphors and abstractions.
- Tend to speak and write in short sentences.
- Trust what has been tried and proven.
- Comfortable with familiarity and practicality.

When communicating with an S:

- Focus on things that are real, factual, and provide specific details.
- Be practical and find ways to bring ideas down to earth.
- Provide concrete examples to support your position or ideas.
- Focus on the past or present prior to sharing future possibilities.
- Present information sequentially.
- Avoid extensive use of metaphors, analogies, or other abstract communication.
- Use words that relate to sensory and real-life images.

N: INTUITIVES

Communication strengths/characteristics: Intuitives are open to possibilities, anticipating and creating change. They are future-oriented and thus will discuss things based on future possibilities and implications moving forward. Intuitives see trends and patterns and are interested in the abstract and theory. They gather information from their intuition and insight and will often use phrases such as "my gut reaction is…" or "based on my intuition…"

People who prefer intuition:

- Focus on patterns, possibilities, and relationships. (i.e., how things fit together)
- Become bored or impatient with too much detail.
- Like to brainstorm and imagine what could be.
- Prefer first to understand the big picture before digging into the details.
- Will ask for the executive summary.
- Trust their intuition and gut often over facts and data.
- Will recall events by "reading between the lines."
- Use metaphors, analogies, and figurative language to convey their message.
- May jump from topic to topic exploring links.

When communicating with an N:

- Consider possibilities, even those that seem far-fetched.
- Provide an overview/executive summary first.
- Do not get bogged down in facts and details.
- Share the main point and then add detail as necessary.
- Show future possibilities of your ideas.
- Be open to change.
- Provide a reality check; help N's link ideas to reality.

T: THINKERS

Communication strengths/characteristics: Thinkers tend to be calm, reasonable, and under control. They provide honest and frank feedback. They analyze, evaluate, and critique. Thinking preferences engage in objective decision-making and clear-thinking processes using defined criteria.

People who prefer thinking:

- Use logic and analysis to spot flaws.
- Will debate and challenge information to understand your logic (natural challengers); need to know "why?"
- Strive for impersonal-objective truth.
- Like to receive and present information objectively, without feelings and emotions.
- Make decisions from their head (logic) using cause and effect reasoning.
- Trust competence and expertise.
- Are tough-minded and impersonal in their approach.
- Generally accept critical feedback without taking it personally.
- Are concerned about things, i.e., bottom line, market share, return on investment.

When communicating with a T:

- Be calm and objective.
- Demonstrate competence.
- Offer frank and honest feedback.
- Provide information logically; be clear, concise, and direct.
- Support your opinions with logical reasoning.
- Show cause and effect relationships; discuss pros and cons.
- Accept critical feedback without personalizing it.
- Refer to best practices, industry standards, and established criteria.
- Focus on task and goal accomplishment and the impact on things.

F: FEELERS

Communication strengths/characteristics: People with a feeling preference are able to empathize and develop rapport with others. They are supportive, nurturing, and interested in people. They can often see and appreciate the perspective of others. Feeling preferences enjoy cooperating, collaborating, connecting with others, and creating a harmonious environment.

People who prefer feeling:

- Focus on individuals' beliefs and values.
- Make decisions from their heart using subjective-criteria.
- Believe that being tactful is more important than being too direct.
- May soften their response to avoid hurting someone's feelings.
- See strengths and positive attributes of others.
- Will often overextend themselves to accommodate the needs of others.
- Like encouragement and positive feedback.
- Like making links and connections with others.
- Are generally warm, supportive, expressive, and affirming.
- Are interested in people and their needs.

When communicating with an F:

- Take time to get to know them and develop rapport.
- Find out what is valued and important.
- Consider the needs of others for harmony and a positive environment.
- Provide feedback gently; critique behaviors, not people.
- Connect first, challenge later; find areas of agreement.
- Be careful to acknowledge; not analyze; feelings and values.
- Show the impact on people.

J'S: JUDGERS

Communication strengths/characteristics: Judging preferences tend to be well-organized and efficient communicators. They are decisive; task and goal-oriented; provide clear expectations and timelines. Judgers like to bring things to closure as quickly as possible and move onto the next task, decision, or project. Theirs is the *joy of closure.*

People who prefer judging:

- Like organized and efficient communication.
- Prefer structured and scheduled interactions.

- Are uncomfortable with open-ended and free-flowing discussions.

- Reach consensus quickly, make decisions, and provide closure.

- Sometimes will make decisions too quickly without enough information.

- Are generally punctual and expect others to be on time.

- Want clear and established expectations, timelines, and objectives.

- Want to have a plan and work the plan; do not like surprises or unplanned changes.

- Tend to make statements and ask closed-ended questions.

- Will use words indicating their desire for closure. (i.e., "always," "never," "let's make a decision and move on")

When communicating with a J:

- Provide structure and clear expectations.

- Narrow and focus your options before sharing them.

- Avoid sharing too many options; focus on what's most important.

- Create and share specific timelines and deadlines.

- Know when to stop exploring.

- Be willing to bring closure and make decisions quicker than you might prefer.

P: PERCEIVERS

Communication strengths/characteristics: Perceiving preferences are flexible and adaptable; willing to respond to the situation as needed. They are open to new information and will generate and consider a wide variety of options. Perceivers generally like to leave their options open as long as possible to make sure they have considered all of the possibilities. Theirs is the *joy of processing.*

People who prefer perceiving:

- Look for new information and will explore multiple options.

- Have a flexible, spontaneous, and unstructured communication style.

- Will often see an unexpected request as an opportunity.

- Are natural change agents.

- Feel boxed in if an immediate decision is requested.

- Without multiple options will either resist deciding, or later regret their decision and/or back out of the decision or situation.

- Ask open-ended questions to help identify and explore options.

- Prefer open-minded discussions.

- Will use words indicating their need to process options. (i.e., "perhaps," "maybe," "we'll see," "let me sleep on it")

When communicating with a P:

- Allow opportunities to explore before deciding.

- Avoid making decisions too quickly or forcing them to do so.

- Share and consider multiple options.

- Ensure you are not making conclusions when speaking.

- Establish mutual deadlines.

- Expect and plan for changes in your schedule.

- Be willing to take initial steps without having a complete plan.

Okay, that was a very quick study of the psychological type theory as represented through the MBTI. I can't do the instrument justice in a short chapter, but I did want to acquaint you with the possibilities that exist if you have some knowledge of personality types. (Can you tell I have a preference for iNtuition? This preference looks for possibilities; or a sense of inner knowing; and tends to be future-focused!) After completing this chapter, you should have a better understanding of how to communicate more effectively to influence and persuade decision makers.

—◦◦◦—

COMMUNICATION STRATEGY

Now let me explain a communication strategy based on the MBTI. This model focuses on the **mental functions** which includes **Sensing**, **iNtuition**, **Thinking** and **Feeling**. The mental functions are used to collect information and then make decisions based on the information collected. Called the "mental functions" because they are things we do in our heads (internally versus externally).

So here is how you can be more effective communicating, both in the spoken word as well as the written word. If you want to influence people, you must **learn to speak their language.** The words we choose to share *our story* will resonate with some and not connect with others unless we have a strategy to address the total audience. To do this, we want to share information from all four of the mental functions of the MBTI. Let me tell you what that looks like, and even the order in which information should be shared for greatest effectiveness (i.e., during a job interview). Hang with me and eventually this will begin to make sense.

(**Note:** This communication strategy is based on the MBTI Z-Model for decision- making.[8] The same model has application to your methodology for effectively communicating and connecting with your audience, whether one person or many.)

HOW TO STRUCTURE YOUR MESSAGE FOR MAXIMUM EFFECTIVENESS

If you want to persuade or influence your audience, whether one person or many, structure your story or message as the following—in the order it is shown:

1. **Share the facts and data (Sensing).** In the interview process this would be sharing your core competencies, your background, experience, key accomplishments, and other relevant data as it relates to the job/position.

2. Secondly, **share ideas and concepts, possibilities (iNtuition),** and other things focused on the future. Here's where you might share ideas about how you can help the company you are interviewing with solve problems and create opportunities for their growth and development.

3. Now you will talk about the **impact on things (Thinking)** such as the bottom line, return on investment, market share, productivity, efficiency, task accomplishment, etc. What have you done in the past for your previous employers or clients, and how can you contribute to helping the interviewer's organization in these areas?

4. Finally, you will also talk about **building relationships (Feeling)** with customers and key stakeholders. What have you done to successfully build strategic

alliances and create customer loyalty? What have you done to build high performing teams? Focus here on the *people* aspect and how you have contributed to creating value for people.

Bottom line, to communicate more effectively, make sure you are addressing your *total audience* if you want to have the kind of impact you desire. The natural tendency is to speak only your preferred language.

If you are a **sensor** and a **thinker** (such as an **IST**J, **EST**J, **IST**P, or **EST**P) you will naturally talk about facts and data and the impact on things, likely forgetting to speak about future possibilities and the impact on people. If you are speaking to another *sensor-thinker* you may be fine, but if not, you may have alienated some of your audience.

If you are an **iN**tuitive and **feeler** (such as an **INF**J, **ENF**J, **INF**P, **ENF**P), your natural focus will be on the future possibilities and people, while your audience may be more interested on facts, data, and the impact on things (return on investment, market share, task accomplishment, etc.). Again, you want to make sure you are addressing your total audience and not alienating anyone.

EXTERNAL ORIENTATIONS (E-I AND J-P SCALES)

Now let's return to the **E** and **I** and the **J** and **P** scales to explore briefly how these preferences might manifest in the interview process. Both are orientations or attitudes to our "external world."

The E-I scale describes our orientation to "energy" we get from others. E's are energized by being around people and I's need time alone to be re-energized after spending time with people. The J-P scale is an orientation to how we like our external world structured and organized. J's appreciate structure and P's appreciate flexibility.

Extroverts (E's) are energized by people and will tend to speak with their body using more exaggerated hand gestures and movement. **Introverts' (I's)** movements are not as exaggerated and an introvert may actually move very little in a job interview. This is good information to know because you will want to mirror, to some extent, the person with whom you are speaking.

Mirroring is done to create rapport. We all do it, often without even thinking about it. For example, when someone smiles at you what do you do? Probably smile back. If you do not smile back, you will be seen as unfriendly. In an interview, if the hiring manager uses a lot of gestures and body language and you sit there like a lump of rocks, she may not feel a connection. A little mirroring movement will be in order, not to manipulate, but rather to better connect. If you are the extrovert and you speak with your hands, and the hiring manager is fairly still, you may want to tone it down a little.

Also, if you are interviewing in the hiring manager's office, take a look around when you first enter. If he is an **extrovert (E)**, he will typically have all sorts of things on his desk and on the walls—photos, college banners, certificates, memorabilia, and so forth. Extroverts tend to share their story with others by placing things in their office space that reflect who they are and what they like. After a quick glance around, you might break the ice with a comment about something you have in common. For instance, perhaps he has a photo of his family with their beautiful golden retriever. I help rescue, rehab, and adopt golden retrievers so I might break the ice by saying something like "What a lovely family you have. I have a golden retriever myself. In fact, I volunteer with a golden retriever rescue." Or perhaps there is a college flag from Syracuse University on the wall. I did not attend Syracuse but two of my cousins did; they both rowed crew there. Commenting on this connection can help build rapport, ease tension, and create commonality.

If the hiring manager is an **introvert (I)** it is likely that he or she will not have much on their walls nor sitting on their desk. Introverts are much more private people; and therefore, you may have to look a little harder to find something you have in common. Still there may be something that catches your attention and you can make a casual comment about it to help break the ice. Don't pry too much, as introverts are unlikely to share a lot with a stranger.

In reality, many of your interviews will not take place in someone's office but rather in a conference or small meeting room. While the external physical clues may be missing, the person you meet with will still give you many clues about their personality and preferences if you know what to look for. I cannot help you too much with that in a short chapter, but the books I have recommended at the end of this section will give you some insight on how to read a person. You can get clues from people by the way they posture themselves, the clothes they wear, body language, the words they use, etc. Check out the book *Type Talk at Work* and you will learn much about reading others, known as "Typewatching."

The **J** and the **P** scale is an attitude or orientation about how we like things structured and organized. Whether you are a **Judger** or a **Perceiver**, always be respectful of time in the interview process (be on time) and be very organized (characteristic of the **J** preference). But also, be open to options and demonstrate flexibility (**P** preference).

The hiring manager may have either a Judging or Perceiving preference. Regardless, you should be on time and show respect for their process to avoid potential misunderstanding or offense.

The MBTI is a powerful and empowering instrument that can help you during the interview process and throughout your entire Career Quest journey. I recommend you complete the instrument if you have not taken it in the past. To find a career coach who is certified in the MBTI check with the Association of Psychological Type International (APTi).[9] If you are in college or the military, your career center may offer the MBTI as part of their coaching services.

 If you are interested in a detailed book on how type preferences show up in the work place, I refer you to *Type Talk at Work*[10] by Otto Kroeger and Janet Thuesen. You also might want to check out a couple of books on careers based on your personality type entitled *What's Your Type of Career*[11] by Donna Dunning and *Do What You Are*[12] by Paul D. Tieger and Barbara Barron-Tieger. A good book on the extroversion and introversion scales for job seekers is entitled *A Job Seekers Guide to Extroversion and Introversion*[13] by Carol Linden. There is no shortage of books and articles out there on the Myers-Briggs instrument.

One more recommended book to enhance your communication skills (but has nothing to do with the MBTI), is a book by John Maxwell entitled *Everyone Communicates but Few Connect.*[14] This book will help you to connect more effectively with others in all circumstances. Definitely a great resource for you during your time in transition and throughout your career.

And finally, one last tip on connecting with others during the interview process. Obviously, you cannot ask the interviewer to take the MBTI instrument in advance so you know more about his or her communication preferences. However, if you know your own personality type you can prepare by anticipating the needs of someone who might be your opposite in preferences. This approach will help you be more prepared to communicate effectively with many different personality types.

"I am not what happened to me, I am what I choose to become."
—*Carl Jung*

✔️ CHECKLIST - BEFORE YOU MOVE ON

☐ Do you know with whom you will be interviewing? If so, have you done some research about the person to have an understanding of their communication style, background, experience, education, etc.? LinkedIn is a great resource for researching the HR recruiter or hiring manager who may be interviewing you.

☐ Based on your research, have you uncovered anything that you may have in common with the interviewer(s) that may help you build trust and rapport? (Be careful not to share with them too much that you found online, or it may feel to them like cyber-stalking! Use the information you have uncovered about them wisely and discretely.)

☐ Did you review the four-step communication strategy to improve your chances of influencing the other party; to achieve the outcome you desire; by giving them the information they need to know and want to hear to be influenced?

Lessons Learned: *Understanding personality type can help you as a job seeker to be more effective in communicating and building rapport with others. The key is to connect with people where they are and to speak their language so they can relate to you and your message.*

CHAPTER 14

THE INTERVIEW PROCESS

F inally, the interview process, something I know you were all looking forward to. Proper preparation is essential if you are to advance in the process and hopefully land the position you desire. You have made it this far so let's get you to the next level.

During an interview, you will get only one chance to make a good impression. Prepare for your interviews with the impression you want to make in mind. Your appearance, your hygiene, the way you shake hands, make eye contact, your body language, and the degree to which you are prepared for the interview are all critical to your success. Your ability to connect with the interviewer(s); how you communicate and present your message; your ability to articulate your value, accomplishments, and why they should hire you; are all crucial factors that will determine, in large part, whether you get the job or not.

One of the first requests you may get in an interview is, "Tell me about yourself." If you did the work I set before you in Chapter 6 you should be well-equipped to respond appropriately. See the end of this chapter for help developing your response to "Tell Me About Yourself." (A template to write down your response can be found in the **Career Tools** section at **www.ProjectCareerQuest.com**.)

Next, many interviewers will start by asking questions based on your resume and the information you have provided. Be prepared! In the summary statement on your resume you stated that you are a "natural people motivator." Okay, tell me how you motivate people? Please, no deer in the head lights look here. You need to have an example prepared to back up *anything* and *everything* on your resume. One slip up and you have lost all credibility. End of interview—lost opportunity!

You have "extensive" project management experience? Be prepared to share with the interviewer an example of your extensive experience. This came up in one of my mock interviews. I asked the individual when was the last time he had developed a work breakdown structure (WBS). He told me he did not know what a WBS was; never heard of one. I told him he could not possibly have "extensive" project management experience if he did not even know what a WBS was. In a job interview he would have lost all credibility and the opportunity to advance in the process. He did have some experience working on projects. I told him to rewrite his summary statement to say, "Experience working on projects including…" It is okay to say you have some project experience but do *not* say you have "extensive" experience (in anything) when you do not. A good interviewer will ask questions to test the validity of what you have included on your resume.

"Good communication skills." Doesn't everyone say that? Prove it. The interviewer will want an example. Can't provide one, you're done—next candidate! Get my point?

I have found that job seekers put lots of things on their resume they think the hiring manager wants to hear, or to match up with key words and phrases, and then think they won't be asked about it during the interview. *Wrong*!

As you move further in this chapter you will find a list of some of the typical questions you may be asked in your job interview. You will also want to have a list of questions you want to ask to determine if the company, culture, position, and compensation are right for you.

Prepare your interview stories (SOAR Stories - Situation, Obstacle/Opportunity, Action, Results, which we will discuss in detail later in the chapter) and be prepared for questions aimed at understanding how you: lead, manage, communicate, relate to others, collaborate, handle conflict, innovate, problem-solve, make decisions, plan, organize, execute, handle ambiguity, cope with stressful situations, manage a variety of personality styles, work under pressure, work with senior management, handle customer complaints, build stakeholder relationships, etc.

ORGANIZING YOUR JOB SEARCH INFORMATION

Before we talk about interviews, let's talk about organizing your job search information so you will be prepared for your interviews. Start by getting a notebook to compile and organize your documentation or use folders on your computer to organize your data. Most likely you may do both. I like having a physical notebook to keep documentation in so I can quickly grab it and flip through the material as needed on a phone call. It's also very portable and doesn't require internet access.

In your binder/file you will want to keep the following information:

- Resume you sent to the company (Some customization will be required for every resume you send)

- Cover letter

- Research notes

- Discussion notes (Including any conversations you have had with company personnel)

- Interview Self-Assessment (Post-interview you will want to capture your lessons learned. I have created a post-interview form for you and have included it in the **Career Tools** section online at **www.ProjectCareerQuest.com**.)

- Anything else relevant to the position and your job search

TYPES OF INTERVIEWS

Now let's address the various types of interviews you may encounter. You may experience one or more than one of these formats in an interview with an employer.

Screening Interviews – These are used to weed out applicants who fall short of the job requirements and preferred experience and to pare down the number of choices for face-to-face interviews. Think of it as *Survivor*. Can you make it past the screening interview(s) to the next step?

You should prepare for screening interviews as you would for a face-to-face. If you attend a *job fair* for example, the companies present are there to screen candidates. Their goal is to identify job seekers they would like to invite for a follow up interview. Telephone and video interviews can be screening interviews used to determine whom the employer will pursue further and who to eliminate. A typical screening interview will last between fifteen to thirty minutes.

Job Fairs – Typically held at businesses, universities, hotels, and other public venues, job fairs are used to screen large numbers of potential candidates and narrow down the field. At a job fair, you may only have the time to present your resume to the attending representative of a particular company. Or you may get a short five to ten-minute interview. Occasionally, depending on the circumstances and their interest in you as a potential candidate, you may get a longer interview on site. Generally, interviews are brief at a job fair.

To prepare yourself for a job fair you will want to review in advance the list of companies who will be attending and prioritize with whom you want to speak. Do your research to know as much as you can about the companies you plan to visit and drop off a resume. When you arrive at the job fair get in line at your #1 choice company first, even if it is the longest line! Next visit your second-choice company and so forth. While you are standing in line, use that time to network with others and gain information and leads.

Be sure to bring plenty of copies of your resume and business cards. Dress professionally—exactly as you would for an in-house interview. Be prepared with your elevator speech, your unique selling points, accomplishment statements, and to respond to the "tell me about yourself" request. Treat whatever time you get like an interview, because it is, no matter how short!

By doing your homework and knowing who will be attending the job fair, you will have the opportunity to customize your resume for the companies you are targeting. Often, along with the companies attending, a list of jobs they are hiring for will also be posted. If you find a job you are interested in, be sure to customize your resume before attending the job fair. Make sure you identify which resume is for which recruiter/company.

Virtual Career Fairs – Not all job fairs are face-to-face. They can occur online as well, allowing you to connect with recruiters around in the world. Job opportunities can be found as well as internships for college students. Virtual career fairs should be approached with the same level of professionalism as a face-to-face job fair. To locate a virtual career fair canvas job boards such as LinkedIn, AARP, and Monster. Google "virtual career fairs" and you will be able to identify upcoming events.

Telephone Interviews – Before getting a face-to-face interview you are likely to get a telephone interview. A telephone interview is a "screening interview" used to eliminate unqualified candidates and move those that are most qualified onto the next step, which might be a face-to-face. Once you have submitted an application, be prepared at any time to get a phone call. This means, be prepared to answer questions about your resume, your accomplishments, and why you would be a good candidate for the position. You should have all your documentation readily available for quick and easy access. This includes a copy of the resume you sent to the company or individual calling you, the cover letter, your market research about the company, and any other relevant information you have collected.

If you get a phone call and you are busy and cannot break away, or perhaps in a vehicle driving, it is okay to ask for another time for the phone interview. Tell the caller you cannot speak at that moment but will call them back in a few minutes or as soon as you can (be specific, i.e., fifteen minutes). Don't delay, call them back as quickly as possible and at the agreed upon time. Be sure to get their phone number and tell them you will call them back. *Do not* ask them to call you. There is a good chance you will not hear from them again. Verify their phone number.

When you are on a phone call with a prospective employer or recruiter, take it *standing* not sitting. Your voice will sound more energetic and enthusiastic and will project better. Also, you might want to consider standing in front of a mirror. I know this sounds strange, but it works. When in front of the mirror look to see that you are smiling. Take note of your facial expressions and posture, and of course stay focused on the interviewer. Looking in a mirror, as strange as that may sound, can have a positive psychological effect on the outcome of the phone interview. Enough said!

Video Interviews – More and more companies are using technology to conduct face-to-face interviews. Skype, Zoom, and other technologies are used to eliminate the need to travel and obviously to reduce costs. I have done several Skype interviews myself for overseas companies who were looking for a trainer in the Raleigh/Durham, North Carolina (Research Triangle Park) area.

Another type of video interviewing besides Skype, Zoom, and other online services, is one where the company sends equipment to you to be connected to your computer with a complete pre-recorded interview. A friend of mine had this experience when she interviewed for a corporate recruiter position. Unfortunately, she was not prepared for the technology or the process and the interview went poorly. Her expectation was that she would be able to start and stop the recording, giving her time to think about her response and then answer. It did not work like that. Once started, the interview proceeded as if she was sitting in front of the interviewer; question asked, her response, move onto the next question.

I share this story with you in the event that someone tells you they are sending equipment for a video interview. Be as prepared as you would for an actual face-to-face. Ask the company you will be interviewing with about the equipment and how the interview will proceed. Have a clear understanding of the process and the equipment so there will be no surprises. Some video interviews are live, and some are recorded with timed responses. Practicing for a video interview is key to doing well.

Case/Technical Interviews – Some companies will invite you to interview and give you a business case to work that reflects a problem or challenge the company or their customers' face. The primary focus of a case interview, sometimes referred to as a technical interview, is not on finding a correct answer but rather on how the applicant analyzes and approaches the situation. The observers will typically be looking for a combination of the following:

- Your problem-solving and creative thinking skills.

- Your decision-making process.

- Your overall approach and how you suggest implementing your proposal.

- Your business/technical skills, commercial awareness, and insight.

- Use of data to quantify your recommendation or outcome.

- Communication and presentation skills to convey your ideas.

- Your ability to influence and persuade others.

- Your ability to think and respond under pressure.

- Your interpersonal skills and professional demeanor.

To be effective in a case interview, be sure to ask probing questions to effectively gather requirements and expectations and to state and clarify any assumptions you might make. And remember to listen carefully.

Panel Interviews – A panel interview is when there is more than one person present during an in-person interview; typically, more than one person will be asking questions. (This can also be done remotely using technology.) What you should know is that everyone in the room during the interview is a potential decision maker. You need to connect with all attendees, not only the person asking the questions. Be sure to give eye contact to everyone. Building trust and rapport with everyone sitting in on the interview is critical. The fact is, the person who says the least during the interview might be the key decision maker.

When asked a question, look first at the person who asked the question and begin responding. Then be sure to glance around at everyone on the panel giving them sufficient eye contact. Finish your response to the question by looking again at the person who asked the question. Repeat this process with every question, always giving eye contact to all members of the panel.

Be observant during this process. Very quickly it may become obvious who supports you as well as who may be harder to persuade. Employers are looking for leaders who can tackle tough problems head on. If you are able to win over the toughest member of the panel it shows your ability to read the audience and problem-solve on your feet. Later when the panel convenes to discuss your interview and candidacy, if you have won over the toughest member of the panel, others are likely to support you as well.

At the end of the interview shake hands with all members of the panel. This is another way of acknowledging all participants. If possible, get business cards from everyone on the panel so you can thank each of them for allowing you to explore career opportunities with their organization. (You may want to send a follow-up letter/email, only to your primary contact, but still share your acknowledgment and appreciation of the others on the panel.)

You can also use the business cards during the interview to help you remember the participants' names by placing the cards in front of you as they are seated around the table. (The Japanese are famous for doing this.) This of course assumes that you collect business cards before you begin the panel discussion. If that is not possible, try to get business cards at the conclusion and share yours as well. I recognize that many companies do not provide business cards for their employees, if that is the case, do your best to get everyone's name and an understanding of their role so you can address them by name during the interview and acknowledge their participation after the interview.

Presentation Interviews – Some companies will invite you for an interview and ask you to make a presentation. Or, if you are an instructor/trainer like me, perhaps you will be asked to teach some material, either your own or material the company provides. I recently did some training and coaching for a large international chemical company. A good number of my students were research scientists. When interviewing with this particular company they were required to make presentations. Not only do you need to know the material, good presentation skills are a must.

I contract with a number of companies to teach a variety of courses and almost always have had to present material during an interview so they could evaluate my teaching style, subject matter expertise, and my ability to manage the classroom. For example, one of the companies I interviewed with (and was hired by) gave me thirty minutes to teach a topic of my choice, project management related. I had fifteen minutes to deliver material and fifteen minutes to facilitate an exercise, address participant questions, and close. The topic I chose to present on was Force Field Analysis, a tool for decision-making and problem solving. I was able to accomplish this and successfully deliver the content in the thirty minutes allotted.

Someone else presenting that same day chose to teach on *Dealing with Difficult People*. Huge mistake! First, he had a hard time delivering the content and making his point clear in the allotted time. His chosen topic was far too complicated for a thirty-minute interview. And second, and more importantly, he chose a topic where he could be easily challenged—and he was. One of the evaluators on the panel, an instructor himself, became the "difficult person" challenging this individual to see how he would handle the situation. The presenter/interviewee failed miserably and was not hired.

If you are asked to make a presentation make sure you know your material inside out and be prepared to be challenged. It's not that the interviewers want to see you fail, but they do want proof that you know what you are talking about and that you can deliver your content with confidence. If you are able to choose your content, choose wisely. Being able to meet your time commitment is almost as important as knowing your content.

Behavioral Interviews – Many of the questions you will be asked during the interview process (on the phone, in person, via video) are likely to be behavioral questions. Behavioral questions are used to determine how you have handled situations in the past and help the interviewer get a feel for how you might react and behave in a variety of situations. Past behavior is a good indicator of future behavior. Behavioral questions tend to start with, "Tell me about a time when…"

For example:

- Tell me about a time when you were on a project team and you had an unproductive team member, what did you do and what were the results?

- Tell me about a time when you did more than was expected?

- Tell me about a time when there was conflict on your team, how did you handle the situation?

(**Note:** We will return to behavioral interviews later in this chapter for an in-depth discussion. All of the interview approaches discussed in this section can and likely will include behavioral interview questions.)

INTERVIEW PROCESS

Now let's address some strategies and best practices for interviewing and some typical interview questions you are likely to be asked. Also, you will want to consider what questions you want to ask the interviewer, or others to whom you are given access.

Before we discuss specific questions for the interview, let's take a strategic look at the overall process. What do you and the interviewer need to know about each other? You want to know if the job, the organization, and the people are a good fit for you. The employer wants to know if you will be a good fit for them. Specifically, you will both want to explore the following:

- Competence
- Commitment
- Compatibility
- Chemistry
- Compensation

Competence - Can you do the job? Do you have the required knowledge, skills, and abilities (KSA's) to be successful in the position? What are your core competencies, what is your educational background, and what training have you had as it relates to the position? These are some of the key things the employer will be looking for. Do you have the leadership skills, people skills, technical skills, communication skills, and/or whatever is required to produce results?

Commitment - Are you willing to make a commitment to the organization? Do you see a future there? Will you be challenged by the work? Employers do not want to hire someone only to have them leave shortly thereafter. Hiring, training, and retraining costs a lot. Employers are looking for someone who will be committed to the position and to them. This is why some people are told they are over qualified. Perhaps the employer sensed the applicant would become bored quickly and move on or use the job as a stepping-stone. While companies no longer make long-term commitments to their employees, they still want employees who are committed to their mission, goals, and success as an organization.

Compatibility - The interviewer will probe to see if you are compatible to their values, organizational culture, and their approach to doing business. And, of course, it should be important to you as well. Do you have similar values to the organization? Will you fit into the organizational culture and their way of doing things? If not, probably not a good fit for either of you.

Chemistry - This is a big one! If the interviewer does not feel chemistry with an applicant, chances of getting hired are slim. The most qualified candidate will *not* always get the job. Often the candidate that had the best chemistry with the hiring manager and others who participated in the process will prevail.

Actually, that's exactly how I got my very first job out of college, not that I wasn't qualified. I flew down to Atlanta, Georgia for my interview for a paralegal position with a major telecommunication company. I prepared best I could (for a twenty-two-year-old with little coaching) and interviewed with one of the senior attorneys. Most of the attorneys were in North Carolina attending a State Bar conference so it was only Mr. C (as I will call him) and me. We went out to lunch and I expected to be asked and answer typical interview questions. They never came and I was somewhat confused. Mr. C proceeded to spend the entire lunch talking about the grapefruit diet he was on and his time at the University of North Carolina in Chapel Hill (I attended N.C. State University right down the road in Raleigh.) To say it was a strange interview is an understatement.

I flew home that same day and told my mother I probably would not get an offer since we never discussed anything related to the position. (Mr. C., had gotten my resume from the paralegal school I attended in Atlanta. I actually never even applied for the position, they reached out to me.) Well, lo and behold, within a week I received a phone call offering me the paralegal job. I was shocked based on my experience in the interview but decided to accept the position.

Later, when I moved to Atlanta and started my job, I was surprised to hear Mr. C. had interviewed many paralegals before selecting me for the position. According to the other paralegals, he was extremely picky and they wanted to know how I won him over. While I was competent to do the job, ultimately it was chemistry that got me hired. We clicked and apparently that's what Mr. C. was looking for in his new employee.

Compensation is the final component of the strategic interview process. Are you willing to do the job for the compensation they are willing to pay? Compensation is pay plus other benefits. When you interview, make sure you have done your homework and you know your value. (Be sure to see Chapter 17 where I discuss in more detail what your compensation package might include.)

"Competence means keeping your head in a crisis, sticking to a task even when it seems hopeless, and improvising good solutions to tough problems when every second counts. It encompasses ingenuity, determination, and being prepared for anything."
—*Chris Hadfield*

QUESTIONS TO ASK BEFORE THE INTERVIEW

The average interview lasts between sixty to ninety minutes, but it could take longer. Before you show up make sure you have asked all the questions and have all the information you need for a successful interview. You want to have a clear understanding of what the interview will entail. Some of the questions you will want to ask before the interview include:

- How long do you expect the interview to last?
- Who will participate in the interview?
- What type of interview process will be used? (Panel, presentation, case study, etc.)
- Where will the interview take place?
- Is there anything special I can do to prepare for the interview?
- Is there anything you need me to bring to the interview?

The last thing you want to do is to show up without fully understanding what the interview process will entail. If you go in with the assumption that there will only be one interviewer and anticipate an hour to an hour and a half interview only to find out it's a panel interview that is scheduled to take five to six hours, you will not be psychologically nor physically prepared. I know people this has happened to because they failed to ask the right questions and the organization failed to provide detailed information about the process. That is simply bad planning on their part, but you will be the one to suffer if this happens to you. If the questions above have not been sufficiently answered, ask them and be prepared for your interview.

BEST PRACTICES FOR INTERVIEWING

Before the interview

- Do your research. Know as much as you can about the company—its challenges, its ambitions, products, services, culture, management, competition, etc.

- Prepare, prepare, prepare! Have a number of stories prepared on a variety of topics that you can pull from during the interview. Use the SOAR (Situation, Obstacle/Opportunity, Action, Results) process described later in this section to ensure your readiness to clearly and succinctly address the questions posed.

- Dress appropriately. Not sure what to wear? Seek the advice of others. Call the company and ask the administrative assistant.

Arriving for the interview

- Arrive ten to fifteen minutes early.

- Be aware that others will be observing you, possibly from the time you enter the parking lot.

- Use any time waiting wisely. Do not spend time on your phone, checking emails, texting, etc. Instead, look around the waiting/reception room to see if there is any literature that you can read. Perhaps you will pick up some new information about the organization that will be helpful to you during your interview.

- Treat everyone you meet with respect and kindness (as you always should), the receptionist, the janitor, everyone. I knew a recruiter who would send the janitor to the hallway before an important interview and ask him to greet the person coming in for the interview. She would later ask him how the candidate treated him.

During the interview

- Take plenty of copies of your resume and other supporting documentation (such as references, publications, and patents) to share as needed.

- Take business cards with you and present one to each person with whom you interview and ask for one of their cards. Getting a business card from the people you meet with will guarantee you have their information for follow-up correspondence. (Many companies no longer provide their employees business cards. If that's the case, ask for an email address which you might be able to get from an administrative assistant, receptionist, or corporate recruiter.)

- Build rapport with those you interview with; maintain good eye contact, a firm hand shake, and find a common connection. (**chemistry**)

- Do not assume the interviewer(s) has thoroughly reviewed your resume. Be sure to share your key accomplishments and selling points as they relate to the position. (**competence**)

- Help the interviewer(s) see how you will fit in with the culture and values of the organization. (**compatibility**)

Concluding the interview

- If you want the job, *ask for it*! (**commitment**)

- Ask about next steps in the hiring process and when the company expect to make a decision.

- Send a thank you email and a hand-written thank you note (within 24 hours).

- Be proactive. Follow up after the interview.

Do not hesitate to follow up after your interview. If you wait for the phone call, it may never come. Many job seekers seem to think a follow-up phone call or email makes them look pushy. No, it's not pushy. It's called being assertive, interested, and proactive. It shows your desire and commitment to working for this organization. Of course, use common sense and allow an appropriate amount of time before you follow up. In some cases that might be a couple of days, a week, or two weeks depending on when the company plans to make their hiring decision. You don't want to stalk them, but you do want to follow up appropriately. Finding a job is not for the passive. It requires taking action.

Please note that one of the *biggest mistakes* many job interviewees make is not expressing their desire for the job. It is worth repeating—**if you want the job, ask for it!**

If you are not comfortable and confident speaking in front of a panel, making presentations, or during a one-on-one interview, you should consider looking into Toastmasters. Toastmasters International[1] is a non-profit educational organization dedicated to helping members improve their communication, public speaking, presentation, and leadership skills. It was through Toastmasters that I developed my platform skills. Many Toastmasters' programs meet at businesses and so attending their programs can also be a great place to network. Meetings generally occur once a week and last about one hour. This is not a huge time commitment but can produce great results, boost your confidence, and significantly improve your interviewing skills.

Several years ago, I had a very qualified candidate, a Ph.D., who was struggling in his job interviews. He had good experience and credentials but a very thick Hispanic accent which he feared was holding him back. He had hired a speech coach without much success. I recommended he try Toastmasters, letting the members know that his goal was to help him slow down and enunciate more clearly. It wasn't too long after that I received an email for him stating he had landed a full-time position with Cisco Systems.

QUESTIONS YOU MAY BE ASKED DURING THE INTERVIEW

For starters, be prepared to address anything that is on your resume. I gave you a few examples at the beginning of the chapter. If you say you are a natural people motivator, you better be able to share some examples.

This is one of the areas where people get themselves into trouble, especially if they had someone prepare their resume with very little input from them. I've seen it happen far too many times. The job seeker doesn't want to take on the stress of developing their resume, so they hire someone to write one for them with their basic information and what they think the employers want to hear. I had a client who wanted me to do that for her, saying the last time her resume was updated the guy who prepared it did it all by himself, without any input from her. I told her I could not do that and would not want her to be in the position of interviewing with a resume that would not truly reflect her accomplishments and credentials. After all, she would have to answer to the resume in the interview. Personally, I consider that type of resume writing unethical, but there are firms out there that will do it and they charge handsomely. These "off-the-shelf" resumes will surely hurt you during the interview process.

Be honest, don't embellish, but also do not be shy or reluctant to sing your praises. After all, your resume is your key sales tool. Often, I have found job seekers leave off valuable information because they did not want to seem like they were bragging. It's not bragging, it's having confidence in your skills, experience, and the value you have to offer a potential employer. Share your accomplishments; that's what is required if you are going to get an interview and ultimately a job offer.

You will be asked many different types of questions during your interview. Most of the questions will fall into the following categories, questions about:

- Your work experiences
- Your accomplishments
- Your education, training, and professional development
- Your innovation and creativity
- Your ability to lead and manage others
- How you manage conflict and stressful situations
- How you work in a fast-paced environment
- Your ability to build relationships with: team members, customers, clients, senior management, and other key stakeholders
- Your goals and objectives such as, "Where do you see yourself in five years?"
- Your problem-solving and decision-making ability
- Your strengths
- Your weaknesses and potential problem areas
- Your compensation expectations

In the **Career Tools** section, at **www.ProjectCareerQuest.com**, you will find a list of some *typical interview questions*. Use these to guide your preparation. I also recommend downloading from the Internet a document called, *The 64 Toughest Interview Questions*.[2] This document does a good job of sharing why the questions might be asked, i.e., what the interviewer is attempting to learn about you, and what strategy you should use to address the question. Find a partner or engage a friend or family member to conduct mock interviews so you will be more comfortable with the process and your delivery will be more natural and fluid.

Three more things I want to address about interview questions and then we will move on to behavioral interviews:

1. Occasionally you may be asked what are considered **sensitive questions** that can actually be illegal and certainly inappropriate. Rarely would you be asked this type of question from a Human Resource professional, most likely from an inexperienced and untrained hiring manager (and they do slip through every once in a while). To address a sensitive question, that you know is inappropriate and possibly illegal, you may want to say something like:

   I am not sure how that question relates to the job responsibilities. Can you help me understand?

An example of an inappropriate, and possibly illegal question, would be a question about your age, religion, race, marital status, plans to have children, sexual orientation, etc. Your best bet if you are asked a question of this nature is to ask a question to understand why it is being asked and its relevance to the job responsibilities. Taking it personally and becoming defensive will not serve you well. Don't lose your cool! You don't have to answer them and often the interviewer will back off when you ask your clarifying question.

2. What about the **weakness question**? That one is always a challenge for job applicants. Be prepared for it and have one to two responses ready should you be asked. Avoid saying your weakness is that you are a perfectionist. How many times do you think hiring managers have heard that one—far too many times, and they won't take you seriously even if you are a perfectionist. Find another response!

Don't make it too flimsy such as, "I'm addicted to chocolate." And don't choose a weakness directly related to the key job responsibilities. If the job requires a lot of organizational skills and you say you have a hard time staying organized, you aren't getting the job. My strategy is to change the word "weakness" to what "challenged" me. For example:

One of the things that really challenged me when I first took over my role as a supervisor was the ability to delegate. Often, I found it easier and faster to just do it myself. However, I realized very quickly that I was not using my time wisely and my employees were not learning new skills as a result. I am no longer uncomfortable delegating work and I delegate when appropriate.

Finally, tell the interviewer what you have done to overcome your challenge and assure them that you are well equipped to meet that challenge now and perform the job effectively.

So, think about it, what has challenged you in the past that you have been able to turn around to a positive? What weakness have you been able to overcome? And for goodness sakes, do not say, "I have no weaknesses." If you use that response you will come across as either arrogant or unaware and you won't get the job! We all have things that challenge us and others may perceive as a weakness. Also, focus on work-related behavioral weaknesses, not on your personality traits.

To identify a weakness to share during your job interview, think back to feedback you have gotten from others you have worked with including colleagues, customers, and your immediate supervisor. Think of feedback you received during your annual performance reviews and how you may have worked to improve your performance in a particular area. But remember to choose a behavioral weakness that you have worked to strengthen so it is no longer a challenge to you nor limits your ability to be successful in the position.

3. Another type of question you will get are questions that can easily and quickly take you down a negative path if you allow it. These are the **negative-type questions**.

   Tell me about a time when you had a disagreement with a co-worker.

   Tell me what you disliked about your previous job.

Be very careful with these questions. Never say anything negative about a former boss, colleague, employee, customer, or your former employer. Find a way to answer the question putting a positive spin on it. Any negative answers will reflect poorly on you. You can find a *lesson learned* in almost everything. Focus not on the negative but rather on the positive lesson you took away from the experience.

Here is one of my personal examples of a positive response to a potentially negative question:

Question - Tell me about a time you worked with, or for someone, whose leadership style was very different than yours and you may not have always agreed with them?"

"Years ago, I had a manager whose personality type, leadership style, and overall approach was quite different than mine—and we certainly had our challenges when we first started working together. However, we learned to appreciate our differences and used them to support each other, making a stronger team. When my boss moved to South Carolina to take over an operations center there, he paid me a great compliment by saying, 'Kerry, after working together for the past seven years I'm not sure whether you learned more from me or I learned more from you.' Although our approach to things could at times be quite different, we learned to bounce ideas off of each other, listen to each other's perceptive, and support each other to meet our project goals and achieve the desired results."

—◦◦◦—

BEHAVIORAL INTERVIEW QUESTIONS

Many of the questions you will be asked during your interview will be behavioral questions, where the interviewer attempts to understand how you would react or perform in a variety of business situations. Behavioral questions may sound like, "Tell me about a time when…." Interviewers are not interested in what you think you would do but rather what you have done in the past that may be indicative of how you would handle a similar situation in the future. (Stay out of the "woulds.") They are looking for specific examples, not theoretical responses. And always make sure your responses are relevant to the position for which you are interviewing.

To prepare for behavioral questions you need to develop **SOAR** stories. SOAR is an acronym that stands for **Situation, Obstacle/Opportunity, Action, Results**. Using this process, you will be able to address what the hiring manager wants to know to make an informed decision regarding your suitability for the position. The primary focus of your response to any interview question is on the action you took regarding a situation and the results you achieved.

The majority, if not all of the interview questions you are asked, should be answered in sixty to ninety seconds, as concisely as possible. When the interviewer says, "Tell me about a time when…," your approach is to first briefly describe the situation, including any obstacles or opportunities you encountered. Next you will describe the action you took and finally share the results of your action, i.e., the outcome.

- **Situation** – brief background information

- **Obstacle** or **Opportunity** – any challenges you faced which could have had either a positive or negative impact (twenty to thirty seconds max for situation and obstacle/opportunity)

- **Action** – describe the role you played in addressing the situation/problem

- **Results** – the outcome from your actions

Again, the primary focus should be on the *action* and *results* that define your *accomplishment(s)*. Keep the description of the situation brief. You should not provide detailed background information. A high-level overview is sufficient. It's been my experience that most job seekers will spend way too much time describing the situation and not enough time articulating their accomplishments (action and results). The background information will not help you get a job, your actions and results will. Focus on your accomplishments! (Be sure that the actions you share describe your role in the situation, not what the team did.)

Write out your SOAR stories, time yourself, and refine your story until it's as clear and concise as possible. Interviewers are busy people. Do not waste their time with unnecessary details.

To refine your SOAR stories, I recommend you practice with an interview partner. Did your story make sense to them? Were your actions and results clearly stated and understood? Did you come across as confident? Were you as concise as possible while still demonstrating your accomplishments and value to your organization? Were you able to share your stories in sixty to ninety seconds?

—◈◈◈—

(Sample SOAR Story)

Question - "Tell me about a time you had a difficult team member, what did you do and what were the results?"

Situation and **Obstacle** or **Opportunity** – *Several years ago I was assigned a major warehouse construction and redesign project in Jacksonville, Florida. When the construction phase was completed it was time to relocate several million dollars' worth of equipment from another facility in South Florida. The warehouse manager assigned a resource to me to receive and relocate the equipment in the building addition. The challenge I faced was that the resource assigned to me had the reputation of being very difficult to work with. I was aware of his reputation and actually had both management and non-management apologizing to me assuming I had been set up for failure.*

Action – *Not having worked with this individual before I started with a clean slate. I did not allow his reputation of being difficult to influence or derail my efforts. I knew, however, I needed to set clear goals and objectives, roles and responsibilities, and expectations with him. I worked to establish trust and rapport with this individual and clearly define the deliverables, deadlines, and my expectations. I also asked him to share with me his expectations and I sought his ideas and expertise as a materials service handler.*

Results – *Ultimately my project was completed on time with no glitches. The individual assigned to the project completed his work as outlined and agreed upon in the plan we established together. I found him respectful, easy to work with, and he met all of my expectations and performance criteria. Having worked in this facility for several months, and knowing this individual's work ethics, I was encouraged to see significant changes in his performance, attitude, and behavior. I set him up for success and as a result the project was a success.*

After responding to the question (in approximately sixty to ninety seconds) the interviewer may ask for more detailed information. In that case, you can provide additional details but still keep your responses relatively short and concise. Provide enough information to answer the question without going on and on with unnecessary detail. Too much information and you are likely to talk yourself right out of the job.

Carefully planning what you will say and how you will say it will greatly increase your confidence and delivery. My recommendation is that you prepare between fifteen to twenty SOAR stories that are relevant to your industry and the position for which you are interviewing.

Topics for SOAR Stories

Some topics you should be prepared to address in your interviews include (but not limited to):

Efficiency - Efficiency is an internal measure of how well a process works. What did you do or contribute to making a process more streamlined and efficient? Did you find ways to eliminate non-value-added steps in a process to create more value for your customers and key stakeholders?

Effectiveness - Effectiveness is a measure of customer or stakeholder satisfaction. What did you do to contribute to effectiveness? How did you improve customer relationships or satisfy a key stakeholder?

Productivity - What did you do to improve and increase productivity?

Cycle time - Did you do anything to help improve cycle time? For example, were you able to reduce the amount of time it took to complete a work activity such as the time to complete a client's order? Were you able to reduce the time it took to complete a process such as the contracting or purchasing process? (closely related to efficiency)

Costs - Did you contribute to reducing costs? Did you find a creative way to cut costs or remove unnecessary and non-value-added costs?

Quantity - Did you do anything to increase quantity, i.e.: increasing the number of satisfied customers, increasing the number of professional certifications in your organization, increasing the number of new clients, number of contracts signed, sales completed, projects delivered on time, number of customers served, etc.?

Quality - Did you do anything that resulted in achieving higher quality of product, services, or results?

Return on investment - How did you contribute to return on investment, the bottom line?

Market share - Did you do something that helped increase market share for your organization, create a new market, or expand an existing market?

Customer satisfaction - How did you contribute to customer or stakeholder satisfaction? Did you turn a negative situation around and win back a previously dissatisfied customer? How did you "wow" a customer?

Customer complaints - How have you dealt with an upset or irate customer? "Tell me about a time when you had an unhappy customer, what did you do and what were the results?"

Employee satisfaction - Did you do anything that resulted in improving employee satisfaction or employee relations?

Employee turnover - Did you take actions that resulted in reducing employee turnover or improving employee retention?

Conflict - How did you manage conflict, either with a team member, colleague, client, or senior management? "Tell me about a time you were in conflict with a team member. How did you handle the situation?"

Ethics - How have you handled situations where you have been placed in an ethical dilemma? For example, "Tell me about a time when you were asked to do something that was in violation of a policy, regulation, or ethical guideline. Or you were under pressure by a customer, colleague, or a manager to take action you knew was wrong."

Diversity - How do you deal in situations with a diversity of personalities, ideas, values, styles, and culture?

Initiative - Be prepared to share a time when you took initiative to do something that was not required of you. "Tell me about a time you took initiative that went above and beyond your job description and responsibilities?"

Professional development - What actions have you taken for your personal growth and development? How has it benefitted you and your organization?

The list above should get you started preparing for your interviews. Practice sharing your SOAR stories with a friend. Practice in front of a mirror. I highly recommend video recording yourself. How did you come across? How was your body language? Any habits or twitches you weren't aware of? Did you use many pause fillers such as "er," "um," "like," and "you know"? I want you to be confident and prepared for your interview. Preparation is key!

Write out your **SOAR stories**. Remember you want at least fifteen to twenty stories to address the topics above and including any others appropriate to your industry. Then practice your responses until you can easily recall them and they feel and sound natural. A template for SOAR stories can be found in the **Career Tools** section at **www.ProjectCareerQuest.com**.

(Other similar acronyms for SOAR you may have heard or be familiar with include: Problem, Action, Results (PAR); Situation, Task, Action, Results (STAR); Situation, Action, Results (SAR); Challenge, Action, Results (CAR). Call it what you want, they are all essentially the same thing. Describe the situation you faced and then focus on your accomplishments that include the actions you took and the results.)

—⟨⟨⟨⟩⟩⟩—

WHAT QUESTIONS SHOULD YOU ASK DURING THE INTERVIEW?

Okay, now it's time to shift to questions you might want to ask during the interview. Remember this is about *your* future! You need to find out if this is a place you want to work. Will you fit in there? Will you enjoy the work? Can you do the work? Do you want to work with these people? Do you have similar values? The focus of your questions should be about:

- Your role in the position and associated responsibilities

- Reporting relationships and decision-making authority

- Resources available to you to accomplish your work and meet business objectives

- Performance measurements and expectations (short-term and long-term)

- Corporate and organizational values and culture including management styles

- The skills and characteristics the company is looking for in the successful candidate (This will help you provide focused responses to demonstrate how you can help them meet their needs and expectations.)

Some of the questions you might want to ask include:

- What are the major responsibilities of the position?

- Is there a job description? If so, may I see it?

- Why is the position open? Is this a replacement or expansion role?

- How long has the position been open?

- What's the turnover in this position?

- Are you interviewing internal candidates for the position?

- What are your expectations for the position?

- What things need immediate attention as it relates to the position?

- What is the most significant contribution you are looking for from me in this position? In the first ninety days? In the first twelve months?

- What skills and characteristics do you expect the successful candidate to have?

- What is the culture of the organization?

- How would you describe the organization's management style?

- Is there a formal appraisal system in place?

- What are the performance criteria for this position and how often is performance appraised?

- Will I be supervising anyone? Whom will I be supervising in this position?

- What are the reporting relationships?

- Will I have a budget? How will it be allocated?

- What are the professional development expectations?

- Does the company pay for training and professional development? How much is allotted on an annual basis?

- Will the department/company pay for certifications and other training related to the position?

- When do you expect to make a decision?

- When could I expect to hear something?

- What are the next steps?

- What is the best way to communicate with you? (Some people prefer email, some phone or text. Let them tell you how to best get in touch with them.)

You should also be prepared with a **closing question** similar to what a sales person would ask to close the deal. More on this under *Concluding the Interview.*

During the interview, take notes or you will not remember everything later. I recommend that you ask the interviewer, "Do you mind if I take notes during the interview?" It is highly unlikely he or she will say "no," but it is always polite to ask.

What to Take to the Interview

Take extra copies of your resume and your list of references to your interview. Do not assume others interviewing you will already have a copy of your resume. If you have been published, and/or have patents, take that information as well. Take anything you think the interviewer will ask for and/or need to make an informed decision. If you are not sure what to take, ask the interviewer or your contact person in advance. And don't forget your business cards.

Body Language and the Interview

In any communication exchange, what you say is not nearly as important as how you say it and what your body language portrays. Body language can be extremely revealing as well as the tone, inflection, and speed of your voice. If you are providing a response with your hand over your mouth you may be viewed as lying. Not making eye contact or having your arms folded across your chest sends a negative message. Speaking too fast may indicate nervousness.

I am not going to go into much detail here about body language and other non-verbal forms of communication, but do your homework. Knowing your own body language, as well as the ability to read other peoples' body language, can be very helpful and insightful. Do you have their attention? You may think so, but their body may reveal otherwise. Are you giving them your full attention? Are you alert, enthusiastic, engaged, or are you slouching and distracted?

I mentioned earlier in the book that you might want to videotape yourself during your practice interviews. In most cases your cell phone will work fine to capture yourself practicing with a partner. Listen and watch for what you say and do, how you say it, tone, inflection, grammar, slang, and filler words such as "ers" and "ums." Watch very carefully your body language. What message are you sending? Do you have any nervous twitches or tics you weren't aware of? Practice with a friend or in front of a mirror until you get more comfortable with the questions and the process. Remember to smile and be attentive and as relaxed as possible

Again, it is worth repeating, the value you will get from joining a Toastmasters International.[3] I have done a number of mock interviews with professionals and college students and the best interviewers, by far, are those who have been on debate teams in college or high school and participate in organizations such as Toastmasters. Not only will the Toastmaster's group give you feedback about what you say, they will also provide feedback regarding your body language and presence. That kind of training makes a world of difference.

—◦◦◦—

CONCLUDING THE INTERVIEW

Be sure to tell the interviewer that you want the position (if you are interested). *Do not walk out of the interview without voicing your desire to get the job and become part of their team/organization.*

Even if you are not interested in the position after concluding the interview, leave on a positive note. You never know when another position will become available within the organization that will be a better fit for you.

Follow up immediately with an email and within twenty-four hours a handwritten thank you note. Your follow up email should:

- Thank the interviewer or interviewers for their time.

- Summarize your key selling points and why you are the best candidate for the position.

- Include any key points you forgot to share during the interview.

- Inform them again of your interest in the position.

- Ask about or suggest next steps if they have not been specifically stated.

I highly recommend that you let the interviewer know you will follow up with them by a specific date or within a specific number of days if they have not provided follow up information. **Successful interviewers are proactive!**

PRACTICE CLOSE

Before concluding the interview, you will want to ask the interviewer(s) a question to see if they have any concerns as to your candidacy for the position. The question might be something like this:

> *Do you have any concerns about my ability to perform the job or any reason to believe I would not make an excellent candidate for this position?*

You may choose to word it slightly different, but do not be afraid to ask about any concerns they may have about you as a candidate/potential employee. If they have any concerns and you walk out of the interview not addressing them, you are very likely *not* to be hired. Better for them to voice their concern(s) and give you an opportunity to address any they may have.

For example, the interviewer(s) may express a concern that you do not have much experience in a particular area. In reality, you might have experience in that area but did not have an opportunity to share any examples. Now you will. **Always ask a closing question** to see where the interviewer(s) stands and if they have any concern(s) whatsoever about your knowledge, skills, or abilities to perform the job.

Too often we go into an interview with our fears and our doubts, instead we should enter with the belief that we can help the interviewer's organization meet their challenges, not with an attitude of arrogance, but rather an attitude of confidence. We often expect that the interviewer wants to see us fail, when in reality they are hoping we are the answer to their problem(s).

WHAT TO WEAR TO YOUR INTERVIEW

In today's diverse work environment what to wear to an interview is much more complicated than in the past. Companies are more relaxed and casual, but don't let that fool you. The majority of companies still expect you to come dressed in business attire, not business casual. Of course, it depends on the industry, and the level of the position. Better to err on the conservative side. You will have only one opportunity to make a good first impression.

Your hygiene and personal grooming are very important. You want your shoes shined, jewelry at a minimum, and nothing too distracting. You should avoid trendy fashions, classic and conservative is generally your best bet. To a great extent, the industry will dictate appropriate attire. The best thing you can do before you decide what to wear is to research the company and their culture. Do not wear perfumes and colognes, this can be irritating to the interviewer and you never know if they might have an allergy to fragrances. If you are not sure what to wear, seek the wise counsel of others.

Preparation + Attitude + Opportunity + Action + Presentation = Success

---

WHAT HAPPENS WHEN THEY REJECT YOU?

Okay, so you prepared, you practiced, you were confident, you thought you connected with the interviewer(s), you sent a thank you note, and you followed up. You were feeling good about your interview and then you got the dreaded "rejection letter."

Looking for a job is not for the faint of heart! Rejection comes with the territory. As qualified as you may be, someone may have been more qualified or had better chemistry with the interviewer. Hard to tell sometimes. However, rejection does not have to be the end of the road. A door of opportunity may still exist.

If you truly felt that you had a shot at the job and it's not clear why you did not get an offer, then I suggest you follow up with the employer. At a minimum, ask them if they could share with you why you were not selected. Is there something they were looking for that you did not have? Is there something you could have done differently that would have made a difference? They may tell you nothing, on the other hand, they may give you some valuable insight that will help you in your next interview. Essentially you are gathering information for your lessons learned.

I recently spoke with a woman who said a recruiter gave her feedback that she came across as "too aggressive." Whatever feedback you get, whether from a recruiter or an employer, accept it as a gift. Never get defensive or try to explain yourself. Thank them for the feedback and store it away for future interviews.

I know several people who have made it to the final two candidates but did not get the offer. For one person, the other candidate got the offer because she had a PMP® certification (Project Management Professional) and he did not. According to the interviewer, the decision to hire the other person was based on the certification, with everything else being fairly equal. It is always good to seek feedback.

Another rejection story is about a friend of mine who had not worked in several years. She was actually pretty occupied trying to get a house ready to sell and so had not focused on her job search as much as she should have. By the time she started interviewing for jobs she was pretty cash strapped. She interviewed for a job she was very interested in and made it to the final two. However, she did not get the offer. When she asked the employer why they had not selected her they replied that the salary requirements she provided were so low they did not think she understood the responsibilities of the position. She low-balled herself right out of a job. My friend proposed a low starting salary thinking it would get her foot in the door. Instead it hurt her. A salary too high will put you out of the ballpark and a salary too low may give the perception that you are not qualified and at the very least, you are uninformed.

REGRET LETTERS

If you receive a rejection letter and you felt strongly that you had a good interview, and a good connection with the interviewer, you may also want to consider writing a "regret letter." A regret letter is an opportunity for you to reach out to the employer once again and thank them for their time and let them know that you are still interested in working for their organization should another opportunity become available. Although you may not have gotten the position you applied for, this does not necessarily mean the employer would not hire you if they had another position with similar requirements.

A friend of mine interviewed with a company and did not get the initial job he interviewed for; however, the employer did reach out to him three more times until they found the right fit. What they saw when they interviewed him was an individual with skills they wanted and needed. It was only a matter of time to find the right position, for the company and for him. So again, if you interview and get the rejection letter, feeling strongly that you were in the running as a finalist, follow through with a regret letter and see what kind of response you get. You never know unless you try. Your regret letter might look similar to this:

Dear Interviewer's Name:

Thank you for the opportunity to interview for the position of (job title) on (date). While I understand you have chosen another candidate for the position, I would like to express my continued interest in working as a (position/job title) for (name of company). I believe that my experience in (highlight one or two key things you know the company is looking for based on your interview) will add value to your organization and help you meet your goal(s) of (mention one or more of the most significant goals the company has that you uncovered in your interview that you can help fulfill based on your knowledge and experience). Should another opportunity become available in (department name) please keep me in mind.

Thank you again for your time and consideration. I will reach out to you in the next couple of weeks to see what new opportunities might exist. I look forward to speaking with you again.

Sincerely,

In the body of the letter you will also want to reiterate *why they should hire you*. Something you should have expressed during your interview. If you interviewed well and felt a strong connection, your regret letter might create another opportunity for you. The employer will know you have a strong desire to work for them and that may impact their future hiring decisions. Go for it! What do you have to lose?

The final story I will share is when a rejection may not be final. One of my business colleagues was working with a job seeker in his fifty's and this particular individual had not worked in over five years. The job seeker's background was in environmental safety. He interviewed with a large corporate entity and felt strongly that he had a good interview. During the interview, he sensed the company needed desperately to hire someone to address pressing regulatory issues they faced. He was hopeful! Days later he got a rejection email telling him he had a good interview but did not meet all of the qualifications they were looking for. They would continue to look for someone who met all their criteria.

The job seeker shared this with my colleague; a retired executive and now career coach; who then encouraged him to make the company a counter-offer. And that he did! This particular individual wrote back to the company the very next day and offered to work for them as a consultant to help address their pressing issues until they could find a candidate who met all of their criteria. What happened next was unexpected. After receiving his counter-offer, the company actually offered him the full-time position. He is now gainfully employed, making a good salary, and the company paid for all of his relocation expenses. (See, people over fifty with an extended absence from the job market can get jobs.) This man was successful because he had a coach who believed in him and he listened to and acted on the advice he was given.

There is opportunity in a rejection letter; opportunity to learn, opportunity to be creative. Don't let rejection stop you in your tracks. Persevere and take some risks. Eventually your persistence and patience will pay off.

KEEPING TRACK OF YOUR INTERVIEWS

In an extended job search project, you may go through dozens of interviews before you find and land the job you've been looking for. In the meantime, you should keep track of all of your interviews: with whom you interviewed, the outcome of the interview, and what you learned in the process. Here are some of the things you will want to track:

- Name of organization and date of interview
- Position title and description
- Name of interviewer(s)
- Name of other key contacts including administrative support
- Overall impression of company and interview (corporate culture, etc.)
- Main focus of the interview and major issues facing the company
- Your main selling point in the interview (value proposition)
- What you did well in the interview
- Where you could improve
- Follow up required (besides a thank you note)
- If you are not offered the position you interviewed for, are you interested in pursuing other jobs within that organization?
- If you are not interested in the position, with whom will you share the job posting?

Even if you do not get the job you interviewed for, you may still wish to pursue a position with that company. You will want to make note of that and work on building a network within the organization if you currently do not have one. If you are not interested in the position nor the organization, is there someone else you know who might be interested? Forwarding jobs onto others who might be interested is a great way to build your network support.

In the **Career Tools** section, at **www.ProjectCareerQuest.com**, you will find an *Interview Self-Assessment* form to help you keep on top of all of your interviews. Be sure to use this tool to capture your lessons learned, next steps, and any information you picked up during the interview that will help you as you move forward in the process. Even if you do not get a follow up interview, there is something to learn from every interview.

—⦿—

TELL ME ABOUT YOURSELF

Be prepared to respond to the "Tell me about yourself" request. Use the format that follows to provide a clear and concise response focused on the responsibilities of the position for which you are applying.

"Tell Me About Yourself"
(Sample)

My profession is: (What's your professional identity?)

I am a Project Management Professional.

Area of expertise: (List your key expertise relevant to the position to which you are applying)

With extensive experience managing and leading complex IT projects from initiating to closing.

Environments where you have worked: (Include industry specific information such as energy, utilities, technology, health care, agribusiness, academia, government, etc.)

I have worked predominantly for Fortune 500 companies but have had experience with a start-up where I wore many hats. Although I work in the private industry, many of my projects have been to support government contracts. I have also worked with Technology and Biotech companies.

Strengths: (Include strengths specific to the job requirements.)

One of my greatest strengths is the ability to communicate effectively with senior management as well as with the technical staff. I have a reputation for building high performing teams and establishing strong stakeholder relationships. I am effective at gathering and understanding customer requirements and delivering successful projects, on time and on budget.

Key accomplishment or distinction: (Include any special skills, awards, or distinctions.)

I have been trained in Agile and Six Sigma and have had my PMP® certification now for almost fifteen years. In fact, when I got my certification I was one of only three PMP's at the large technology company I worked for at the time. I continue to advocate for the certification and follow best practices of project management. Also, I am fluent in French and German, which has helped me in many of my international projects.

What you are looking for in a new position: (Include the main reason why you are interested in the position.)

The primary reason I am interested in this position is the opportunity to…

Now it's your turn. Fill in the **"Tell Me About Yourself"** template and practice your answer until it becomes natural.

"TELL ME ABOUT YOURSELF"

My profession is:

_____

_____

_____

_____

I have expertise in:

_____

_____

_____

_____

I have worked for:

_____

_____

_____

_____

My strengths include:

_____

_____

_____

_____

My key accomplishments/awards/distinctions include:

_____

_____

_____

_____

I am looking for a position that:

_____

_____

_____

_____

✔️ CHECKLIST - BEFORE YOU MOVE ON

- ☐ Have you reviewed a list of frequently asked interview questions so you can be as prepared as possible?
- ☐ Have you created and rehearsed fifteen to twenty SOAR stories for your interviews?
- ☐ Are you confident and prepared mentally to sell yourself? What makes you unique; why should they hire you? Why do you want the job? Why do you want to work for their company?
- ☐ Are you aware of your body language and words you may use that could be distracting or annoying (filler words such as er's, um's, etc.)?
- ☐ Do you have all the information you need before you leave for your interview: location, time expectations, process, participants, etc.?
- ☐ Do you have all the documentation you need for your interview such as extra copies of your resume, list of references, list of publications, etc.?
- ☐ Have you done your research on the company and the person(s) with whom you will be interviewing?
- ☐ Do you have your list of questions prepared and ready to ask?
- ☐ Have you thought about how you will conclude the interview and the question or questions you will ask to clarify the next steps?
- ☐ Do you have your "closing" question prepared?
- ☐ Have you selected an appropriate outfit to wear to your job interview? Are your shoes neat and clean and your appearance polished?
- ☐ Do you have thank-you notes so you can send one out immediately after the interview?

Lessons Learned: *Refine and nail your message. Practice with a friend or in front of a mirror, repeating your SOAR stories over and over again, until you are comfortable and confident delivering your message. The ability to sell yourself is key. Practice, practice, practice!*

PART 4

MONITOR
AND CONTROL

Staying the Course

CHAPTER 15

MONITOR, CONTROL,
AND COURSE CORRECTION

All projects follow a natural course: **Initiation, planning, execution, monitor and control,** and **closeout**. Monitoring and controlling results is something that should be done throughout the project, from initiation to closeout—beginning to end. Where your results are less than satisfactory, you will want to determine why, what you can do to improve, and what is it going to take to get the results you want.

Your job search project requires constant monitoring of what you have done, how it's been done, what results you've gotten, and are they the results you want. Are you meeting your objectives and achieving your goals? If not, why not? What needs to change?

For example, if one of your goals is to have a relatively short job search project, then you must continuously monitor results to ensure you are progressing as planned, at least as it relates to those things you have some control over. For some of you, your project will be intentionally longer, as you spend more time to explore possibilities. Time may not be as critical to you as the quality of results. On the other hand, for some of you time may be one of the most important factors.

Let's focus here on the planning and executing phases of your project. Some of the questions you will want to explore to get a feel for how well you are doing include:

PROJECT PLANNING

- Did I create a Project Charter to guide me on my journey?

- Have I completed a work breakdown structure (WBS) of all the activities I need to undertake in my job search project?

- Have I determined what resources I will need?

- Have I identified my project stakeholders? Have I reached out to them and engaged them effectively?

- Have I identified who I need on my team and what role(s) they will play? Is my team in place and supporting me?

- Have I anticipated the roadblocks and other challenges I will face? Am I dealing with them appropriately?

- Have I done my upfront risk assessment for opportunities and threats in my job search project? Do I have a strategy to address them? Have I been addressing the risks as they occur, both threats and opportunities?

- Have I identified my potholes and other barriers to my personal productivity? Am I dealing with them appropriately?

- Have I clarified my career objective(s)?

- Do I know myself: my strengths, core competencies, values, priorities, likes, dislikes, interests, etc.?

- Have I done my research to determine how my industry may be changing, what skills will be required of me in the future, if I want to stay in the same industry, etc.?

- Have I reached out to key resources to help guide me in the planning process?

PROJECT EXECUTION

- Am I working my plan?

- Am I focused and productive?

- Do I have a daily agenda and prioritized activities? Do I work them as planned?

- Am I spending my time on the Internet wisely, producing good results?

- Do I follow through on my commitments?

- Am I honoring my time commitments to others?

- Have I identified my communication strategy and developed the necessary documents to implement my strategy?

- Do I have a personal marketing plan that I can give to people I meet at networking events and send to my established contacts?

- Have I been utilizing my marketing plan to gain information on potential opportunities and to obtain additional leads and suggestions?

- Do I have a binder or other way to file all of the documentation and communication I have with various individuals and organizations? (Resume, Marketing Plan, market research, information on key players, conversation notes, etc.)

- Am I using social media effectively? Is my resume posted on various job boards?

- Is my LinkedIn profile up-to-date and consistent with my overall communication strategy?

- Am I using my social media contacts (LinkedIn for example) to find valuable marketing information and job leads?

- Am I updating my resume on a regular basis to ensure it remains high in the Google searches so it will be seen by recruiters and hiring manager?

- Am I attending networking events weekly (in person or via the web) that are helping me advance my job search project?

- Do my interactions with others produce valuable information?

- Am I effectively building relationships?

- Have I contacted recruiters and executive search firms?

- Am I being contacted by recruiters and hiring managers? If not, what can I do to improve my chances of being found on the Internet, LinkedIn, and various job boards?

- Have I conducted informational interviews to uncover potential job leads and business opportunities?

- Am I contacting and scheduling meetings with hiring managers each week?

- Do I follow up from an informational interview and/or job interview with a thank you email and/or thank you note?

- Am I positive in my interactions with others?

- Do I show gratitude to those who help me?

- Am I helping other job seekers along the way?

- Am I taking care of myself?

- Am I taking care of my family and other personal commitments?

MONITOR & CONTROL

After asking yourself the questions listed above, and others you might think of, determine what action is necessary to get (and keep) your project on track to achieve your desired results. I can offer you little advice at this point, not knowing where you are or what you have done or not done. But I do advise you to use your trusted and valuable team members to help you take any necessary corrective actions. Reach out to them for candid feedback, coaching, guidance, and direction. It is easy at times to get off track. What's important is that you recognize when you are off course and take the necessary steps to regain control of your project. As I have said before, you do not need to do all of this alone, seek the wise counsel and support of others.

—◦◦◦—

And while we are talking about *staying the course*, I want to address again the emotional aspects of the job search process. I feel like I would fail you not to bring this up again at this point.

I have seen it time and time again where people start to lose their way when they are not getting the results they want as fast as they want. They start to lose traction and interest in their job search. This can lead to frustration, disappointment, and even apathy.

Perhaps you have been getting interviews but no offers. Instead, a lot of rejection letters. No one likes to be rejected, but with so much competition in the job market these days it is likely to happen. Do not let the rejection shake your confidence (yeah, easy for me to say). Shake it off and ask yourself, "What did I learn from this experience and how can I apply these lessons to future interviews and other aspects of my job search moving forward?" See the *Interview Evaluation* form that I have provided to you in your toolbox which you can find online at **www.ProjectCareerQuest.com**. Use the form to document your lessons learned and to assess what you can do to be more effective in future interviews.

Not knowing where you live or what the job market is like in your area, your project may not be moving as you would like, even if you are doing all of the right things. Don't be too hard on yourself and please, please don't let the gremlins get the best of you. Negativity will not help advance your job search efforts.

If you are struggling with self-esteem and confidence, it is time for a dose of encouragement. Reach out to encouraging friends and family and other team members who can give you some fresh perspective, insight, and the encouragement you need to keep going. *Remember, it takes persistence, perseverance, and patience to be successful!*

FAILURE TO LAUNCH

If you are failing to make progress in your job search project then you are likely falling into some *potholes* or perhaps listening to the *gremlins*, (which we discussed in Chapter 2). Take a look at the following checklist to see if any of these things sound familiar. If so, then you have some course correction to do!

_____ Bad attitude/negative mindset

_____ Procrastination

_____ Bad or unproductive habits

_____ No clarity, no vision; not knowing what you want

_____ Poor time management

_____ Expecting others to find you a job

_____ Excuses

_____ Lack of preparation

_____ No follow through

_____ Not utilizing job search tools

_____ Ego

_____ Not networking

_____ Not on the "radar screen"

_____ Not building relationships

_____ Negative talk (self or others)

_____ Not tapping into your resources for support

_____ Other? _____

"We can't direct the wind, but we can adjust the sails."
—*Thomas S. Monson*

CHECKLIST - BEFORE YOU MOVE ON

☐ Are you reviewing how you are doing on a regular basis? Is your approach and strategy for your project effective?

☐ Do you need to make some adjustments? If so, what?

☐ Are you gathering your lessons learned along the way and using them to improve your performance and results?

☐ Are you successfully navigating your obstacles?

☐ Are you removing or adjusting for your roadblocks?

☐ Are you avoiding potholes?

☐ Are you managing the gremlins and engaging in positive self-talk?

 Lessons Learned: *Monitoring and controlling your efforts and actions are critical to keeping you on target to meet your career goals and achieve your desired results. Monitor your relationships, your productivity, your activities, and your outcomes. Without reviewing your results on a regular basis, you can quickly get derailed and lose momentum. Turn to your team when you need encouragement and use your lessons learned to make the corrections you need to get back on track.*

CHAPTER 16

NEGOTIATING YOUR COMPENSATION PACKAGE

You are almost there. You have a job offer and now it's time to negotiate salary and other compensation. You have done a lot of work to get where you are, but you still have some very important work to do. Many people fall short when it comes to negotiating their total compensation package, that's salary and beyond. Preparing for your negotiation is almost as important as preparing for your interview. Don't fall short here or you will sell yourself short!

THE NEGOTIATING PROCESS

Anytime you negotiate, you want to "begin with the end in mind" by selecting your negotiating approach. Do you compete or do you collaborate? I think you know the answer to that. Collaboration is about achieving a wise outcome for both parties based on "interests."[1] If you want an offer and signed employment contract, collaboration is the approach for you!

To prepare for your negotiation, you need to consider your interests as well as the employer's interest. What's important to you and why? And from the employer's perspective, what's important to them? Be prepared to address both. Always make sure you have a compelling reason for asking for something in the negotiation.

Remember our discussion on Maslow's *Hierarchy of Needs* in Chapter 6? All *interests* are based on *basic human needs*. When you prepare for your negotiation, think about what interests you are trying to satisfy (i.e., safety and security, affiliation, self-esteem, etc.) and what does that look like? What would you need to meet your interests and achieve a wise outcome for your Career Quest? And what need(s) is the employer trying to satisfy? You should have identified their needs by this point in the process. Now you have to be prepared to address those needs as you ask for and agree to the terms of your employment contract.

Let's look at the negotiating process as it relates to a job offer. There are actually three areas to negotiate: 1) **the job itself**, 2) **salary** and, 3) **other non-cash compensation**. Besides salary and the benefits package, what is it that you need to find job satisfaction with this organization? Don't forget about the responsibilities and structure of the job itself.

As part of your preparation process, I suggest you go online and research best practices for negotiating employment contracts. The Harvard Business Review has numerous articles on negotiating strategies and things you should take into consideration, as does Glassdoor.com and other sites. An online search will provide you with lots of information and strategies to educate and empower you to be a more effective negotiator. Negotiating is not something that many people look forward to, but it is a critical and necessary part of the job search process and your ultimate job satisfaction.

NEGOTIATING SALARY

Before you begin negotiating salary and other forms of compensation, research the marketplace to determine a salary range and other non-cash compensation that is appropriate for your level of experience, expertise, and industry. You will need to be prepared with a salary range that you are willing to accept. Most large organizations have pre-established ranges and will attempt to bring in new employees at or below the midpoint of the range. I have provided you with a list of websites, later in this section, where you can research salary for various jobs and industries.

The salary discussion with a company that has given you no indication of the salary for the position advertised is like playing a game of chess—it takes a lot of skill to determine your next move! You do not want to come in too low nor do you want to come in too high. This is why doing your research is critical. If no data is readily available for the position you are applying for, see what comparable jobs pay in that industry.

Also, do not exaggerate your previous salary. Providing false information is not the way to start what you may hope to be a long-term collaborative relationship; and it is simply dishonest. When a company contacts your previous employer, they can typically get confirmation that you worked there and sometimes your previous salary. This usually depends on your former employer's policies. (I do believe this practice of providing salary information is changing.)

Yes, we would all like to make more money than our last position but that may not always be the case. There are many factors to be considered:

- How much experience do you have as it relates to the position?

- Is it a new industry for you?

- How long have you been looking for a job?

- How competitive are you for this position?

- Will this position be a good stepping-stone for your career?

- What will you do if you do not take this job/position? What's your best alternative?*

(* Best Alternative-Authors Roger Fisher and William Ury refer to this as your **BATNA**—Best Alternative to a Negotiated Agreement.[2] Your BATNA is your walkaway position. It defines what best alternative you have if you *cannot* reach an agreement with the other party to the negotiation. Knowing your BATNA protects you from making a poor decision and keeps you open to exploring possibilities.)

WHAT ARE YOUR SALARY EXPECTATIONS?

What do you do when the employer asks you, early in the process, "What are your salary expectations?" Many applicants will respond, feeling pressure to do so. But I caution you not to discuss salary until you understand the responsibilities of the position and the employer's expectations.

The employer's interest in asking you your salary expectations early in the process may be to make sure they are not wasting their time interviewing someone whose requirements and expectations are too high. On the other hand, they may be fishing to see how low they can bring you on board.

Answering that question too early will make it difficult for you to negotiate effectively later. In the first place, and most importantly, you don't have all the information you need to accurately assess fair compensation. To do so, you need an understanding of the job requirements and the employer's expectations beyond what was shared in a job description or online advertisement. And secondly, once you disclose your desired salary or salary range, your actual offer may be tied to those numbers even if the company could have brought you in at a higher rate.

Also, if you have no information about the salary range being considered, you may put yourself in the position of coming in too low and being seen as not capable of performing the job. A salary too high or too low could eliminate you as a candidate. Or you get stuck with a salary way below what the job should pay and what you are worth!

Without a total understanding of requirements and expectations, you are not in a position to discuss *fair compensation*. As I have always taught my project management students, **requirements drive everything!** Before discussing salary, you should understand the *total scope* of the position.

Never, never go into a job interview or enter a salary discussion without having thought through your worth, the value you would bring to the employer's organization, and what the market is paying for your level of expertise and experience. You do not want to have regrets later that you under-sold yourself. Taking a reactive approach will not serve you well. Information is power in a negotiation. You want to negotiate from a position of strength. Do your homework, be prepared!

Negotiating for compensation should occur after job requirements and expectations have been clarified and an offer has been extended. But still you must be prepared to address the salary question anytime in the process. I recommend you use the following approach regarding salary discussions:

1. **Delay** - Initially you will want to postpone any discussion about salary (and even a salary range) until you know more about the position, job requirements, what you would be accountable for, expectations, reporting authority, responsibilities, etc. It is not unreasonable to say something like:

   I would need to know more about the position and what I would be accountable for before discussing salary. However, I would expect to be fairly compensated in terms of current market salaries and commensurate with responsibilities.

2. **Inquire** - If the topic comes up again prior to you having all the information you need to make an informed decision, ask the interviewer what they typically pay someone with your knowledge, skills, and experience. Also inquire about the range for the position. If you provide information about salary before you are

totally prepared, you may have to live with the consequences. Inquire and hopefully the hiring manager (or corporate recruiter) will give you the range. Now you have something to work with.

Even if you have done your homework and you have a good sense about what fair compensation would be in the industry, you still assume the risk of coming in too high or too low. Instead of taking that risk and playing the guessing game, ask them for their range for the position. (Public sector, i.e., government positions, universities, and public institutions, are required to post a salary range. Private industry is not.)

What is the range you typically pay someone with my background and experience?

3. **Disclose** - And finally, if asked again your salary expectations prior to getting an actual offer, provide a range, not a specific number. Once you have a clear understanding of the job responsibilities and other expectations associated with the position, you should be able to reveal your salary range.

   Based on what you have told me about the job responsibilities and expectations, I think a range from...to...would be acceptable.

   Be sure you can live with the low end of the range and that the range you have provided is based on solid research.

A number of years ago I had a decorator's license, having studied Interior Design at the Art Institute in Atlanta, Georgia. Do you think I would give a client a price to do their decorating or design work without first understanding what they wanted to be done and their expectations? No way, of course not. And neither should you.

Project Managers (that's *you* as you move through your job search project) should always understand the total scope of the project before providing cost estimates/pricing. Until you have a full understanding of what is required to do the work successfully you are not in a position to talk salary.

If you are working with a recruiter, they will want to know a salary range before moving forward so they don't waste your time or the employer's time. Remember, recruiters are paid by the employer. They will always have the employer's best interest in mind. My recommendation is that the range you provide a recruiter should be wider the less you know about the position and the responsibilities. With more specific information, you will be able to tighten the range.

Doing your homework and asking questions is key to success. And when it comes to determining your starting salary, **do not be afraid to negotiate**. According to a study conducted in early 2018 by staffing firm Robert Half, and reported by the Society of Human Resource Management (SHRM),[3] on average only 39% of people surveyed indicated negotiating their salary during their last job offer. The study showed that 46% of men said they negotiated salary and only 34% of women negotiated. Gender and age were both a factor in who was most likely to negotiate their compensation. Most of those who did not negotiate regretted it later. Many workers could be earning more income by being informed about their market value and negotiating accordingly.

WHERE DO I FIND SALARY INFORMATION?

Internet - There are many online salary calculators, I have listed a few of the sites below. There may also be some local websites for jobs in your area that will include salary information.

Occupational Outlook Handbook - Published by the U.S. Bureau of Labor Statistics. This handbook is revised every two years and will provide earnings, a general job description, training needed, etc.

Trade and professional journals - Do an online search and you will find a list of trade publications and professional journals that are industry specific.

Professional and industry associations - An internet search will yield a whole list of professional and industry associations that regularly publish salary information.

Networking - Talk to your network contacts, many of them can give you an idea of salary ranges, although be sure to do your own research.

Sites to research salary:

> www.glassdoor.com
> www.salary.com
> www.salaryexpert.com
> www.payscale.com
> www.salarylist.com
> www.LinkedIn.com/salary

www.bls.gov (Bureau of Labor Statistics, see Occupational Outlook Handbook)

www.opm.gov (U.S. Office of Personnel Management - manages the U.S. government civilian workforce)

The Economic Research Institute

Job boards (Career Builder, Indeed, ZipRecruiter, Monster, Dice, etc.)

These are just a few sites you can use to research salary. Do an online search and you will find there are many resources available to you.

There are actually no limits on what you can negotiate. Be creative and focus on the interests of both parties as you ask for what you think is fair and reasonable under the circumstances. Be prepared to support your requests by illustrating value to the employer. Your approach should be win-win!

The extent that you will be successful also depends on the nature of the position and level of the job, as well as the hiring policies of the company. Do your research on the company and throughout the industry looking at standard practices. This does not imply that you must follow a standard practice. Your circumstances, skills, ability, experiences, etc. may be very different and unique. Take those things into consideration when planning your negotiating strategy. Be sure to **have a strategy.**

Women often complain that men make more money for doing the same work. One reason being is that men tend to ask for more and are more likely to negotiate, thereby achieving better results. Studies have shown that men tend to use a more active negotiating approach by directly asking for a higher salary. Women tend to use a more indirect approach by emphasizing self-promotion. In other words, they don't ask for a higher salary but might instead re-emphasize a key selling point. **Don't be afraid to negotiate—don't be afraid to ask!** If you don't ask, it won't be offered.

Case in point—not too long ago I was at a client site delivering a resume and interviewing skills workshop. The Human Resource manager had flown in from out of state and asked if she could sit in on the training. Of course I said "yes." (What else could I say?) I also encouraged her to add her insight and support to my presentation. When we got to the discussion on negotiating, I told the attendees not to be afraid to negotiate for more salary and additional compensation if they felt the offer they received was not in line with their expectations and what they felt they were worth based on their research. At that point, the HR manager shared some invaluable insight with the employees (all of whom would be laid off in the next thirty to ninety days).

She told the group that when she offers new employees a compensation package, she is only authorized to offer them the *standard package*. But then she added that she is also authorized to negotiate with candidates for more than the standard compensation package, *if they ask* and their request is reasonable.

I was so glad she was in the room that day to support and validate what I was telling them. Hearing that information from their Human Resource manager added additional credibility and reinforced my message. For many people, negotiating salary and other compensation can be quite uncomfortable. I believe that what the HR manager had to say changed many of their perspectives on negotiating. I could sense a shift in their attitude about negotiating terms of employment based on her comments. Hopefully they left the training session feeling more empowered and encouraged to negotiate their worth.

She also told them not to be afraid to ask for additional compensation based on the fear that the HR manager (or hiring manager) would withdraw an offer. She said that in the twenty plus years that she had been hiring employees she had only twice withdrawn an offer. Both times she considered the requests unreasonable. By the time she gets to the point of negotiating salary and other compensation she has already invested too much time to withdraw an offer without good cause.

"If you don't ask, the answer is always NO."
—*Nora Roberts*

BEYOND SALARY

Many people believe that salary is the only thing to be negotiated in the hiring process, but in reality, there are many things that can be negotiated. Beyond salary, things you will want to take into consideration as part of your total compensation package include:

WORK SPECIFIC:

- Scope of responsibility
- Decision-making authority
- Reporting relationships

- Budget, resources, and support
- Working location (i.e., telecommute, remote)
- Flexible workday
- Job sharing
- Job description*
- Job title*
- Performance
- Training, certifications, and professional development
- Employment contract
- Start date
- Automobile expenses (company car, expenses in lieu of a company car)
- Air travel (First class, Business class, VIP lounge privileges, etc.)

(***Note:** Negotiating job title and job description may be applicable for senior level positions, or if you are interviewing at a smaller or startup company. Many larger organizations will not negotiate job title or job description, although some may. Always worth the effort, especially if you feel the job title they are proposing would look like a step down from your previous position, even if it is not.)

Recently a client of mine accepted a project management position with a small CRO (clinical research organization). The job title the company proposed was Project Manager. Her title with her current employer (as she was still working) was Senior Project Manager. She felt that for future employment the Project Manager title would look like she had taken a lower level position, even though it was comparable to what she was currently doing. She negotiated for the Senior Project Manager title and the company agreed to her request.

BENEFITS AND BONUSES:

- Medical plans (Including dental, eye, counseling, deductible, choice of providers, etc.)
- Insurance (Life, Disability, Accident, etc.)
- Stock options
- Pension plans

- Vacations
- Paid holidays
- Educational assistance programs
- Professional memberships
- Club memberships and dues
- Bonuses (including a signing bonus)
- Company product/discount programs
- Child care
- Student loan repayment program
- Relocation expenses

Some companies even let their employees bring their dogs to work as a benefit these days. Now *that* would have been a key selling point for me! That was not even imaginable when I worked in the corporate world. How times have changed and continue to change. When negotiating your total compensation package think about what's important to you and your job satisfaction AND career development.

You will find in the **Career Tools** section, at **www.ProjectCareerQuest.com**, a template to help you list and prioritize your *total compensation package* for your negotiations.

"Salary negotiations shouldn't be limited to just salary.
Salary pays your mortgage, but terms build your career."
—*Christopher Voss*

GUIDELINES FOR NEGOTIATING

- **Have a strategy and a plan going into the negotiation.** Be proactive, not reactive.

- **Enter the negotiation with confidence.** Have your data ready and your logic in order. Prepare, prepare, prepare!

- **Do not be afraid to negotiate.** Your salary and compensation package depend on it. If you don't ask, you won't receive. How you negotiate will be a reflection of what you will be like as an employee. Negotiate reasonably and professionally.

- **Create the desire to hire you.** "An experienced salesman doesn't sell; he creates a situation where the customer is eager to buy." (Unknown) To get the best salary offer you must create the desire to hire you. Emphasize your unique selling points and how you can help the company meet their goals and objectives.

- **Prioritize your needs from your wants.** You are likely not to get everything you want, so be prepared with an understanding of what you *need to have* to accept the position and feel good about your decision.

- **Do not share your salary requirements too early in the process.** Salary should not be negotiated until you have a *full* understanding of what you will be responsible for in the position and any additional expectations the employer may have. Also, doing so too early in the process may cause you to lose leverage.

- **Negotiate cash compensation first.** This would include bonuses, profit sharing, stock options, commissions, pension, etc. Then follow up with other non-cash benefits.

- **Negotiate non-cash compensation, focusing on those that are most important to you first.** This may include things such as vacation time, professional membership, automobile expenses, and educational assistance to name a few possibilities.

- **If you cannot get the salary you want, focus on future incentives** such as a bonus, performance incentive, a six-month review, or other added benefits.

- **Keep your conversations about money objective**. It is easy to get caught up in the emotions of what you think you are worth and what you want. Do your homework in advance. Be prepared to justify your rationale and your requests with logic and supporting data.

- **Never exaggerate your previous or current salary.** This information can be (in some cases) easily accessed and you will ruin your chances of getting hired, not to mention you would be creating a relationship based on deceit.

- **Do not let a lower salary keep you from accepting a job that can position you well in the future.** Always take into consideration the non-cash compensation you will receive, the reputation of the company or organization, and the opportunities you will have working for them. Many organizations with great reputations and *hiring appeal* pay lower than industry standard. But they also position a good employee for many opportunities in the future, both within and with other competing organizations. Sometimes *getting your foot in the door* is exactly what is needed to catapult your career. Don't get stuck in your *position* but rather focus on your *long-term interests*.

- **Do not accept an offer on the spot**. This is an important career decision you are about to make. No matter how good the employer's offer sounds, ask for time to think about the offer. It is always better to step away for twenty-four to forty-eight hours to think over the proposed terms and compensation. Stepping away gives you time to reflect on the offer, lends to better objective decision-making, and takes some of the emotions out of the process.

  Rarely would an employer pull an offer at this point in the hiring process, so don't be afraid to ask for a day or two to think through the proposed terms before making your final decision. Give yourself time to make sure you have not missed anything and to ensure you will be satisfied with the offer and the opportunities within the organization. An internal recruiter friend of mine said that people who accept an offer on the spot often appear needy. You do not want to appear needy or desperate, nor do you want to make a decision you will later regret.

CLOSING THE DEAL

- Agree on a decision date and be sure to give your response by that date.

- If you have multiple offers, buy yourself as much time as possible.

- If you need to let the company know you are interviewing with another organization (and perhaps have an offer on the table) do so, but be sure to express your interest in the position within their organization. This may result in the company upping their offer. (It is not advisable to share the name of the other organization, mostly for their privacy.) You need to navigate this situation very carefully so it does not appear that you are employing competitive tactics. Be as transparent as you can be to provide information to the prospective employer so you can both make a decision in your best interests.

- Do not stop your job search until you have a written offer in hand, things can quickly get delayed and fall through. I have seen this happen to job-seekers many times.

- It is always best to get an offer in writing. Not doing so will put you at risk. If the company does not offer you anything in writing, you can follow up with a written confirmation of your acceptance of the position, confirming the terms of agreement.

Last word of advice—Talk to others who have recently been through the process of landing a new position and negotiating a compensation package. What were their experiences? What worked well for them. What did not work? Remember your circumstances will be different, but learning from others will give you more knowledge and confidence for your negotiating success. Engage in lessons learned!

I have read many books on negotiating but my "go to" books on negotiations are by Roger Fisher and William Ury, *Getting To Yes*[4] by Fisher and Ury and *Getting Past No*[5] by Ury. The strategies discussed in the books are timeless and apply to day-to-day negotiations as well as to complex negotiations. They teach a collaborative approach *focused on interests* and *achieving a wise outcome for both parties*. Most of you negotiate daily (even if you do not recognize it) and thus becoming an effective negotiator will serve you well throughout your career.

CHECKLIST - BEFORE YOU MOVE ON

☐ Have you done your market research? Do you know what a fair salary is for some-one with your experience and credentials? Do you have a salary range established based on reliable data?

☐ Have you prepared your negotiating strategy? Do you know what you *need* and what you would *like* to have?

☐ Have you prioritized what you want as part of your total compensation package?

☐ Do you know your value and worth to the employer?

☐ Are you prepared to advocate for yourself?

☐ Do you have a strategy to handle the salary question if it is asked before you are prepared to address it?

☐ Have you spoken to others who have recently gone through a similar transition to learn from their experiences and lessons learned?

 Lessons Learned: *Don't be afraid to negotiate your total compensation package. If you don't ask you won't receive. Have a strategy, a plan, a range, and know your value. Do your research to determine fair compensation for someone with your experience and credentials.*

PART 5

CLOSE OUT

Preparing for New Challenges

CHAPTER 17

CLOSING OUT YOUR JOB SEARCH PROJECT

If you've made it this far—**CONGRATULATIONS**! Your persistence, perseverance, patience, and hard work have paid off. Perhaps you have already started your new job or you have an anticipated start date. Regardless of where you are, there are still things that should be done to successfully close out your job search project.

Before you start telling your family, friends, and those who have assisted you along the way, make sure you have a signed employment contract in hand or other documentation that includes your job offer.

True story—several years ago a job seeker from California interviewed for a job in the Durham, North Carolina area and was offered a position with a small clinical research organization. He sold his house, packed up the wife and kids, and moved across the country. He arrived on a Monday morning to his new place of employment and checked in with security, identifying himself and providing the name of his boss so he could access the facility. Unfortunately, the person with whom he had interviewed was no longer with the company, and neither security nor anyone else had information regarding his employment. Bottom line, he moved across the country with *no* employment contract and *no* job. Not an enviable position to be in!

That being said, let's examine some of the other **things you should do to successfully close out your project**:

- Close out any outstanding offers you may have with other companies or organizations. This should be done as soon as you have made your decision to take another position and have an employment contract. Not doing so will look bad for you and will delay the other organization's process of finding a candidate. Always be gracious in declining an offer with another company and thank them for the opportunity to interview with them. As the expression goes, "Don't burn your bridges." Not notifying corporate recruiters or hiring managers, when a candidate has accepted another position, happens far too often. Be respectful of the other company's time and their need to fill a position.

- If you have been working with a recruiter or executive search firm, notify them of your change of status. Thank them for their support and referrals and let them know how to contact you in the future.

- Notify friends, family members, and others who have assisted you along the way that you have landed a position. Let them know you have found a job and are ready to start your new career and thank them for helping you on your journey. With the exception of close family members, you should wait to notify most of your contacts until you have actually started your new job. Be sure to let them know how to get in touch with you—keep your network alive!

- Do your end of project lessons learned. What did you do well and where could you improve for possible future career/job changes? What did you learn about yourself during your career transition project? In today's job market, you never know when you may encounter this journey again—there are no guarantees and few long-term commitments. *Learn from your past and be prepared for your future!*

- Close out and update your project files. The files you kept in a binder or in files on your computer may come in handy for future searches.

- Sometime after being in your new position you will want to update your LinkedIn profile. I recommend waiting two to three weeks before doing so until you settle into your position, you are clear on your role and responsibilities, and you are sure this job is going to work out.

- Ask yourself if there is anything else you need to do to complete your job search project. Not knowing your journey, I cannot say for sure that I have included everything you need to do. You would know best.

- Thank those who have been instrumental in your success: recruiters, coaches, volunteers at job seeker groups, family members, friends, former colleagues, neighbors, etc. A THANK YOU and an update will go a long way. Sending a thank you note to those who helped you on your journey is not only common courtesy, it will also benefit you in the long run.

- Use your knowledge of the career transition process to give back to others. Now it's your turn to support someone else in their job search project.

- And finally, don't forget to **celebrate your success**. You've worked hard and you deserve it!

Common sense is not always common practice—thanking those who have helped you on your journey is the right thing to do.

CHECKLIST - BEFORE YOU MOVE ON

☐ Do you have a signed employment contract?

☐ Have you closed out any outstanding offers with other companies or organizations?

☐ Have you notified any recruiters or search firms you have been working with about your change of status?

☐ Have you done your end of project lessons learned?

☐ If you have started your new job, have you notified friends, colleagues, and others who have helped you on your journey?

☐ Have you updated your LinkedIn profile?

 Lessons Learned: *Closing out your job search project includes compiling and documenting your lessons learned and keeping your networks alive by recognizing and thanking those who helped you be successful.*

CHAPTER 18

THE JOURNEY CONTINUES

You started a new job, **congratulations**! A new beginning—but still there is so much to be done. Now you must successfully **navigate the first ninety days and beyond**.

You interviewed, you got the offer, you started your job, and now you need to build credibility, relationships, and a network in your new organization. You will need to establish yourself and earn the trust and respect of your colleagues. You were hired based on your resume, your interview, your reputation, and recommendations. Now you need to demonstrate your worth to your new employer. Your primary goal in the first ninety days should be to:

- Create value for the employer—meet and exceed their expectations.

- Build key relationships—establish yourself as a team player.

- Build trust and your reputation—become an asset to the organization.

Who are the decision makers? Who are the influencers? What can you do to quickly assimilate into the culture, add value, and make a positive impact?

Now is not the time to settle in and blend into the background. What you do or don't do will be evaluated, your performance observed. You were hired with a purpose in mind: to help them meet their challenges, to create new opportunities, to solve problems, to cut costs, bring in new business, improve productivity, deliver successful projects, train personnel, coach, mentor, and lead others. Now it's time to deliver!

Someone will be evaluating your performance. Are you meeting and exceeding their expectations? Do your own assessment. Stay on top of your performance.

It's a new job, a new organization, new personalities, new boss, new colleagues, new customers, new challenges; a lot to learn. At times it might seem overwhelming, so don't be afraid to ask for help and seek feedback from others. Seek opportunities to learn new things and create value wherever you can.

If the job you landed is a temporary or contract position, and it is your goal to get on with the employer as a full-time employee, remember the importance of networking. As I said previously, you do not want to settle into the background. Seek opportunities to get noticed. Volunteer for challenging and high-profile assignments whenever possible. Set your goal to be a full-time employee and then do what needs to be done to achieve that goal. Your performance, your mind-set, your approach, your contribution, and who you get to know, will be determining factors in your ability to achieve your goal.

Outline a **strategy for your first ninety days**. What will you do to build credibility, relationships, trust, and network within your new organizations? What high profile assignments or projects can you volunteer for? What will you do to create value for your new organization? Give these questions serious thought and develop a plan of action.

Be thankful for each new challenge.
Challenges are gifts that help to build your strength and character.

And while it may seem that your Career Quest journey has finally come to an end, it is anything but over. The days of long careers with one company have come and gone. As reported earlier in the book, the average tenure in the job market today is slightly over four years. (Less for millennials; based on U.S. job market statistics.)[1] That in itself would indicate that you need to be prepared for your next career move, voluntary or otherwise.

"Change is inevitable. Growth is optional"
—*John C. Maxwell*

While change is inevitable, growth is *not* optional if you want to remain employable!
Now that you have landed a position, started your own company, purchased a franchise, or otherwise found your path, you will need to focus on your personal and professional growth. There are no permanent positions in today's world, only stepping-stones to your next career opportunity.

"The only job security we have is our individual commitment to personal development."
—*Kevin Turner*

Be vigilant, be prepared, be strategic, and take charge of your career moving forward. Don't wait until the next layoff to "up your game" and improve your skills. Think strategically. "What do I want to do next? What's my next career move? What skills will be required?"

Hope is NOT a strategy! Hoping this is your last career move and becoming complacent can prove to be a big mistake. As much as you don't want to hear this, being laid off in the future is a very real possibility. I suggest you don't wait for that to happen. Be prepared! Here are some questions to think about so you can take appropriate action to be prepared in the future. The goal is to remain highly marketable and employable:

- What's my next career move? (internally or externally)
- What skills will be needed? Do I possess those skills?
- What do I need to do to get the skills I may need in the future to achieve my career objectives?
- What assignments can I volunteer for to help develop my skill sets?
- With whom should I be strategically networking to prepare me for future assignments and opportunities? (internally or externally)

- What professional organization(s) can I get involved with to network and advance my career?

Things will continue to change. That's guaranteed. There will continue to be mergers and acquisitions. There will continue to be downsizings and reductions in force (RIFs). There will continue to be realignments and outsourcing. Companies will continue to look for ways to do more with less. Technology will continue to impact the need for *human resources* to complete work, in many cases reducing the need for headcount. These things are guaranteed.

What's not guaranteed is that you will remain an asset to your organization and employable unless you have a plan for your ongoing growth and development. You must invest in yourself to remain competitive and ready for your next transition, whenever that may be. *Survival of the fittest* applies in today's workforce—more so than ever before!

If you prepare, if you plan, if you are constantly seeking opportunities to learn and grow, if you are stretching to gain new knowledge and skills, you will survive the next major career shift. Your preparation and growth, both personally and professionally, will make you more adaptable and resilient to the changes guaranteed to come! Growth is optional—it will only occur if you have a *plan* and take *action*.

What will you do to ensure that you continue to grow in knowledge and skills and continue to add value to your employer, your customers, your team, your stakeholders, your family, *and* yourself?

"If you don't design your own life plan, chances are you'll fall into someone else's plan. And guess what they may have planned for you? Not much."
—*Jim Rohn*

So, don't wait for the next layoff, merger, acquisition, or outsourcing. Don't wait until you are exasperated and frustrated in your nine-to-five job. Take action **NOW** to design and plan what you want your future to look like. Take action **NOW** to move forward strategically and develop your full potential.

Some of the tools I mentioned earlier in the book that can be used to help you map out a plan and chart your course include **mind maps**, **vision boards**, and my absolute favorite tool, **Force Field Analysis** (FFA). Force Field Analysis is a tool to help problem solve, analyze forces that either help or hinder a change you want to make, generate ideas, make decisions, and develop a plan of action. Check out these tools in the **Career Tools** section at **www.ProjectCareerQuest.com**. Continue to use these tools to map out your future and plan your growth strategy.

"The difference between where we are and where we want to be is created by the changes we are willing to make in our lives."
—*John C. Maxwell*

One of the laws in John Maxwell's book, *The 15 Invaluable Laws of Growth*[2] is **The Law of the Rubber Band**.[3] The subtitle of this chapter is: *Growth Stops When You Lose the Tension Between Where You Are and Where You Could Be.* Too many people are willing to settle for average lives, the "comfortable life" as author and motivational speaker and teacher Brendon Burchard refers to it. When we stay in our comfort zone it leads to lives of mediocrity.

If you have faithfully been on this journey of **Project Career Quest** from chapter one until now, I am betting that you want more than mediocrity. (I could be wrong, but if you stuck it out this long, I doubt it!) The law of the rubber band says we have to S-T-R-E-T-C-H to reach new heights of performance, growth, and overall fulfillment in life.

A rubber band itself offers no value unless you stretch it. Try it. Put a rubber band in your hand and see what it can do for you. Lay it on your palm and see if it offers you any value.

Now stretch that same rubber band and the possibilities of what you can do with it are endless. When stretched that same rubber band can be used to hold your hair back (assuming you have some), it can bind something together, can be used as a toy or a weapon (like a sling shot). You can put a rubber band around your wrist as a reminder of something. You can use super-sized rubber bands to exercise with. Rubber bands are used on braces to help straighten teeth. You can use a rubber band to hold up your socks, and the list goes on and on if you use your imagination.

You see, the value in a rubber band is when it is stretched. Your value to yourself, your family, your employer, your friends, your community, is also when you stretch—beyond your comfort zone to your performance zone.

"If you plan on being anything less than you are capable of being,
you will probably be unhappy all the days of your life."
—*Abraham Maslow*

 One of the best books currently on the market regarding growth and personal development is John Maxwell's book, entitled, *The 15 Invaluable Laws of Growth.*[4] I highly recommend you purchase this book and use it as a tool to further your growth and development needs. *Life is a journey, not a destination.*[5] While you may have arrived at your current position, the journey continues and you will want to be prepared. (And yes, I did recommend this book already in Chapter 2—just wanted to make sure you did not miss out on this wonderful resource!)

Two other books I would highly recommend on developing your human capacity and understanding what motivates people to reach for higher levels of success include: *No Limits*[6] also by John C. Maxwell and *High Performance Habits*[7] by Brendon Burchard.

 CHECKLIST - BEFORE YOU MOVE ON

☐ Do you know all the key players in your new organization and how you interface with them?

☐ Have you learned your job responsibilities and are you performing them up to your manager's expectation?

☐ Have you explored areas where you can add value to your new organization?

☐ Have you sought help and feedback when needed?

☐ Do you have a strategy for personal growth and development?

Lessons Learned: *Just because you have landed does not mean your work is over as it relates to your job search project; you still need to prove your value to your new employer. Job security is created when you constantly seek opportunities to learn, grow, and stretch beyond your comfort zone.*

"God's gift to us: potential. Our gift to God: developing it."
—*Author Unknown*

AUTHOR'S NOTE TO THE READER

I hope our time together with *Project Career Quest* has been fruitful for you and that I have helped you answer the question "**NOW what**?" There are **N**ew **O**pportunities **W**aiting if you know how to find them.

I am confident that you will be successful if you: follow the process, complete the exercises, take the assessments, dig deep, listen to your heart as well as your head, approach your Career Quest with a positive mindset, and surrounded yourself with people to support you on your journey. How could you not be?

Will all your work be done? Of course not! But you should be well on your way to making significant progress on your journey to meaningful and satisfying employment. Wishing you a fulfilling life where you use your special talents and gifts to make a positive contribution to the world.

Your Guide,
Kerry Ahrend

"The purpose of life is not to be happy. It is to be useful, to be honorable, to be compassionate, to have it make some difference that you have lived and lived well."
—*Ralph Waldo Emerson*

Appendix 1

Best Practices
for Successful Career Transition

I want to leave you now with a summary of some best practices for successful career transition. This is not an extensive or all-inclusive list, but hopefully a quick reminder of what it takes to find success on the journey I refer to as **Project Career Quest**.

Mindset and Approach:

- Keep a positive mental attitude.

- Do not isolate yourself or try to go it alone.

- Do not keep your job search a secret.

- Anticipate your roadblocks and potholes and come up with a plan to deal with them.

- Do not listen to the gremlins. Avoid negative self-talk and negativity from others.

- Take care of yourself: physically, mentally, and emotionally.

Project Planning and Executing:

- Manage your job search like a project.

- Have a plan and work the plan.

- Create a daily schedule and adhere to it.

- Do not put off the important. Plan to spend 80% of your time in job search mode focusing on Quadrant II activities. (*First Things First*, Stephen R. Covey)

- Do your risk assessment. What are your opportunities and potential threats to your job search project? Develop a mitigation strategy to prepare for and overcome the threats and seize the opportunities.

- Be proactive; take action and don't wait for someone else to make the first move.

- Follow up and follow through.

ENGAGING OTHERS:

- Network, network, network!

- Engage others in your job search project; build your support team.

- Develop a personal Marketing Plan to help you engage and get input from others.

- Build quality relationships and keep your networks alive.

- Consider using a search firm and working with a recruiter, they have more contacts and relationships with employers than you do. Leverage those relationships. (Do not, however, expect them to find you a job. It's still your project.)

- Communicate with your target audience (hiring managers) in the most effective way for them. Learn to speak their language and always address your total audience.

- Give back by helping others where you can add value.

COMMUNICATING YOUR VALUE:

- Know yourself and your value—you MUST if you are to sell yourself.

- Focus your resume on what the market is buying and the skills you have to meet what is needed.

- Write your resume in a way that it sets you apart and gets you noticed, highlighting your value proposition and unique qualifications.

- Have your accomplishment stories ready for job interviews. (SOAR Stories)

EFFECTIVE INTERVIEWING:

- Refine and nail your message. Practice it over and over again until you are comfortable and confident delivering your message.

- Build a relationship with the interviewer. Focus not only on your spoken words but on your non-verbals as well. (Good eye contact, firm handshake, attentive posture, etc.)

- Listen actively and engage in two-way communication with your interviewer.

- Never criticize your former employer, boss, business colleagues, customers, or suppliers. Always keep your discussion positive.

- Ask appropriate questions including next steps.

MONITORING AND ASSESSING PERFORMANCE:

- Do lessons learned throughout your project. Ask yourself what went well and what you could have done better. Make corrections as needed.

- Be certain to do lessons learned after each job interview so you can continue to refine your interviewing skills.

- Don't be afraid to ask for feedback from hiring managers, recruiters, and others you engage with along the way.

APPRECIATION AND HELPING OTHERS:

- Pay it forward; help others along the way.

- Send thank you notes and follow-up emails.

- Show gratitude throughout the process. Your success depends upon it.

PROJECT CLOSING AND BEYOND:

- Don't stop your job search until you have a written offer in hand.

- Always get an offer in writing.

- Close out any outstanding offers you have with other companies.

- Notify those who have helped you along the way of your new position. (Generally best to wait until you have started your new job.)

- Once in your new position, be sure to add value to the organization.

- Continue to focus on your personal growth and development.

Appendix 2

5-Star Lessons Learned

To help you recap what we talked about in the book, I have compiled here all of the **lessons learned** that were scattered throughout the chapters. I hope you will now take some time to jot down your lessons learned and will continue to capture lessons learned throughout your Career Quest journey.

1. Keep it positive and let people know you are looking for your next career opportunity and ask for their support. Do not isolate yourself and seek help as needed.

2. Your thoughts will influence your attitude, your attitude your behavior, your behavior your results. Maintaining a positive mental attitude is critical to success.

3. Be aware of the roadblocks, potholes, and gremlins you will face on your journey to find meaningful employment and have a plan to address them. Also look for the benefits along the way, there are many!

4. You will face many challenges as you approach and carry out your job search project. Identify your challenges and develop a plan to address and overcome them. You can do this, one step at a time. It is natural and inevitable that you will go through the stages of adjusting to change. Take note of where you are on that journey and seek help as needed. Awareness and the right attitude are critical to making progress and ultimately achieving success.

5. Projects have distinct processes with specific activities to be completed in each of the processes. Project planning is critical to a successful job search project. Planning is defining what to do; Executing is implementing according to the Plan; Monitoring and Controlling is making sure the Plan is working and getting the desired results—adjusting as needed. A proper project Close Out includes thanking those who help you deliver a successful project and updating them with your current status.

6. Effective project managers understand in advance what it takes to bring in a project successfully. Finding a job or new career requires a lot of knowledge and planning. Having a clear vision of what it will take to complete the career transition journey and a detailed roadmap are key to success.

7. Building a team to support your job search efforts is critical to a successful transition. Finding others who can help you navigate the job market and other challenges you will face along the way will keep you on track and productive.

8. Knowing yourself and what you want to do next can be one of the most challenging aspects of the job search process. However, if you are to be successful you must dig in and get to know yourself. You will need to gain clarity on your career objectives to be able to sell yourself and your value to others, and most importantly your value to yourself. If you do not value yourself, you will be unsuccessful convincing others of your value.

9. If you want to discover your passion you must be willing to move beyond your comfort zone and try new things. Also, you must look inside your heart to reveal those things that matter most to you. Only then will you discover your passion.

10. Career transition offers an opportunity to explore a number of different paths. You don't have to be defined by your previous job or career. You have options and can reinvent yourself if desired.

11. If you have lost your job, lost your way, or lost your enthusiasm for what you were doing, it does not mean that your options are limited. Start exploring and asking others to help you brainstorm options. Examine your options and eventually you will find an opportunity that's right for you.

12. Getting your message out effectively requires having a communication strategy and plan that is consistent with your overall career goals. You must have a thorough understanding of your market and be able to articulate your accomplishments and value to a prospective employer.

13. Networking can happen anywhere and anytime. Sometimes when you least expect it a job opportunity can present itself.

14. Networking is about building quality relationships and is one of your most valuable tools in career transition. Networking can be face-to-face or online and opportunities to network present themselves daily. Anyone can network successfully, especially if they focus on the other person and not on themselves and practice active listening.

15. Working with a recruiter or search firm has many advantages. They have built relationships with employers and you will want to tap into that. Be sure that you understand the dynamics of the relationship, expectations, and any paperwork that you sign!

16. Social media is a powerful tool for networking, marketing your personal brand, and communicating your value to others.

17. Understanding personality type can help you as a job seeker to be more effective in communicating and building rapport with others. The key is to connect with people where they are and to speak their language so they can relate to you and your message.

18. Refine and nail your message. Practice with a friend or in front of a mirror. Repeat your SOAR stories over and over again until you are comfortable and confident delivering your message. The ability to sell yourself is key. Practice, practice, practice!

19. Monitoring and controlling your efforts and actions are critical to keeping you on target to meet your career goals and achieve your desired results. Monitor your relationships, your productivity, your activities, and your outcomes. Without reviewing your results on a regular-basis you can quickly get derailed and lose momentum. Turn to your team when you need encouragement and use your lessons learned to make the corrections you need to get back on track.

20. Don't be afraid to negotiate your total compensation package. If you don't ask you won't receive. Have a strategy, a plan, a range, and know your value. Do your research to determine fair compensation for someone with your experience and credentials.

21. Closing out your job search project includes compiling and documenting your lessons learned and keeping your networks alive by recognizing and thanking those who helped you be successful.

22. Just because you have landed does not mean your work is over as it relates to your job search project. You still need to prove your value to your new employer.

23. Job security is created when you constantly seek opportunities to learn, grow, and stretch beyond your comfort zone.

Now that you have reviewed all the lessons learned from the book, take time to jot down your lessons learned and remember to capture them as you continue on your **Career Quest** journey. If you consistently gather lessons learned and reflect on your experiences, your journey will only get better and better and SUCCESS will be yours!

MY LESSONS LEARNED ON MY CAREER QUEST JOURNEY...

_____

_____

_____

_____

_____

_____

_____

_____

_____

_____

_____

_____

APPENDIX 3

NOTES

INTRODUCTION

1. PMP® is an industry-recognized certification for project managers that can be earned by leading and directing projects and passing a rigorous four-hour exam developed and administered by the Project Management Institute (PMI).

CHAPTER 2: JOB SEARCH REALITIES

1. PMP, CAPM, CISM, CPA, CTP, MCP, CCNP, PM, SPHR are just a few professional business certifications that are earned based on experience, training, and having successfully passed an exam. Certifications are highly valued by employers and can give a job applicant a competitive edge.

2. The *Law of Attraction* is the belief that we can attract either positive or negative things and experiences into our lives based on what we focus on. "It is the Law of Attraction which uses the power of the mind to translate whatever is in our thoughts and materialize them into reality." (TheLawOfAttraction.com, assessed August 10, 2019)

3. James Allen, *As A Man Thinketh*; (Revised and updated version–New York, NY: Penguin Group, 2008)

4. The *hidden job market* is a term used for job openings that are not publicly advertised. In part, this is due to an employer's desire to reach out to their employees and other reliable sources to fill positions with qualified candidates.

This approach is almost always less costly, more efficient, and generally more effective in finding *quality* candidates versus a *quantity* of applicants. To identify unadvertised job openings requires much networking on the part of the job seeker.

5. Applicant Tracking Systems (ATS) are used by employers to process job applications, screen applicants, and manage the hiring process.

6. Viktor Frankl, *Man's Search for Meaning,* (Boston, Mass: Beacon Press, 2006. First published in 1946.)

7. The *Boiling Frog Syndrome* is an analogy used here to describe what happens when an individual remains in a job that they should have escaped from long ago. Put in a pot of water with a source of heat turned on, a frog's body will adjust as the temperature of the water rises. However, when the water reaches the boiling point, the frog is no longer able to adjust his body temperature nor jump out of the pot because it has lost all its strength by this point. What killed the frog is not the boiling water but rather the frog's inability to decide when it was time to jump out.

8. John C. Maxwell, *The Fifteen Invaluable Laws of Growth;* (New York, NY: Center Street, 2012)

CHAPTER 3: JOB SEARCH CHALLENGES

1. An encore career is "…work in the second half of life that combines continued income, greater personal meaning, and social impact." (Wikipedia, accessed July 31, 2019)

2. The Employment Security Commission is a state government agency that matches jobs and workers in the local job market and provides unemployment compensation to support unemployed workers.

3. Kubler-Ross Model as originally developed described the five stages of grief in the case of a terminal illness. The model was originated by Swiss-American psychiatrist Elisabeth Kubler-Ross in her book *On Death and Dying* in 1969.

4. Elisabeth Kubler-Ross, *On Death and Dying;* (New York: The Macmillan Company, 1969)

CHAPTER 4: ORGANIZING YOUR JOB SEARCH PROJECT

1. PMP® is an industry-recognized certification for project managers that can be earned by leading and directing projects and passing a rigorous four-hour exam developed and administered by the Project Management Institute (PMI).

2. The Project Management Institute (PMI) is a global nonprofit professional organization for project management. They are headquartered in Newtown Square, Pennsylvania, USA. In the Project Management Body of Knowledge, more commonly referred to as the PMBOK® Guide, PMI identifies the five process groups as Initiating, Planning, Executing, Monitoring and Controlling, and Closing.

3. The Project Management Institute (PMI) is a global nonprofit professional organization for project management. They are headquartered in Newtown Square, Pennsylvania, USA. In the Project Management Body of Knowledge, more commonly referred to as the PMBOK® Guide, PMI identifies the ten Knowledge Areas of project management.

4. Stephen R. Covey, A. Roger Merrill and Rebecca R. Merrill, *First Things First*; (New York: Simon & Schuster, 1994)

5. The Eisenhower Principle is said to be how the American General, and 34th President of the United States of America, Dwight D. Eisenhower, organized his workload and priorities.

6. Stephen R. Covey, A. Roger Merrill and Rebecca R. Merrill, *First Things First*; (New York: Simon & Schuster, 1994)

7. The Eisenhower Principle is said to be how the American General, and 34th President of the United States of America, Dwight D. Eisenhower, organized his workload and priorities.

8. Dave Ramsey, *Total Money Makeover*, (Nashville, Tenn.: Thomas Nelson, 2013)

9. Dave Ramsey, *Financial Peace University*, is a nine-lesson course offered through many churches and nonprofits to teach people how to pay off debt and build wealth. For more information see https://www.daveramsey.com/classes. Material is also available online.

CHAPTER 6: GETTING TO KNOW YOURSELF

1. Tom Rath, *Strengths Finder 2.0* (New York, NY: Gallup Press, 2007)

2. The Clifton StrengthsFinder Assessment, formerly known as Strengths Finders 2.0, looks at thirty-four strengths and sorts them into four domains: Strategic Thinking, Executing, Influencing, and Relationship Building.

3. Abraham Maslow's *Hierarchy of Needs* is a motivational theory that looks at five levels of basic human needs.

4. Myers-Briggs Type Indicator® (MBTI) is the most widely used personality inventory in the world. It was developed by Katharine Briggs and her daughter Isabel Briggs Myers in collaboration and is based on the work of the Swiss psychiatrist Carl Jung. The MBTI has wide application in career coaching and personal development.

5. Association of Psychological Type International (APTi) is a nonprofit international membership organization whose members seek to extend the development, research, application, and ethical use of type theory.

6. The Center for the Application of Psychological Type (CAPT) is a not-for-profit organization located in Gainesville, Florida that promotes MBTI research and the accurate understanding and ethical use of the MBTI instrument. They also certify trainers and coaches to administer the instrument. CAPT was co-founded by Isabel Briggs Myers and Mary McCaulley, Ph.D. https://www.capt.org

7. The Myers-Briggs Company is the current publisher of the Myers-Briggs Type Indicator® (MBTI). They specialize in personality, career, and professional development assessments. https://www.themyersbriggs.com

8. Donna Dunning, *What's Your Type of Career: Unlocking the Secrets of Your Personality to Find Your Perfect Career Path* (Palo Alto, CA: Davies-Black Publishing, 2010)

9. Paul Tieger, Barbara Barron, and Kelly Tieger, *Do What You Are: Discover the Perfect Career for You Through the Secrets of Personality Type* (Boston: Little, Brown and Company, 2014)

CHAPTER 7: DISCOVER YOUR PASSION

1. Passion is defined as, "…a powerful and compelling emotion or feeling." https://www.dictionary.com, accessed August 1, 2019.

2. Richard Chang, *The Passion Plan: A Step-by-Step Guide to Discovering, Developing, and Living Your Passion* (San Francisco, CA: Jossey-Bass Publishers, 2000)

3. Ibid.

4. Dr. Tony Colson, *Unlocking Your Divine DNA* (Powell, Ohio: Author Academy Elite, 2017) https://www.tonycolson.com

5. The *caged life*, as described by Brendon Burchard in his book *The Charge,* is a life where we feel imprisoned, restricted, disengaged, perhaps trapped in a dead-end job. Life and work are unfulfilling and may feel meaningless.

6. The *charged life*, as described by Brendon Burchard in his book *The Charge,* is one where we are filled with energy and enthusiasm, we are engaged, empowered, and living our best life.

7. Brendon Burchard, *The Charge: Activating the 10 Human Drives That Make You Feel Alive* (New York, NY: Free Press, 2012)

8. The *caged life*, as described by Brendon Burchard in his book *The Charge,* is a life where we feel imprisoned, restricted, disengaged, perhaps trapped in a dead-end job. Life and work are unfulfilling and may feel meaningless.

9. The *comfortable life*, as described by Brendon Burchard in his book *The Charge,* is where we may feel engaged and thankful for our lives but at some point may wonder, "Is this all there is?" Or we may start to question what happened to our ambition and drive. We've become comfortable with all of the trappings of success and yet still may find ourselves unfulfilled.

10. *The charged life*, as described by Brendon Burchard in his book *The Charge,* is one where we are filled with energy and enthusiasm, we are engaged, empowered, and living our best life.

11. Kary Oberbrunner, *Day Job to Dream Job* (Powell, Ohio: Author Academy Elite, 2018) https://dayjobtodreamjob.com

12. Dr. Tony Colson, *Unlocking Your Divine DNA* (Powell, Ohio: Author Academy Elite, 2017) https://www.tonycolson.com

CHAPTER 8: NEW OPPORTUNITIES WAITING

1. *edx.org* offers numerous courses, programs, and degrees from major universities including Harvard, Massachusetts Institute of Technology (MIT), Boston University, Berkeley, The University of Texas System, and a number of international universities. Many of the courses are self-paced and free.

2. The Service Corp of Retired Executives (SCORE) is a U.S. based nonprofit volunteer organization dedicated to educating and mentoring entrepreneurs and small business owners to promote the formation, growth, and success of small businesses. SCORE offers live and recorded webinars every week providing small business tips and strategies. Local SCORE chapters have volunteers who help thousands of entrepreneurs start and grow their businesses each year. SCORE also has an online Business Learning Center.

3. Small Business Development Centers (SBDC) is part of the Small Business Administration (SBA). Its mission is to promote entrepreneurship, small business growth, and the U.S. economy. Local SBDCs provide face-to-face business consulting and training on a variety of topics for new and existing businesses. https://www.americassbdc.org

4. Small Business and Technology Development Centers (SBTDC) is a business and technology service that provides management counseling and educational services to small and mid-sized businesses. https://www.sbtdc.org

5. SBA.gov is the Small Business Administration. The SBA is a government agency that supports American small businesses. The SBA connects entrepreneurs with lenders and funding to help them plan, execute, and grow their business. https://www.sba.gov

6. U.S. Bureau of Labor Statistics is a unit of the U.S. Department of Labor and is responsible for measuring labor market activity, working conditions, and price changes in the economy. This bureau produces vital statistics about jobs and unemployment. https://www.bls.gov

7. The contingent work force is made up of workers who do not work directly for an employer. Consultants, freelancers, independent contractors, and temporary contract workers (temps) can all be considered part of the contingent work force.

8. Standard Occupational Classification System (SOC) is a federal classification system used by U.S. federal agencies to classify workers into occupational categories. This information is then used to understand skills, education, and

training needs of the various occupational classifications, among other things. https://www.bls.gov/soc

9. Occupational Information Network (O*Net) has an online database containing detailed information on over 1000 occupations to help the job seeker, workforce development, researchers, students, and Human Resource professionals. It is considered to be a tool for career exploration and job analysis. The O*Net provides information on the knowledge, skills, and abilities (KSA) required to perform various occupations. https://www.onetcenter.org

10. A portfolio career is when a person divides their skills, talents, and time between a diversity of roles and perhaps even industries. For some, a portfolio career, versus full-time employment with one employer, offers them a better work-life balance.

11. An encore career is "…work in the second half of life that combines continued income, greater personal meaning, and social impact." (Wikipedia, accessed July 31, 2019)

CHAPTER 9: COMMUNICATION STRATEGIES AND TOOLS

1. PMP® is an industry-recognized certification for project managers that can be earned by leading and directing projects and passing a rigorous four-hour exam developed and administered by the Project Management Institute (PMI).

2. Six Sigma is a methodology and toolset to help organizations analyze and improve their processes to achieve breakthrough improvements.

3. Agile methodology is a results-focused approach to software development. It allows teams to analyze and improve their product throughout its development. The process is designed to respond quickly to ever-changing technology requirements no matter how early or late in the project.

4. SCRUM is an agile process framework most frequently used by software development teams to structure and manage their work.

5. CISCO certification is one of many certifications that can help build a technology career and add value to an employer.

6. Microsoft certification is one of many certifications that can help build a technology career and add value to an employer.

7. A *base resume* is one that the job seeker develops for a particular type of position or industry and will then customize for each position for which they apply. For example, if you are both a trainer and a business consultant, and use a resume to get work, you would have a base resume for training positions and a base resume for consulting positions. As a position/job is identified, the base resume can be modified/customized for the specific position.

CHAPTER 10: NETWORKING FOR RESULTS

1. The *hidden job market* is a term used for job openings that are not publicly advertised. In part, this is due to an employer's desire to reach out to their employees and other reliable sources to fill positions with qualified candidates. This approach is almost always less costly, more efficient, and generally more effective in finding quality candidates versus a quantity of applicants. To identify unadvertised job openings requires much networking on the part of the job seeker.

2. Community organizations are a great place for the job seeker to network while serving others and adding value to their community.

3. Women in Bio (WIB) is a nonprofit organization committed to promoting careers, leadership, and entrepreneurship for women in the life sciences. Activities focus on educating, mentoring, networking, and creating opportunities for leadership. https://www.womeninbio.org

4. Myers-Briggs Type Indicator® (MBTI) is the most widely used personality inventory in the world. It was developed by Katharine Briggs and her daughter Isabel Briggs Myers in collaboration and is based on the work of the Swiss psychologist Carl Jung. The MBTI has wide application in career coaching and personal development.

5. DiSC is a behavior profile used to understand oneself better as well as others. Widely used for team building, leadership training, to enhance communication, and build relationships. DiSC is published by Personality Insights. https://www.personality-insights.com

CHAPTER 11: WORKING WITH RECRUITERS AND SEARCH FIRMS

1. Applicant Tracking Systems (ATS) are used by employers to process job applications, screen applicants, and manage the hiring process.

CHAPTER 13: UNDERSTANDING PERSONALITIES AND COMMUNICATION STYLES

1. Myers-Briggs Type Indicator® (MBTI) is the most widely used personality inventory in the world. It was developed by Katharine Briggs and her daughter Isabel Briggs Myers in collaboration and is based on the work of the Swiss psychologist Carl Jung. The MBTI has wide application in career coaching and personal development.

2. Katharine Briggs and Isabel Briggs Myers were the coauthors and co-creators of the Myers-Brigs Type Indicator® (MBTI).

3. Carl Jung was a Swiss psychologist whose theory on psychological type is reflected in the Myers-Briggs Type Indicator®, an instrument that seeks to promote the constructive use of differences.

4. Association of Psychological Type International (APTi) is a non-profit international membership organization whose members seek to extend the development, research, application, and ethical use of type theory. https://www.aptinternational.org

5. The Myers-Briggs Company is the current publisher of the Myers-Briggs Type Indicator® (MBTI). They specialize in personality, career, and professional development assessments. https://www.themyersbriggs.com

6. The Center for the Application of Psychological Type (CAPT) is a not-for-profit organization located in Gainesville, Florida that promotes MBTI research and the accurate understanding and ethical use of the MBTI instrument. They also certify trainers and coaches to administer the instrument. CAPT was co-founded by Isabel Briggs Myers and Mary McCaulley, Ph.D. https://www.capt.org

7. Association of Psychological Type International (APTi) is a non-profit international membership organization whose members seek to extend the development, research, application, and ethical use of type theory. https://www.aptinternational.org

8. MBTI Z-Model is a useful and applicable process for job seekers to communicate and connect with others more effectively. Developed as a decision-making model, following the same process can help job-applicants structure their message in a more effective way to facilitate the decision making of the interviewer/hiring manager.

9. Association of Psychological Type International (APTi) is a non-profit international membership organization whose members seek to extend the development, research, application, and ethical use of type theory. https://www.aptinternational.org

10. Otto Kroeger with Janet M. Thuesen and Hile Rutledge, *Type Talk at Work: How the 16 Personality Types Determine Your Success on the Job* (New York, NY: Dell Publishing, 2002)

11. Donna Dunning, *What's Your Type of Career: Unlocking the Secrets of Your Personality to Find Your Perfect Career Path* (Palo Alto, CA: Davies-Black Publishing, 2010)

12. Paul Tieger, Barbara Barron, and Kelly Tieger, *Do What You Are: Discover the Perfect Career for You Through the Secrets of Personality Type* (Boston: Little, Brown and Company, 2014)

13. Carol Linden, *The Job Seekers Guide for Extroverts & Introverts* (Raleigh, NC: Font Publications, 2014) https://www.effectivewithpeople.com

14. John C. Maxwell, *The 15 Invaluable Laws of Growth* (New York, NY: Center Street, 2012)

CHAPTER 14: THE INTERVIEW PROCESS

1. Toastmasters International is a nonprofit educational organization that operates worldwide to promote effective communication, public speaking, and presentation skills. Meetings are held weekly at various businesses and meeting locations. Dates, times, and locations can be found by doing an online search. https://www.toastmasters.org

2. The *64 Toughest Interview Questions* can be located on the Internet and provides the job seeker with a list of questions to assist them in their interview preparation. Along with the questions is some insight on what the interviewer might be looking for and how to structure your response.

3. Toastmasters International is a nonprofit educational organization that operates worldwide to promote effective communication, public speaking, and presentation skills. Meetings are held weekly at various businesses and meeting locations. Dates, times, and locations can be found by doing an online search. https://www.toastmasters.org

CHAPTER 16: NEGOTIATING YOUR COMPENSATION PACKAGE

1. *Interests*, as used in context here, refers to a motivating factor that will cause someone to decide on a *position*. A position is *what* someone wants; the interest is the reason *why*. For example, if you ask your boss for a 15% raise (what/position), the reason behind asking for the raise is the why or your interest. Interests can be tied back to basic human needs such as for safety, security, inclusion, and self-esteem.(See Maslow's *Hierarchy of Needs*)

2. Roger Fisher and William Ury authored *Getting to Yes* and used the term BATNA to describe a negotiator's best alternative if they fail to reach an agreement with the other party. BATNA stands for best alternative to a negotiated agreement.

3. Study conducted by staffing firm Robert Half, as reported by the Society of Human Resource Management (SHRM). https://www.shrm.org/resourcesand-tools/hr-topics/talent-acquisition/pages/salary-negotiations-are-not-happening.aspx

4. Roger Fisher and William Ury, *Getting to Yes* (New York, NY: Penguin Books, 1991)

5. William Ury, *Getting Past No* (New York, NY: Bantam Books, 1993)

CHAPTER 18: THE JOURNEY CONTINUES

1. U.S. Bureau of Labor Statistics is a unit of the U.S. Department of Labor and is responsible for measuring labor market activity, working conditions, and price changes in the economy. This bureau produces vital statistics about jobs and unemployment. https://www.bls.gov. See USDL-18-1500, September 20, 2018.

2. John C. Maxwell, *The 15 Invaluable Laws of Growth* (New York, NY: Center Street, 2012)

3. *Law of the Rubber Band* is one of John Maxwell's 15 laws for growth as described in his book *The 15 Invaluable Laws of Growth*. The law of the rubber band describes when you lose the tension between where you are and where you could be.

4. John C. Maxwell, *The 15 Invaluable Laws of Growth* (New York, NY: Center Street, 2012)

5. "Life is a journey, not a destination" is a quote credited to the American philosopher, journalist, and poet Ralph Waldo Emerson.

6. John C. Maxwell, *No Limits* (New York, NY: Center Street, 2017)

7. Brendon Burchard, *High Performance Habits: How Extraordinary People Become That Way* (Carlsbad, CA: Hay House, 2017)

FEEDBACK AND SUCCESS STORIES

My goal in writing *Project Career Quest* is to educate, empower, and encourage the reader as they set out on their **Career Quest** journey. I look forward to hearing your feedback and experiences using the tools and strategies provided. Please visit my website at **www.KerryAhrend.com**. I would love to hear your success stories as well as your challenges. Thank you for purchasing the book and I wish you a successful career transition wherever that may take you.

"...but they who wait for the Lord shall renew their strength; they shall mount up with wings like eagles; they shall run and not be weary; they shall walk and not faint."
—*Isaiah 40:31*

ABOUT THE AUTHOR – KERRY AHREND

Kerry Ahrend is a career coach, trainer, speaker, and certified Project Management Professional (PMP®). She has traveled extensively throughout the United States, Canada, and internationally delivering training and performance improvement interventions to Fortune 500 companies, government agencies, non-profits, and small entrepreneurial enterprises in the best practices of project management, leadership development, team building, communications, negotiation skills, conflict resolution, and business process analysis.

For over twenty years Kerry has worked with individuals and organizations to increase skills and competencies and help people meet their challenges with confidence. For the past ten plus years Kerry has used her knowledge of how to plan, execute, and deliver successful projects to coach those in transition. As a career coach, she has worked with one of the leading providers of career transition services in the world. She works with professionals and those in transition to assess their skills, strengths, core competencies, and other essential information to help map out a strategy to achieve their career goals.

Kerry has a Master's Degree in Human Resources Training and Development; a Master's Certificate in Project Management from George Washington University; a Project Management Professional (PMP®) certification; and is a certified trainer, speaker, and coach with the John Maxwell Team.

On the personal side, Kerry is an animal advocate and volunteers with several dog rescue groups (she's a cat lover too!) She fosters, fundraises, and coordinates events. She has worked with Special Olympics North Carolina (SONC) for over 18 years and participates in other volunteer activities through her church, alumni association, and other charitable organizations. Volunteering to help those in need is a passion of Kerry's and one of the inspirations and motivation for writing *Project Career Quest.*